A Nation in Denial

A Nation in Denial

The Truth About Homelessness

Alice S. Baum and
Donald W. Burnes

Westview Press
BOULDER • SAN FRANCISCO • OXFORD

Copyright © 1993 by Alice S. Baum and Donald W. Burnes

Published in 1993 in the United States of America by Westview Press, Inc., 5500 Central Avenue, Boulder, Colorado 80301-2877, and in the United Kingdom by Westview Press, 36 Lonsdale Road, Summertown, Oxford OX2 7EW

Library of Congress Cataloging-in-Publication Data
Baum, Alice S.
  A nation in denial : the truth about homelessness / Alice S. Baum and Donald W. Burnes.
    p.   cm.
  Includes bibliographical references and index.
  ISBN 0-8133-8244-0. — ISBN 0-8133-8245-9 (pbk.)
  1. Homelessness—United States.   2. Homeless persons—United
States.   I. Burnes, Donald W.   II. Title.
HV4505.B378   1993
362.5'0973—dc20   92-42265
                                                                              CIP

Printed and bound in the United States of America

The paper used in this publication meets the requirements
of the American National Standard for Permanence of Paper
for Printed Library Materials Z39.48-1984.

10   9   8   7   6   5

This book is dedicated to Button, Ralph, Brenda, Tim, Donald, Loraine, Richard, Charles, Jimmy, Donald, Steve, Edith, Ted, Shannon, Patricia, Arthur, Archie, Joe, Zollie, Henry, Jerome, and the other homeless people with whom we worked and from whom we learned the importance of telling the truth.

Contents

Figures

Preface

On August 24, 1992, Hurricane Andrew hit southern Florida and Louisiana and left in its wake an unparalleled path of destruction and devastation. The costliest natural disaster in U.S. history, Hurricane Andrew damaged or destroyed 137,500 homes, leaving an estimated 250,000 people literally homeless.

Something deep in the American psyche is touched when devastation and disaster strike members of our society. The nation's immediate response to this disaster epitomized the powerful American tradition of citizens assuming responsibility for helping members of society who are in trouble. Calls for donations of goods, money, and services were met with such generosity that officials were initially overwhelmed with the task of distributing and accounting for all the contributions. Roads leading to devastated communities became gridlocked with vehicles from around the country filled with people wanting to help, trained relief workers ready to volunteer their expertise, and shipments of food, clothing, medical supplies, building materials, and even ice. In the November/December 1992 issue of *Psychology Today,* John Carnes, a psychologist helping families cope with the traumatic effects of the hurricane, reported seeing more U.S. flags being displayed in affected communities than he had seen at the height of Desert Storm.

The homelessness created by Hurricane Andrew presents a stark contrast to that of the men, women, and children whom Americans have called "the homeless" since the early 1980s and confirms the need to reexamine "homelessness" in America today. Although the problem for both groups is described as being without homes, the impediments that prevent "the homeless" from establishing independent and self-sufficient lives are much more complex than the lack of housing that they share with the hurricane victims. The people who lost their homes to the hurricane needed exactly the kinds of emergency help that have been provided to America's homeless for more than a decade: temporary shelter, food, clothing, and financial assistance. The tragedy of homelessness in America in the 1980s and 1990s is that this kind of help has proven to be insufficient to address the multiple problems of the vast majority of the people called "the homeless."

Just three months after they were constructed, the last of the tent cities was closed and most hurricane victims had either found alternative housing or had moved into mobile homes provided by the federal government as interim housing. Ironically, on the same weekend in late October 1992 that the last of the emergency shelters in the tent cities in Florida was being dismantled, about 600 people in Omaha and Lincoln, Nebraska, slept out-doors in freezing temperatures to draw attention to homelessness in America. One participant told a local television reporter that spending only one night on the streets was an insignificant sacrifice compared to the years that America's homeless people have suffered in shelters and on the streets. Why is it that most of the people who lost their homes to Hurricane Andrew resettled into new housing in just three months, while hundreds of thousands of others remain homeless for years?

Complete economic and psychological recovery from the tragedy of Hurricane Andrew will take energy, money, and enormous stamina, but the expectation is that in time most hurricane victims will rebuild their homes and their lives. Why is it that so many people in this nation do not have the same expectation for America's "homeless"? Why has there never been the same sense of urgency to help "the homeless" reconstruct their lives as was evidenced in the days and weeks following Hurricane Andrew? Why does America persist in describing the problems of "the homeless" in terms of poverty and lack of housing, when the evidence overwhelmingly suggests that other problems prevent "the homeless" from working and maintaining permanent housing? Why is there a sense of fatalistic inevitability that America's "homeless" will always have marginal lives, dependent on shelters, soup kitchens, and clothing distributions? Why is it that, despite the tradition of deep concern for the needy in our society, the problem of homelessness has proven so intractable?

We have written this book to answer these complex questions.

Alice S. Baum
Donald W. Burnes

Acknowledgments

In writing this book, we received help and support from many friends and colleagues who shared their insights and knowledge with us. We wish to thank them all. However, several of them deserve particular mention.

Carolyn Douglas, our good friend and colleague, read every word of several drafts of our work. She always provided invaluable comments and constructive suggestions and edited our drafts with extreme patience and an unflagging commitment to the truth. Without her support and wisdom, we would never have finished this book, and we are deeply indebted to her.

Dr. Robert Koff, a longtime friend and colleague, read our next to last draft and, as always, asked penetrating questions that forced us to clarify our thinking. His careful reasoning helped us write a better book.

Several other friends and colleagues deserve a special note of thanks. Irving Shandler, president of the Diagnostic and Rehabilitation Center in Philadelphia, and Daniel Steffey, former assistant to the mayor of Portland, Oregon, were both generous with their time, knowledge, and insights. Irv made time in his very busy schedule at the DRC to meet with us, arranged a lunchtime seminar with executive staff members, and arranged meetings for us with several members of the project staff. We were awed by Irv's commitment to his very difficult work, and we learned a great deal from him and other members of the DRC staff about maximizing opportunities for homeless men and women to achieve sobriety and recovery from drug addictions. Dan provided substantial assistance in our extensive visit to Portland, helped us make arrangements to visit the many impressive component projects of the Portland Model, and shared with us his profound optimism about truly helping the homeless.

We are indebted to Barbara Deard who patiently transcribed the six hours of taped interviews that are the basis for Chapter 4. Without her assistance this chapter could not have been written.

Two members of our families, David G. Baum and Raymond Burnes, also deserve our thanks. David created our graphics with skill and expertise. Raymond, always the teacher, read the entire manuscript and carefully called errors and omissions to our attention.

The editorial staff at Westview Press provided the most professional help for which writers could ask. Katherine Streckfus edited our work with extreme sensitivity to the subject and helped turn our manuscript into a truly readable document. Shena Redmond paid dedicated attention to detail and oversaw the completion of our work with great talent and expertise.

Finally, we wish to thank our book agent, Gail Ross, who believed that this book was important and needed to be published, and Barbara Ellington, the editor at Westview Press who agreed with her.

A.S.B.
D.W.B.

Introduction

In the early 1980s, America became aware of the homeless. Although homelessness was not new to this country, the sight of men, women, and children living on the streets and in shelters was shocking to a nation that only twenty years earlier had declared War on Poverty. Now, despite public outrage, media attention, and political debate about homelessness, the American public seems no closer to understanding the problem or its causes. Moreover, despite all the time, energy, and money spent to address the issue, the United States has come no closer to relieving the misery on the streets or even to having viable ideas about what to do.

While the 1980s were marked by compassion for the homeless, the 1990s seem to have become the decade of antihomelessness. Most people are showing less sympathy for the homeless than before, and officials regularly sweep street people from downtown areas. As public attention shifts away from homelessness and turns to other domestic issues, the United States seems ready to admit that it has failed the homeless and, having tried to provide help for so long with so few results, the general public seems to feel it has little else to offer.

It is our belief that, in fact, American society has never really tried to help today's homeless, because, for the various reasons we will explore in this book, people have been unwilling and unable to admit the truth about the nature of homelessness in America today and have therefore failed to pursue appropriate remedies. Instead, policymakers and advocates have used the horror of homelessness to advance a variety of political agendas that have less to do with homelessness than with the nationwide shift away from policies intended to eliminate persistent and lingering poverty in America.

When homelessness first became an issue of national concern, the U.S. political scene was changing dramatically. The electorate had sent a conservative governing majority to Washington with a mandate to cut taxes, to scale back government's intrusion into local affairs, and to enact massive reductions in the amount of money spent to help America's dependent poor. Many social analysts and advocates for the homeless made the convincing case that these changes in federal policy were directly linked to the increase in homelessness. They further asserted that homelessness was a manifestation of the crumbling social safety net that had, however inadequately, kept most of the poorest Americans from total destitution for generations. Homelessness, thus defined, required structural solutions: policies that assured full employment at increased wages, that restored funding for social welfare programs, and that created additional affordable housing subsidized by more generous federal funding. At the very least, the homeless and the hungry had a right to emergency shelter and food.

In 1986, we began work at a church-based organization created to help the poor and homeless in Washington, D.C. Our first task was to improve the emergency programs already in place: an emergency food pantry, an emergency financial assistance program intended to pay overdue rent and utility bills, and a job placement program. Our second task was to add transitional programs such as job readiness training, budget management, adult education, and referrals to permanent housing where possible. We believed that these programs would help our clients overcome the poverty and homelessness that were the result of massive cutbacks in social programs, changes in the postindustrial job market, and most important, the deplorable shortage of affordable housing. For three years, in our respective roles as executive director and substance abuse counselor, we worked with many of the homeless people who sought help at our center. As we came to know them, they shared the stories of their lives with us, we met members of their families, we hired several to work with us at the center, and we developed close and trusting friendships with many.

Our daily experiences over this three-year period presented startling contradictions to our initial views about their needs. We were confronted by problems that were not directly related to the structural, economic, and social forces that were so frequently cited and that provided the content of the political debate about homelessness. What we saw instead were people frustrated and angered by personal lives out of control. They were entrapped by alcohol and drug addictions, mental illness, lack of education and skills, and self-esteem so low it was often manifested as self-hate.

Through these experiences we learned a lesson that many people find very hard to accept, namely, that the help that many well-intentioned people were trying to provide to these troubled human beings was, in fact, of little or no help at all. We learned that helping the poor and the homeless without admitting the truth of their situation often increases their misery, their sense of isolation, and their hopelessness and does little to help them make the changes in their lives that can empower them to break the cycle of homelessness.

Meanwhile, newspapers, magazines, books, and television programs reported stories of homeless two-parent rust-belt families temporarily down on their luck or of homeless individuals who had recently been laid off from permanent employment. These stories led policymakers, politicians, and advocates to frame the issue as one of people not having homes and therefore being "homeless." None of these descriptions bore any resemblance to the people we knew. Nor were they consistent with the emerging research, which documented that up to 85 percent of all homeless adults suffer from chronic alcoholism, drug addiction, mental illness, or some combination of the three, often complicated by serious medical problems.

Denial

Ronald L. Rogers and Chandler Scott McMillin, in their book *Free Someone You Love from Alcohol and Other Drugs* (1992), defined denial as "the inability to recognize a problem in the face of compelling evidence." America is in deep denial about homelessness. There is compelling evidence that the primary issue is not the lack of homes for the homeless; the homeless need access to treatment and medical help for the conditions that prevent them from being able to maintain themselves independently in jobs and housing.

Denial takes many forms. Some advocates fear that admitting the extent of substance abuse and mental illness among the homeless would generate a backlash of retribution against those whose plight they are trying to relieve. Many are afraid of "blaming the victim" for their condition of homelessness and prefer to present the issue in strictly economic, political, and systemic terms. Some researchers, afraid of being criticized for "medicalizing" the problem, develop contorted explanations of homelessness that often bear little relationship to their own findings and thus undermine the very nature of scientific inquiry.

Policymakers and the general public may be fearful about acknowledging problems for which there are few guaranteed remedies and that are so pervasive in society that overcoming them seems beyond reach. Finally, among advocates as well as in policymaking circles and in the general public, some people are wedded to the social remedies designed over the past twenty-five years and prefer to focus on those few homeless people who can immediately benefit from job training, education, transitional and low-income housing, and community or political organizing. Regrettably, many seem to be unaware of the ability of homeless alcoholics to get sober, of homeless addicts to recover, and of the homeless mentally ill to benefit from treatment, medication, therapy, and rehabilitation and therefore accept these conditions as ones about which nothing can be done.

Paradoxically, during the same years that this country has stubbornly refused to acknowledge substance abuse and mental illness among the homeless, middle-class Americans have enjoyed greater access to increasing numbers of residential and in-hospital treatment programs for alcoholism and addictions and have been using health insurance and employee assistance programs to pay for them. When alcoholism, drug addiction, mental illness, and domestic violence strike family members, most families do everything possible to provide treatment and support, while society leaves those most disabled by these problems to their own devices because it is unwilling to acknowledge the role these problems play in their lives.

Not only are we a nation in denial, but our denial is selective.

Toward an Honest Understanding

If policy debates about homelessness continue to be misguided and uninformed, the problem of homelessness can only continue unabated. Our purpose in writing this book is to inform the future debate so that it will be based on a more honest understanding of the homeless, who they are, and what needs to be done to help them escape from the tragedy of crippled lives. In the following pages, we review scientific research, but this book is not primarily a review of the scientific literature. We analyze many political perspectives and reports, but we have not written a policy manual or a political treatise. Readers who are expecting a policy blueprint for solving the problem of homelessness will not find one, even though we include model policies and examples of programs that work. Our firm belief is that before America can develop effective policy, Americans must first come to some basic agreement about the nature of homelessness today and its real causes.

As we began to write this book, we came to understand the importance of the stories of the homeless people with whom we had worked. Although we have changed their names and altered some of the details to protect their privacy, we have included their stories so that they too can be part of our effort to overcome the denial about homelessness. In most cases, we knew these men and women well, having spent extensive time with them as we tried to understand their situations and their real needs. In one case, we asked a man we call Franklin to tell us about his experiences at a Washington, D.C., shelter; we have used the transcript of his six hours of conversation with us as the basis for Chapter 4.

These stories are not like the romanticized tales found in the media and the popular literature; they are neither fictions created for the purpose of illustration nor reports based on one-time interviews. Rather, they are individual stories that were revealed to us over time. For example, William taught us what it means to be "on the stick," that is, what it means to be homeless; like so many of the homeless, he needed alcohol treatment and health care to help him solve the problems that kept him entrapped in joblessness and despair.

When we first met William, he had just been asked to leave the rooming house—again—because he was drinking—again. Before he could try to find work, William needed surgery on his leg, which had been injured in an alcohol-related accident several years ago. One night, his buddy died while they were drinking in an aban-doned car. William and his friends were sorry that Jimmy died, but they knew that either he or some other member of their bottle gang would die soon. Someone always died; someone always had one more drink, the one that proved to be the last. William was a homeless alcoholic, and homeless alcoholics know people who die.

Unfortunately, there are few victories among the stories we share with the readers of this book, because the help that was needed was rarely available, and in most cases, these individuals' lives are still filled with alcohol, drugs, and mental illness. We have dedicated this book to these men and women, even though some have died since we started our work.

A necessary first step in developing an honest understanding about homelessness is to look realistically at what the research reveals and what our experience has told us about the homeless. This is the purpose of Part One, where we describe homelessness as it is today in detail. In Chapter 1, we talk about who the homeless are, examine the alcoholism, drug addiction, and mental illness that fill their lives, and discuss how these problems affect their physical health and their ability to work. The picture that emerges is a compelling one.

Chapter 2 introduces the connection between homelessness and the baby boom, the population explosion that has overwhelmed society's institutions in new ways with each decade. We examine the extent to which the baby boom was more than merely a demographic phenomenon by looking at the social and political forces of the era—in particular, the counterculture—that challenged the value systems of settled society and endangered its most troubled members, many of whom joined the ranks of the homeless. Chapter 3 continues our examination of the baby boom era but focuses instead on the emergence of the underclass in America's inner cities—people living in increasingly deserted inner cities where hopelessness, poverty, drugs, and crime are inextricably connected to multigenerational welfare dependency, family violence, and in some cases, homelessness.

Having completed a review of the basic problems, in Chapter 4 we spend a day with Franklin, who describes the difficulty of trying to maintain his personal dignity in a system that paradoxically seems to dehumanize the very individuals that it seeks to help. Franklin makes real the daily horrors of a life filled with alcohol, drugs, mental illness, and a system that is completely unprepared to respond to the medical and social needs of seriously impaired human beings. In Chapter 5, we review the components of that system—the services now in place to help the homeless. By understanding the inadequacy of our efforts to help the homeless, readers may begin to see why America is becoming frustrated, angry, and even bored and why people seem to be walking away from a monumental social problem that shows no sign of diminishing.

In Part Two, we step back to place homelessness in a historical and social context. In Chapter 6, we review the history of homelessness from colonial days, through the exploration of the West, the gold rush, the industrialization of the late nineteenth century, and the Great Depression. We look at the struggle to empower America's disenfranchised poor that began in the 1960s and changed the way society addresses social policy issues by focusing on economic and social systems instead of personal problems—a change in focus that often produced unintended consequences for the homeless by fraying the decades-old safety net of skid row and other institutions that had developed to meet the needs of the most disadvantaged Americans.

The analysis of the past 350 years leads us to an examination of the past decade and, in Chapter 7, we turn our attention to the politics surrounding the plight of the homeless. At the center of the politics of homelessness was the homelessness movement, a group of political and social activists on the Left who were searching for a new cause as the Vietnam War and Watergate receded from America's consciousness. These advocates for the homeless enlisted the media to persuade America that the homeless, like other Americans, are victims of the postindustrial economy of the Reagan years. These individuals redefined homelessness to mean needing only shelter and housing, thus confusing poverty with disabling conditions. Our examination of the politics of homelessness leads to an exploration in Chapter 8 of the extent to which the homelessness movement influenced the research community during the 1980s. We examine how the movement caused many analysts to shy away from acknowledging the extent of substance abuse and mental illness as causes of homelessness and how the movement compelled analysts to focus instead on issues and solutions better suited to the problems faced by America's working poor. In this examination, we raise a central question: If poverty is the cause of homelessness, why are there so many very poor people in the United States who are not homeless?

For an answer to this question, we turn to Part Three, where we present a more reasoned analysis of homelessness and encourage different strategies for addressing this profound social problem and the personal problems that help to cause it. Chapter 9 begins with a review of the most universal characteristic of homelessness, the alienation of homeless people from society and its institutions. We then describe how the stigma surrounding alcoholism, drug addiction, and mental illness leads some into homelessness. Finally, we examine a variety of major shifts in attitudes and policies that have helped to increase homelessness: deinstitutionalization of the mentally ill, decriminalization of alcoholism, gentrification of both skid row and of treatment services, and the extent to which the population explosion of the baby boom exacerbated the effects of all of these policies.

In Chapter 10 we lay out a new agenda for responding to homelessness. We begin by arguing that the word "homeless" should not be used because it deceives us and does not inform our thinking about the complexities of modern homelessness. We identify some promising programmatic approaches currently being used by substance abuse treatment professionals and by psychiatrists and other mental health professionals committed to working with homeless individuals and families, taking into account the special complexities that homelessness introduces into the processes of treatment, follow-up care, and long-term rehabilitation.

If there is one unifying theme in this book, it is that America's homeless, the people living in shelters and on the streets, deserve better treatment than they are receiving. We stand firm in our belief that in order for our society to begin to solve the problems of homelessness, it must stop making distinctions between the deserving and the undeserving poor and must stop denying the extent of alcoholism, drug addiction, and mental illness among the homeless. Unless the nation overcomes this denial, the homeless will continue to suffer lives of misery and desperation. Denial and indifference to the truth about the homeless have already exaggerated the divisions between the "haves" and the "have-nots" in our society; staying on the present course will only divide us further. Since the earliest days of our democracy, American ideals have included not only equality and justice, but also a commitment to share responsibility for the common good. Ultimately, the quality of life for all Americans depends on our ability to recognize that everyone shares in the destiny of homeless men, women, and children, our most needy citizens.

PART ONE

Homelessness Today

1

Who Are the Homeless?

The term "homeless" is actually a catch word, a misnomer that focuses our attention on only one aspect of the individual's plight: his lack of residence or housing. In reality, the homeless often have no job, no function, no role within the community; they generally have few if any social supports. They are jobless, penniless, functionless, and supportless as well as homeless.[1]

Every day, in cities and towns across the country, men and women dressed in rags walk the streets aimlessly, oftentimes talking to visions, and frequently begging for money. They are often carrying plastic bags or pushing shopping carts filled with their worldly possessions. Sometimes they curl up on a bench or in a doorway under filthy blankets or tattered coats. If someone gives them money, they may respond with prayers of thanks and blessing; others continue to stare off into space, seemingly untouched by efforts to help.

These people are called the homeless, but they are obviously more than just people without homes. They are dirty and sometimes frail; when they talk to visions, they show the signs of mental illness or drug addiction, and the smell of alcohol that infuses their clothing reveals their drunkenness. But most people seem incapable of acknowledging what they see or of talking about what they know to be true. Reinforced by what they read in the newspapers and see on the nightly news, many people feel sorrow and sometimes pity; when they are accosted by panhandlers, some may feel anger or even fear; at worst, groups gather to celebrate the lonesome deaths of the least fortunate by holding candlelight services on heating grates, saying they "died with dignity." This is denial.

For more than a decade, America has experienced a love-hate relationship with the homeless. On the one hand, many people want to reach out and help these destitute and troubled men, women, and children; on the other, they are frustrated because, despite so many public and private efforts, nothing has eliminated or even decreased homelessness. To do so, the American public must start telling the truth, by no means an easy call to action. Many will continue to be overly cautious for fear of "blaming the victim" or "medicalizing the problem"; others will view the problems as too complex and the remedies as too expensive. Unless this nation proceeds with new clarity, however, homelessness will continue to be one of the great unsolved social problems of our time.

A necessary first step is to learn who the homeless are and what problems confront them. Unfortunately, media reports about homelessness are often not very specific, and therefore not very helpful. The academic and professional research community, however, has made a concerted effort to investigate the nature and causes of homelessness in the United States. This research literature offers reasonably consistent information about the homeless, despite the difficulties of studying a population that is by definition transient and frequently hard to interview or engage in conversation.[2] Most important, this literature provides the knowledge that is needed to develop realistic policies and programs that have some chance of addressing the problem.

The Many Faces of Homelessness

There is no single way of describing homeless individuals, even though the term "homelessness" suggests that there is a single defining characteristic, that is, being without a home. The homeless population includes single men, single women, and families, most of which are headed by a single parent, usually a woman. The homeless are white, African American, Hispanic, Asian, and Native American. They are refugees and aliens, parolees, runaway youth and children, Vietnam veterans and other traumatized individuals, a few elderly people, and former hippies and flower children. They live in cities, suburbs, and rural areas. They are alcoholics, drug addicts, and mentally ill persons; some suffer from a combination of all three of these problems, and many have other serious medical problems. Some are victims of domestic violence; others are victims of other people's alcohol and drug habits. Finally, some are homeless because of an immediate economic crisis or a disaster over which they have no control, such as the death of a loved one. Anna, for example, became homeless when someone close to her died, but her situation was also complicated by other problems.

> Anna became homeless because her pimp was murdered. While he lived, she wore furs and rode in a Cadillac; when he died, all she had left were the memories, scars, and her heroin addiction. She began her new life on the streets, graduated to a barracks shelter for women, and impressed people enough to be accepted into a "drug-free" transitional night shelter. Anna was required to obtain counseling and medication (for her mental illness) at a Washington, D.C., public mental health clinic. On the strong recommendation from the shelter, we hired her to work at our center.
>
> When we first met Anna, she was struggling to maintain her appearance of stability. As she got to know us and understood that we worked with alcoholics and drug addicts without denying their addictions, she opened up and began to tell her story. At first, she told us that she was clean and trying hard to stay clean. Perhaps

she was, but from what we could tell, she had no support in trying to overcome her addiction. We saw pressure mounting as Anna was required to look for an afford-able apartment, which she was to share with other women "graduating" from the shelter. She was terrified because she had no money for the rent deposit. The shelter had required her to establish an escrow account as soon as she had an income, but when she told shelter staff members tales about sick relatives and long-lost children whom she needed to see, she had been permitted to raid the account. As her stress mounted and her mood became more and more somber, we became convinced that she was using drugs; perhaps she had never stopped. Despite the limited resources for drug treatment, particularly for women, we attempted to collaborate with the shelter staff in helping Anna seek treatment; however, they had already decided that she had become too disruptive to remain at the shelter and had told her to leave. We hung in with her for another week, giving her just enough time to steal money from our office, and then we too had to fire her. A short while later, Anna was in jail. After her release, she found her way to another shelter.

During our last conversations with Anna she both said and acted as if she was trapped and very angry. She was angry because she had failed to "pull off" her new life—conning people into supporting her (enabling her) with shelter, food, and money so that she could continue to live with her heroin addiction. At the same time, she was angry that she had been unable to respond to the challenge of quitting her habit and untangling the web of lies, misery, and addiction that enveloped her.

The New Homeless

Many current reports focus on the changes in the homeless population and the differences between today's homeless and the traditional white male "skid row bum" of past years. By the standard of the old skid rows, it is true that today's homeless are younger; the average age of the homeless popula-tion is low to mid-thirties.[3] Less than 5 percent are elderly, primarily because the homeless, particularly the substance-abusing homeless, die some twenty years earlier on average than the rest of us.[4] Minorities are over-represented in today's homeless populations; nationally, slightly more than half of the homeless are members of minority groups.[5] To avoid creating new stereo-types, however, it is important to remember that the actual racial composi-tion of the homeless population in any one place reflects local and regional population trends—major metropolitan areas on the East Coast have high proportions of homeless African Americans; Minneapolis has many homeless Native Americans; in southwestern cities such as Los Angeles and Phoenix there are greater concentrations of Hispanics among the homeless; and in the Northwest, some cities report that most of their homeless are white. Finally, while homelessness occurs in rural and suburban areas, the rate of homelessness is substantially greater in cities.[6]

Despite the differences from the old skid row stereotype, the vast majority of America's contemporary homeless population continues to be single men.[7] In the words of Howard M. Bahr, one of the leading historians on homelessness in America, "the 'new' homelessness is much like the old. Most homeless people are still multiproblem men."[8]

> *Mr. Ordway was only fifty years old, but he looked seventy-five. His face was lined, his hair was white, and his trembling hands were shriveled. He walked haltingly with the help of a cane and often stumbled as he came into the day center looking for food or, more likely, for money. In an effort to control his "budget," Mr. Ordway had agreed to turn over his monthly disability check to the day center so that his caseworker could pay his bills and ration his weekly allowance; but, needing money to buy vodka, he came in almost every day to ask for more money. He had a hacking cough that shook his body, making it hard for him to speak. Mr. Ordway's memory had long since ceased to serve him, and he was often unsure of just what day or year it was. He had no family that he could tell about, except for his mother; Mr. Ordway had not seen her for years but hoped that she prayed for him despite the trouble he said his drinking had caused her. The only friends he had were drinking buddies, many of whom deserted him when his cash ran out. No matter how hard the counselor tried, Mr. Ordway refused to get the help he needed—help to stop drinking, help to relieve the pain in his legs, help to stay alive—even though he was a veteran and could easily have been admitted to the local VA hospital. Nothing much mattered to him anymore; as long as he could get a bottle every day and keep from freezing in the winter, he wanted to continue to exist in his own way. Since he felt he had lost everything already, he had nothing more to lose.*

Approximately one-third of single homeless men are veterans, and veterans, particularly those of the Vietnam War, are more likely to be seriously troubled by substance abuse problems and psychiatric or trauma disorders than other homeless men.[9]

One of the most confounding issues in discussing the composition of the homeless population is whether to report the number of homeless individuals or the number of homeless household units; there is no generally accepted standard, and the choice is often motivated by the desire to emphasize the size of one or another portion of the homeless population, usually families. Some studies refer to all individuals—counting each adult and every child. Others refer to homeless households—counting children accompanied by at least one adult as one household. The way these numbers are reported affects our understanding of who the homeless are.

Using the household measure, 90 percent of all homeless households are single unattached adults; 81 percent of the single adults are men and 19 percent are women.[10] These statistics ignore important nuances in the actual composition of the homeless population; many women who are counted as single are actually mothers who have lost their children to the foster care system or have left them with relatives or friends.[11] The remaining 10 percent of homeless households across the country are families—adults accompanied by young children.[12] Although these data seem inconsistent with reports that homeless families make up almost a third of the total homeless population, in fact, the difference depends on how family members are counted. When counting every individual, family members represent 23 percent of the total of all homeless people; 8 percent are adults and 15 percent are children.[13] To further confuse the issue, a number of good local studies report substantially higher numbers of families than the national average,[14] suggesting that when making policy or planning services, it is important to take local and regional variations into consideration. These studies also suggest that generalizations about the homeless based on information derived from a single location must be made with great care. This is a caution that many popular accounts of the homeless fail to heed. For example, New York City has an exceptionally high proportion of families among its homeless compared to the rest of the country;[15] it would be a mistake for someone familiar with New York's homeless population to assume that families were as large a part of the homeless population elsewhere.

Families, Runaways, and Homeless Youth

Perhaps the most troubling dynamic concerning homeless families occurs when the distinction between homeless families and homeless youth becomes confused. As Oregon's Tri-County Youth Services Consortium report suggested:

> Homeless teen parent families are a unique population because they are both adult and child. . . . Teen parents most at risk of homelessness come from families of severe dysfunction. They share with their own parents histories of substance abuse, criminal involvement, unemployment, health and mental health problems, multiple domestic partners, domestic violence, overcrowded living quarters, and emotional/physical/sexual abuse.[16]

Research confirms that multigenerational domestic violence is a primary characteristic of homeless families; parents who have suffered abuse during their own childhoods tend to repeat familiar parenting styles, thus perpetuating the cycle of substance abuse and sexual and physical violence that often leads to homelessness, including homelessness among youth.[17] Hard as it may be to accept, homeless youth often find homelessness and the violence of the streets a better alternative than their home situations. They are "running *away*: away from neglect, away from physical and sexual abuse, away from rigid or unstable families" (emphasis in original).[18] Once on the streets, homeless youth turn to prostitution and crime to support themselves, and the vast majority abuse drugs and alcohol.[19] Without help, these youngsters are likely to become the next generation of homeless adults.

Alienation and Disaffiliation

Despite the diversity within the homeless population, homeless people share an important and distinctive characteristic: They are almost totally alienated from people and society's helping institutions. We would like to believe that homeless people are "just like us, but have had a really bad break," but it isn't true. Substance abuse, mental illness, health problems, and even economic crises affect many people who are still able to function in jobs and maintain their housing. Most people, even the poorest in our society, have friends, family, and neighbors who can help in times of crisis; they belong to churches, unions, clubs, and have formal and informal associations with other groups. Migrant workers, for example, have no permanent residence, but they do have supportive relationships through work, family, and community, and even though their lives are often harsh and their living quarters marginal, they are not homeless. Homeless people, in contrast, lack social support systems, often because they have used them up by making too many demands on them or because their emotional problems make them fearful of close contact and enduring relationships with others. According to Howard Bahr, "Homelessness . . . is a condition of disaffiliation, a lack of bonds, a pathology of connectedness, and not an absence of proper housing."[20] Said another way, homelessness "is a metaphor for profound disconnection from other people and institutions."[21] A man named Mike lived this metaphor.

> When we met Mike, he had lived on the streets for two years, drinking and learning to strike first in a fight because he was so small. At the age of thirty-nine, he had never married, had no friends, and even though he was in the same city as his family, he never saw them. Mike had worked for short periods as a secretary, a telephone operator, a grocery clerk, a janitor, and a counterperson, but he always quit or was fired because he alienated his coworkers and hated being supervised. All of his jobs had been "people jobs," but he complained about people—he was afraid of them because he was frail and was sure they would abuse him if they had the chance.
>
> When Mike got sick, he wouldn't see a doctor or contact his family. When he got too sick to avoid doing something any longer, he went to a clinic and was diagnosed as having tuberculosis; but he wouldn't go to a hospital. When public health officials threatened to have him forcibly hospitalized, he found an unheated room where he could sleep on a battered couch. Every few days, members of the church next door took him meals; Mike insisted that they leave them on the landing outside his door.

The nature and extent of the isolation among the homeless is well documented. More than half of all homeless adults have never been married, and an additional third are separated, widowed, or divorced. Furthermore, the homeless tend to have little contact with the families and friends they do have. In one study, 75 percent of the homeless individuals interviewed had no family relationships or friends, while in other studies more than half of the homeless had no contact with family or friends, even though in many cases these family members or friends lived in the same city.[22] Based on his study of the homeless in Chicago, for example, Peter H. Rossi reported that more than three-quarters of homeless single mothers would not choose to return to their families, and most of these women believed that their families would not want them back.[23] Rossi also reported that, even though more than half of the adults in his study had children, 91 percent did not have their children with them.[24]

The majority of homeless people are so alienated from society's systems and institutions that they do not use the social benefits for which they are eligible, including welfare, disability benefits, veterans' benefits, Medicaid, and food stamps.[25] Although many writers have argued that the reduction of benefits during the 1980s contributed to the increase in homelessness, ample research shows that many homeless people are too troubled to find or make use of benefit programs that are still in place. This extraordinary underutilization of benefits suggests that services designed to help homeless people must take into consideration not only the institutional barriers to obtaining services, such as residency and eligibility requirements, but also the isolation, fear, and reluctance to make contact with others so characteristic of the people called the homeless.

Alcoholism: A Continuing Problem

The clearest example of our nation's denial about homelessness is the extent to which most people believe that the "new homeless" are not like the "skid row bums" of years past. By focusing on families, youth, racial diversity, the declining age of the homeless, and even their social isolation, society tries to ignore the fact that alcoholism continues to be the most significant problem connected to modern homelessness.[26] The truth is that "the traditional, older Skid Row alcoholic has been joined, *not replaced,* by newer arrivals to the ranks of the homeless" (emphasis added).[27] The rate of alcohol abuse among today's homeless, in fact, is about the same as it was on skid row.[28]

Most recent research shows that the homeless suffer from alcoholism at rates six to seven times that of the American population in general.[29] Pamela J. Fischer and William R. Breakey, two leading researchers who have studied alcoholism among the homeless, have suggested that the most rigorous research shows that up to two-thirds of the homeless suffer from alcoholism;[30] however, given the wide variations in the research, the general consensus is that approximately 40 percent of homeless adults have significant alcohol problems. Like the general population where more men than women suffer from alcoholism, more homeless men than homeless women suffer from alcoholism, with serious problems affecting 52 percent of the men and 17 percent of the women.[31]

> *Sammy was a World War II veteran who worked as a truck driver and a blast furnace operator until the "furnace jumped out" at him one day when he was drunk on the job. When we met Sammy, he was living on disability payments,*

sometimes sleeping on the streets or passing out in alleys, and was often in trouble
with the police. He attended alcohol group meetings as a condition of his parole,
which was periodically revoked when he drank too much and got into fights.
During meetings, Sammy shared stories with other "old timers" about drinking the
alcohol captured from straining shoe polish through bread or laughed with other
truck drivers about late night escapades, including the time he couldn't find his
18-wheeler that he "misplaced" when he was drunk. His favorite stories were about
his drinking adventures during the war when he was stationed in the Philippines.
There, Sammy and his buddies kept a still going with potato peelings; when those
ran out, they drank "torpedo juice," the liquid propellant drained from captured
torpedoes. Sammy had high blood pressure and diabetes and suffered from fainting
spells on hot summer days. He was often sober when he came to the group meetings,
but he was also often very drunk.

Several comparative studies provide clear evidence that homeless alcoholics
are more seriously disabled than both alcoholics who are not homeless and
homeless people who are not alcoholics. A Los Angeles study found that compared with their domiciled counterparts, homeless alcoholics were heavier
drinkers, were less likely to be married, were more likely to be divorced, and had
fewer children. They lost jobs due to drinking more often than alcoholics who
were not homeless, had histories of more fights, and had more arrests, more
symptoms of physical deterioration, and more health problems related to heavy
drinking.[32] Similarly, a statewide study in Ohio found that the alcoholic homeless were more disabled than the nonalcoholic homeless. In this study, the alcoholic homeless were homeless twice as long as the nonalcoholic homeless; they
were less likely to have had a permanent full-time job and it had been longer
since their last job had ended; they were in poorer physical health; and they were
more likely to show signs of both depression and anxiety.[33]

Anyone familiar with the potential ravages of alcoholism will not be sur-
prised that homeless alcoholics have serious and multiple health problems,
many of which are life threatening. These include cardiovascular, gastrointes-
tinal, and neurological disorders, including high rates of hypertension, liver
disease, and epilepsy. Many people often assume that the serious physical
health problems caused by alcoholism come only with old age. Unfortunately,
this is a myth. We first met Elaine when she was twenty-four, when a social
worker at a local hospital, searching for a place for Elaine to live so the hospital would not have to release her to the streets, called the church where our
office was located. One of the few things Elaine could remember was the
name of the church.

Elaine had lived on the streets since she was twelve. She was already a late-stage
alcoholic who suffered from severe memory loss, liver damage, and other physical
impairments caused by continued drinking. Her one friend was Peter, a homeless
alcoholic who probably loved Elaine and tried to take care of her the best he could.
Every few months, Elaine experienced an episode of pancreatitis, internal hemor-

rhaging, or seizures, and Peter called an ambulance to take her to the hospital, where he visited her every day.

Elaine's only piece of identification was a birth certificate that listed her as "baby girl Wheeler." Without a documented first name, it was impossible to obtain other forms of identification. Peter brought Elaine's birth certificate to us so that we could try to correct it; despite our many efforts and those of hospital social workers, including searching for baptismal records and asking the local school district to search its records, there was no way to verify that Elaine was the person listed on the certificate. The school district found the records of an Elaine Wheeler who had been born in the same neighborhood as our Elaine, but the date of birth was different, leading us to suspect that Elaine was using a cousin's name without realizing it. She couldn't remember very much about her family but told us that she thought they were all dead. We tried but were unable to locate any family members to swear that her birth certificate was valid.

Without formal papers, Elaine could not be enrolled in the Medicaid program to pay hospital expenses. Nevertheless, various local hospitals treated her medically and then, unable to find a treatment or other residential program in which to place her, released her back to the streets where, with Peter's help, she found places to stay. But she continued her cycle of drinking, suffering medical crises, calling an ambulance, entering a hospital, and often being released to our day program.

Because of their deteriorated physical condition, homeless alcoholics experience grossly elevated rates of infectious disease, such as venereal disease and tuberculosis; the homeless nationwide suffer from TB at a rate some hundreds of times higher than the population at large.[34] Malnutrition, a common complication of alcoholism, is exacerbated by the state of homelessness, just as hypothermia and respiratory ailments, common conditions connected with homelessness, are exacerbated by alcohol. According to a major study on health problems among the homeless, "chronic alcohol abuse is a direct cause of many of the physical disorders and a contributing factor in many others."[35] Furthermore, homeless people have mortality rates 3.1 times higher than the expected rates for the American population as a whole, and they die, on average, twenty years earlier than would be expected.[36] According to the authors of the report on the Health Care for the Homeless (HCH) project, "Alcohol is the direct cause of death in at least 16 percent of the cases reviewed, and a contributory factor in perhaps half of them."[37] Not surprisingly, the HCH project also reports that the nonalcoholic homeless also suffer from elevated rates of physical health problems.[38]

Health problems are not the only problems aggravated by alcoholism. Homeless alcoholics who are drunk or passed out are often victims of theft and brutal physical or sexual attack, both in shelters and on the streets.[39] Finally, as we will discuss more fully in Chapter 9, despite the legal efforts to decriminalize alcoholism, homeless alcoholics continue to have frequent encounters with the criminal justice system and are frequently arrested for public drunkenness, disorderly conduct, and fighting.[40]

Although none of this may be surprising, it is surprising that the American public is so unwilling to admit that so many of the homeless suffer from alcoholism and that its consequences take such a heavy toll. To contend that a majority of the homeless are not "skid row bums" because *only* 40 percent are alcoholics not only understates the problem;[41] it also prevents developing help for people whose addiction to alcohol is killing them. Homeless alcoholics can respond to treatment, particularly if the treatment is geared to their special needs. They need not be left to suffer, to be arrested, or to die without help.

Drug Abuse: A New Phenomenon

There is even more denial associated with drug use among the homeless than with alcoholism. During the same decade that homelessness became an important issue on America's social and political agenda, attitudes about illegal drugs—from marijuana to heroin, from PCP to cocaine and its derivative, crack—changed dramatically as people became more aware of the consequences of drug use. The drug-related deaths of such celebrities as basketball star Len Bias, movie star John Belushi, and others finally extinguished America's fascination with recreational drug use; the national "Just Say No" campaign and the "War on Drugs" transformed the tolerant attitudes fostered in the 1960s and 1970s. The American public is now appropriately horrified by the disasters caused by drugs: street violence, gangs, and the epidemic murder of young African American men involved with drugs; the connection between shared needles and AIDS; and, perhaps most heartrending, the tragedy of boarder babies, those infants who are born addicted and left behind in hospital nurseries, abandoned by their mothers too caught up in their own addictions to be burdened by their newborn babies. Individuals and whole communities across the country have made clear that a new standard prevails—drugs are illegal, dangerous, and wrong.

In the face of these attitudes, it is no wonder that those who want to maintain popular support for the plight of the homeless do not want to associate homelessness with the scourge of drugs, its illegality, and its violence. Reports that might otherwise reveal drug use among the homeless are often not told or are told in sanitized ways. When Robert Hayes, the founder of the Coalition for the Homeless, was quoted as saying that alcohol and drug use among the homeless is "our dirty little secret,"[42] he might have added that drug abuse is the dirtiest secret.

Our experience with the Mayor's Homeless Coordinating Council in Washington, D.C., provided firsthand experience with both the incidence of drug use among the homeless and the unwillingness to publicly acknowledge it.[43]

At one meeting of the council, the vice president, a leading local business executive, reported about his recent visit to a motel where the city sheltered homeless families.

He had gone there to identify twenty families who could be moved into the subsidized apartments he had located in response to a mandate from the council. Much to his surprise, of the twenty mothers he interviewed, only six were interested in moving from their squalid quarters. In disbelief, the vice president asked the social worker in charge why his offer was so soundly refused. She told him that 85 percent of the mothers were addicted to crack cocaine, and since the motel and its grounds served as an open-air drug market, the women refused to move because it would make obtaining drugs more difficult. After they heard this report, several council members tried to convince the council to adopt a strongly worded recommendation urging the city to stop random attempts to move families from shelters without first addressing the need for drug treatment; however, declaring that moving families out of shelters was a top priority, the council quickly dismissed the issue of drugs, refused to discuss the proposed recommendation, and continued to discuss ways of finding more housing.

Drug abuse has now become almost as much a feature of the homeless population as alcohol was on the old skid rows,[44] and it disproportionately affects the "new homeless," including minorities, especially African American men, homeless families, homeless youth, and the younger victims of mental illness. Perhaps because researchers are cautious about labeling people as being involved in criminal activities such as the use and distribution of illegal drugs, or because of the difficulty in identifying drug use other than through self-reporting, few studies have focused exclusively on drug abuse among the homeless. Nevertheless, there is increasing agreement that up to 20 percent of the homeless are addicted to drugs, and Fischer and Breakey in their review of recent research reported that almost half of all homeless adults suffer from drug disorders.[45] According to a 1992 report by the New York City Commission on the Homeless, 80 percent of the men in barracks-style shelters and 29 percent of residents in family shelters tested positive for drugs, mostly cocaine.[46] Unlike alcohol abuse, drug abuse is equally common among both homeless men and women.[47] Fischer and Breakey reported that the rate of drug abuse among homeless female heads of families is four times greater than among housed poor mothers.[48] Furthermore, reliable anecdotal information suggests that drug addiction, particularly to crack cocaine, affects a majority of some segments of the homeless population, including pregnant women and women with children.[49] It is therefore not surprising that a recent government study found that drug trafficking is a serious problem in many welfare motels that shelter homeless families.[50]

The advent of crack has been devastating and is intimately related to the increase in homelessness, especially family homelessness. Crack cocaine is perhaps the most invidious of all illegal drugs—it is cheap; it is readily available; its effects are almost instantaneous; it does not require the use of needles, making it much more attractive to women, who typically are fearful of injecting themselves; and it is one of the most addicting drugs ever observed by

medical researchers. Crack addicts give up work, family, and financial responsibility to spend time feeding their addiction, and addicts and their families are
joining the ranks of homeless people in increasing numbers. Irving Shandler,
president of the Diagnostic and Rehabilitation Center (DRC), an inner-city
treatment agency that has worked with alcoholics and addicts for twenty-five
years, said, "Mothers forget they are mothers when addicted to crack. Families
are destroyed; domestic violence and child abuse are synonymous with substance abuse. It is no coincidence that as cocaine addiction increases among
women, women as a new group among the homeless is on the rise."[51]

> *Arlene was a crack addict who had just given birth to her third child. She and her
> children lived in the cramped quarters of the motel that served as a family shelter.
> Arlene's older children had been in and out of foster care; they were taken away
> from her whenever social workers found clear evidence of either physical abuse or
> neglect or when it was clearly apparent that Arlene was on a drug binge. When
> Arlene entered a drug treatment program she was plagued by worry about the fate
> of her children and left the program before completing treatment. Back at the
> motel, Arlene left her children alone in the room most of the time. She regularly
> asked church volunteers for more supplies for the children than she needed. Her
> social worker suspected, but could not prove, that she routinely traded her food
> stamps for drugs and sold the various items donated by the church—diapers, baby
> food, clothing, school supplies—to get drug money.*

In a California study that compared poor families in stable housing with
homeless families, homeless mothers were more likely to be drug abusers, to
be involved with drug-abusing men, and to have had mothers who used
drugs.[52] Other studies have reported that close to 100 percent of homeless
youth use or abuse drugs and that drug use starts, in some cases, as early as
age eleven. As in society at large, drug use among the homeless is a phenomenon related to age: Homeless people over the age of forty tend to use
alcohol, while homeless people under the age of forty tend to use drugs or
both drugs and alcohol.[53] As would be expected, drug use is highest among
homeless individuals in their late teens and twenties.[54]

As in the case of alcohol abuse, drug use among the homeless leads directly
to serious physical health problems, especially those associated with intravenous drug use and the sharing of needles. Skin lesions and skin ulcers,
hepatitis, sexually transmitted diseases, and other infectious diseases are
common, and the incidence of AIDS and HIV infection is increasing dramatically among the homeless population. These health reports are especially
troubling because drug-abusing homeless women have significantly higher
rates of pregnancy than drug-free homeless women.[55]

Our purpose here is not to be pejorative or moralistic about either alcoholism or drug abuse and certainly not to "blame the victim." Rather, in
light of the significant research regarding the extent of alcohol and drug

abuse among the homeless, we contend that denying the existence of these addictions can only lead to the failure to meet the needs of these disabled individuals. To make matters worse, many services for the homeless, including emergency shelters for single adults and families, refuse to admit those who are drunk or actively using drugs, and only a few programs offer the homeless actual treatment for substance abuse.[56] The result is that very disabled and dangerously sick people are often left without shelter, primary health care, or help in overcoming their addictions.

Mental Illness and the Revolving Door

A disease like schizophrenia is very unpleasant. No one would ever sign up for it.[57]

The nation's denial of mental illness among the homeless is different from its denial of alcoholism and drug abuse. Most people are willing to admit its existence, but few are willing to try to understand the extent and the nature of the problem or to develop appropriate responses. A clearly inappropriate but common response is described by E. Fuller Torrey, a psychiatrist who has worked with the homeless mentally ill: "Some of the same mentally ill individuals who once used [Manhattan State Hospital] as hospitalized patients, now use it as shelter residents. The difference is that now there are no nurses, no doctors, no medication and no treatment."[58]

Although the most facile popular reporting about homelessness suggests that legions of deinstitutionalized mental patients roam the streets of our cities, a 1988 General Accounting Office report stated that there are actually no reliable national estimates about the extent of mental illness among the homeless.[59] Most researchers agree, however, that at least one-third of the homeless suffer from severe and persistent chronic psychiatric disorders such as schizophrenia and manic-depression; the proportion may be as high as one-half.[60]

These psychiatric disorders are conditions that modern psychiatry can treat. However, the homeless mentally ill frequently do not use available treatment and hospitalization services. Some are fearful of involuntary commitment; others are too disorganized to make or keep appointments; and some fear losing their children. In addition, according to a National Mental Health Association Conference Report, "Many don't believe they're mentally ill, or they don't want to go to places where there are other people who they identify as being mentally ill."[61]

Robert, for example, mentally ill and homeless in his mid-thirties, was the son of a middle-class Texas family and still had a checking account at a local Texas bank. He refused to get in touch with his family or to use his money. Robert's story reveals both the horrors of mental illness and how, with patience, it is possible to provide real help.

Robert wore his down parka year-round, not to keep warm but to hide his body. He wouldn't shower for fear of exposing his body to ridicule; Robert had a deformed foot that affected his posture, forcing him to bend and lean over in order to stand up. We regularly provided a look-out in the shower room so he could bathe with the assurance that no one would see him. He was usually silent, but when he talked, we could tell he was educated. Robert had lived on a mattress in an abandoned lot for almost three years; his "voices" told him to live out of doors, but he was often afraid and cold. For a few days one year, he stayed at Savior House, a medical facility for the homeless, but he left when the doctor offered to make a special shoe for his foot. He insisted that there was nothing wrong with him, either physically or mentally; his "voices" told him not to let anyone do anything "to" him.

Robert roamed the streets picking up bits of trash—bottle tops, bits of broken glass, scraps of paper—which he brought as gifts to a volunteer at the day center. He did not ask for money, but on Sundays, he sat on the steps of the church and collected as much as $200 a day, which he "banked" at the day center. One winter when the weather was very severe, Robert refused to use his savings for renting a room or an apartment. During a week when the temperature never went above 10 degrees, a mental health outreach worker was able to convince him to go into a community facility for the mentally ill. When the court appointed a conservator for Robert, we turned over Robert's savings, some $1,800. His funds were in pennies, nickels, dimes, and $20 bills.

The homeless mentally ill are the most likely to be "revolving door" patients—patients discharged before they are ready to live independently and without adequate connections for follow-up care. They often fail to stay well, are readmitted, and discharged again, often to the streets, to repeat the cycle. "After a while, they stop taking their medication, they neglect their nutrition, they let their lives unravel, they become disorganized, and they eventually find their way back to the hospital, to jail, or to the street."[62] Some 20 percent commit suicide.[63]

Some common perceptions about the homeless mentally ill are correct. For example, the stereotype of the ubiquitous "bag lady" is confirmed by research that shows that single homeless women are more likely to be mentally ill than single homeless men.[64] Not often acknowledged, however, is the extent of mental illness among women accompanied by children, that is, homeless families. Although homeless mothers are not as likely to have been hospitalized for mental illness as other homeless women, they are five times more likely than women in the general population to be suicidal and severely depressed.[65]

According to some observers, there are more homeless mentally ill on the streets than there are in shelters;[66] as one remarked, "The streets [have become] an open-air asylum."[67] Sometimes romanticized as "grate people," these street people are often the mentally ill who have been abandoned. Some are refused beds at shelters because of their odd appearance or behavior;

some are so disaffiliated and disoriented that they refuse shelter when it is available; and others may have fallen through the cracks of the treatment system because mental health clinics frequently refuse to treat people who are drinking and addiction detoxification centers often reject those who appear to be mentally ill. These exclusionary practices are especially devastating, considering that as many as 40 to 50 percent of the homeless mentally ill also suffer from alcoholism or drug addiction or both or use alcohol or drugs to self-medicate their psychiatric symptoms.[68]

The combination of substance abuse and mental illness presents particular challenges to professionals and volunteers. Substance abuse by the mentally ill exacerbates psychiatric symptoms and greatly complicates accurate diagnosis, particularly because many behavioral manifestations of alcohol or drug use mimic mental illness, especially schizophrenia.[69]

Gloria carried a disability card verifying her status as a diagnosed schizophrenic— a diagnosis that was made when she was on an alcohol and cocaine binge some years earlier. She was nevertheless regarded as a relatively stable member of the community and therefore a good person to serve as a representative of the neighborhood on various committees. Increasingly, Gloria failed to attend meetings, and when she did attend, she was often close to irrational. As she became less and less functional, her substance abuse problems could no longer be ignored. She lost her job with a community organization, and her friends and colleagues began to feel squeamish when she came around. Eventually, Gloria admitted herself to a substance abuse program, but she was soon discharged because of her continued denial of her addictions. For Gloria, being labeled schizophrenic was far better than being labeled an alcoholic or a drug addict. She returned to the streets, where she was often seen battered, sick, and drunk.

"Dually diagnosed" individuals—those who are mentally ill and abuse alcohol and drugs—have more family conflicts, are more socially isolated and less trusting, and have higher rates of arrest and incarceration than those homeless people who suffer from mental illness but do not use alcohol or drugs.[70] One of the least appropriate resting places for the homeless mentally ill is a jail cell, although many spend considerable amounts of time in jail. Despite knowledgeable reports that the mentally ill are often not violent, their bizarre behavior frightens shelter workers and volunteers who tend to use the police and jails as a last resort.[71] As a result, jails have become the "most enduring asylum" for the homeless mentally ill;[72] according to one report, some 600,000 mentally ill individuals are incarcerated in county and city jails every year.[73]

Although not strictly a problem of mental illness, mental retardation is also found among many of the homeless. According to one study, the rate of adult mental retardation among the homeless may be as much as two to three times greater than that of the general population.[74] The incidence of developmental disabilities and delays among the children in homeless families, a subject to which we will return in Chapter 3, is alarming.

The problems confronting the homeless mentally ill are severe, and by many accounts, the mental health system is not presently designed to offer sufficient help. Some advocates for the mentally ill have called for a variety of reforms and improvements in services so that this disabled population can receive humane and appropriate treatment as well as long-term supervision and care when needed. Here again, action is impossible unless people are willing to acknowledge the severity of the problem and the barriers to treatment. Not only is our society failing the homeless mentally ill now, but it is even less prepared for a new generation of mentally ill young adults, who, as we will show in Chapter 2, are more numerous, more likely to use alcohol and drugs, and twice as likely to commit suicide.

Employment Patterns of the Homeless

Cookie was a homeless alcoholic and heroin addict who bragged about having been in every prison in the United States and who proudly showed the scars from various knife fights he survived in prison. After escaping from a penal halfway house, he lived intermittently with his sister and her four children. When he was drinking or had hustled enough "change" to do drugs, he spent time in the "old neighborhood," sleeping with his buddies in abandoned buildings or in cars. Cookie talked a lot about "getting straight," but he failed to keep his appointments to enroll in a treatment program. Finally, after almost a year of counseling, Cookie entered a city-run detox program but was identified as an escaped prisoner and had to return to prison to finish his sentence. He was released nine months later, clean and sober, and wanted a job so he could pay his sister the rent she demanded as a condition of his living with her. His problem was that in his thirty-five years, he had never worked and didn't have the vaguest idea about how to look for a job or about what kind of work he could do.

In trying to understand the reasons for the increase in homelessness over the past decade, many reports refer to changes in the job market and the high unemployment that accompanied the recession of the early 1980s. In light of the serious disabilities of the vast majority of homeless people, however, it is not surprising that homelessness is not specifically related to employment cycles. Most of the homeless have been without jobs substantially longer than they have been homeless and "have lived on inadequate personal incomes literally for years before becoming homeless. Few of the homeless were precipitated abruptly into homelessness by the loss of a job."[75]

Despite media reports that grossly exaggerate the extent of employment among the homeless, national and local data present a clear picture of their troubled work histories. One-third of the homeless have been totally jobless for more than two years; 60 percent have not worked at all in more than a year; and only 5 percent currently have full-time, steady employment. Heads of homeless families have work patterns similar to those of single homeless people. Those who do work tend to work in unskilled or low-skilled jobs and are more likely to be employed as day laborers or on a part-time basis than in full-time, permanent work. As would be expected, multiproblem homeless adults who live on the streets and those with substance abuse problems or mental illness work less than those with fewer problems.[76] According to one study of more than 1,000 patients in an alcohol detoxification center, most of whom were homeless, 94 percent were unemployed and half reported that their primary source of income was panhandling and hustling.[77]

The Mobility of the Homeless

Just as the term "homeless" inappropriately implies a homogeneous group of people, "homelessness" seems to imply a constant condition; in fact, the living situations of many of the homeless change frequently and the experience of homelessness is different for different subgroups of this population. Three useful categories distinguish between the varied patterns of homelessness: temporary homelessness, chronic homelessness, and episodic homelessness.[78]

Between 10 and 20 percent are temporarily homeless, that is, homeless because of a single problematic event like a fire, a medical crisis that over-burdens an already tight budget, or an economic crisis caused by sudden unemployment. The temporarily homeless are the least disabled subgroup among the homeless and are usually homeless for short periods.

Almost half of the homeless are chronically homeless because of the severity of their disabilities. These people have been homeless for considerable lengths of time. Recent national surveys and a number of local studies report that 50 percent of the homeless have been homeless for almost a year or more and 20 percent have been homeless for four years or more.[79] Single men over the age of forty, particularly those with long histories of alcohol abuse and other health problems, have been homeless for the longest periods—some for up to fifty years.[80]

The remaining third are episodically homeless, drifting in and out of homelessness because of their tenuous ability to maintain themselves in stable housing. We knew many men and women whose patterns of homelessness were typical of the episodically homeless; Slim was one of them.

Slim was always on the hustle to get some change to buy marijuana. He knew he was smart and was sorry he had not taken advantage of the various scholarships he had been offered while he was still in high school. Now, he was, according to his own words, "nothing, a street bum." He lived either on the streets, at a shelter, or with his girlfriend, who shared his drug habit. From time to time, Slim worked and was proud of himself. At one job, he was able to move to a supervisory position after just one month, but he just couldn't keep it together and resigned so he "wouldn't have to face the hassle of [his] boss telling [him] what to do all the time." He tried going to detox a few times, but under pressure from his girlfriend, he would quit and start smoking dope again. He always ended up back on the streets and back on the hustle.

The episodically homeless use shelters or spend short periods of time in transitional housing. They enroll in alcohol detoxification or treatment programs, sometimes as a way of getting out of the cold, and many spend time in mental hospitals and jail, only to return to either the streets or shelters. Homeless people with histories of psychiatric problems coupled with use of alcohol and drugs are the most likely to have recurrent episodes of homelessness.[81]

Families are homeless for the shortest periods of time but are also likely to have recurrent episodes of homelessness.[82] Because shelters and motels are clearly inappropriate living quarters for families, shelter workers are inclined to move families into more suitable housing as quickly as possible. Because there are very few programs that provide sufficient support services, including treatment for addictions, to ameliorate the underlying problems that precipitate family instability and homelessness, however, homeless families are frequently unable to sustain themselves in unstructured situations and therefore become homeless again. According to Ellen L. Bassuk, a leading researcher on homeless families, "Sheltering facilities [are] just brief stops in patterns of instability and family disruption."[83]

In the past, homelessness has been synonymous with transiency, and throughout this nation's history, Americans have been suspicious of transients, particularly when they are economically dependent and make claims on community resources. Today, some local government officials are concerned about attracting large numbers of homeless people from other parts of the country by providing better than average services and shelter. In fact, the research shows just the opposite. The vast majority of homeless people are longtime residents: More than 75 percent have lived in the same city for at least one year, and more than 60 percent have been in those cities for ten years or more.[84] A major exception is younger homeless adults with serious chronic psychiatric disorders who also abuse drugs and alcohol. These troubled individuals migrate from city to city, not so much in search of services or shelter as in search of an escape from their problems.[85] Unlike their earlier counterparts who drifted in search of work or adventure, today's drifters are often the most seriously disturbed among the homeless. We will return to a more complete discussion of this group in Chapter 2.

Our Denial

The downward drift into homelessness, often precipitated by substance abuse, family instability, domestic violence, or mental illness, is accompanied by the loss of family and friends, the absence of work, and perhaps most important, the loss of independence and the capacity to sustain what most people take for granted as ordinary living. Once on the streets or in shelters, the homeless face days and nights filled with uncertainty, alcohol and drugs, mental illness, physical disabilities, victimization, and crime. They become entrapped in a cycle in which they are shuttled between prisons, jails, mental hospitals, and alcohol and drug detoxification units.[86]

And yet, American society maintains its denial, despite the overwhelming and devastating misery. By focusing on the newer additions to the ranks of the homeless, the general public tries to deny alcoholism. Those who sympathize with the homeless avoid the issue of drugs because they do not want to stigmatize the homeless as participating in illegal activity. Although most people acknowledge the fact that mental illness exists among the homeless, they refuse to recognize its seriousness, its chronicity, and the extent of its incidence. The media, and people in general, rarely talk about how sick and physically disabled the homeless are. Finally, since somehow the working poor seem more deserving of sympathy, the media grossly exaggerate the employment of the homeless.

But denial, comfortable as it may be, generates powerlessness. Only when policymakers and their constituents accept the truth—that somewhere between 65 and 85 percent of the homeless population suffer from serious chronic alcoholism, addiction to drugs, severe chronic psychiatric disorders, or some combination of the three[87]—will our society be able to develop programs and services that have any real potential for helping these most unfortunate Americans break the degrading cycle of homelessness.

2

The Baby Boom
and Homelessness

As devastating as the portrait of homelessness described in Chapter 1 may be, it is incomplete. The downward spiral precipitated by alcohol and drug abuse, domestic violence, family instability, and mental illness provides only part of the explanation for the growing ranks of homeless people. There is yet another group of the homeless, one that is large and perhaps the fastest growing. This is the generation of young adults, born in large numbers during the baby boom, who have reached the age for the onset of serious mental illness and whose attitudes and behavior reflect the various social movements of the 1960s and 1970s. Their experience includes homelessness too, but the complex dynamics of their homelessness warrant separate examination.

Between 1946 and 1964, almost 76 million babies were born in the United States. When demographers predicted an increase in births in the years immediately following the end of World War II, no one predicted that the explosion of births would continue for nineteen years and would affect families in all parts of the nation and in all social classes and races. These baby boomers crowded maternity wards, nurseries, schools, little league teams, scout troops, colleges and universities, job markets, hospitals, jails, prisons, and housing; eventually they will overwhelm nursing homes and then cemeteries.[1] Currently, some of them are crowding shelters and soup kitchens serving the homeless.

The Pig in the Python

War babies. Spock babies. Sputnik Generation. Pepsi Generation. Rock Generation. Now Generation. Love Generation. Me Generation. Hippies. Yippies. The Woodstock Nation. The Big Chill Generation. Yuppies. Dinks. Grumpies.[2]

The 75.8 million babies born during the nineteen-year period from 1946 to 1964 represented an increase of almost 53 percent, or 26.2 million babies, over the preceding nineteen-year period. During the nineteen years immediately following the baby boom, almost 66 million babies were born, some 10 million fewer than had been born during the baby boom.

Amazingly, it was the generation born during the years of the Great Depression—fewer in numbers by far but flush with the victory of World War II, made secure by the expanding postwar economy, and excited about the future—who married and gave birth in record numbers. In the eight years prior to the start of the baby boom, on average, fewer than 2.8 million babies were born each year. In the first eight years of the boom, mothers gave birth to an average of 3.7 million babies each year. Then, starting in 1954 and continuing for eleven years until the end of 1964, more than 4 million babies were born every year. When the boom stopped, the number of babies born each year dropped back to 3.8 million in 1965 and declined annually until 1968. Births then increased slightly for two years, and starting in 1971, declined every year until 1973, when they leveled off for four years at about 3.15 million, as shown in Figure 2.1. The steady increase in the number of babies born each year since 1976 is often called the "echo boom," referring to the fact that the baby boomers themselves have started giving birth. As Leon F. Bouvier and Carol J. De Vita have observed:

> The baby boom generation, born between 1946 and 1964, has been called the most "over-defined group of our times." It has been blamed for the nation's ills, credited with its successes, observed, studied, analyzed, and scrutinized by writers, academics, planners, policymakers, business marketers, and the popular press. . . . As America's largest generation in history, the baby boom has reshaped U.S. society.[3]

The baby boom was a population bulge unique in history, and like a pig being swallowed by a python,[4] it moved inexorably from birth through its teen years into young adulthood, challenging American society and its institutions by the ever-burgeoning demands it placed on them. By tracking the baby boom, it is easy to understand the sequential impact these large numbers of people have had on society. For example, in 1950, the 2.9 million babies born in 1945 entered kindergarten. Just one year later, the 3.4 million five-year-olds born in the first year of the baby boom required an additional 500,000 kindergarten spaces. In 1952, the number increased by another 400,000; thereafter, the numbers kept increasing, forcing schools to expand exponentially for more than a decade to accommodate the ever-increasing numbers of children headed their way. The entire elementary-school population grew from 23 million in 1950 to 37 million in 1970.[5] In order to provide space for the baby boomers, thousands of elementary, junior, and senior high school buildings sprang up all over the country. California, for example, opened one new school building every week in the 1950s.[6] Nevertheless, new construction could not keep pace, and double shifts became commonplace. By 1964, the first wave of the baby boomers

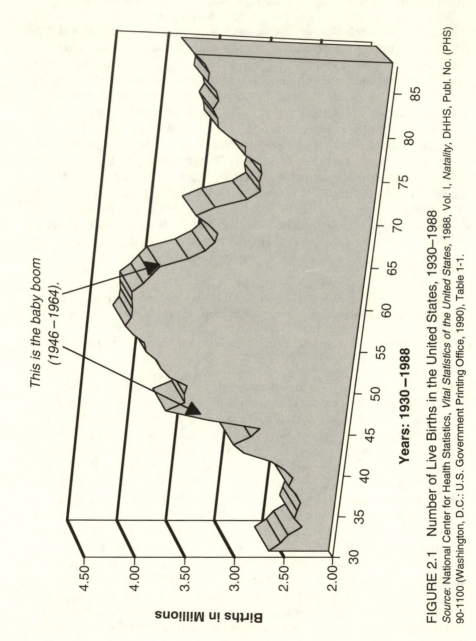

FIGURE 2.1   Number of Live Births in the United States, 1930–1988

Source: National Center for Health Statistics, *Vital Statistics of the United States,* 1988, Vol. I, *Natality,* DHHS, Publ. No. (PHS) 90-1100 (Washington, D.C.: U.S. Government Printing Office, 1990), Table 1-1.

arrived on college campuses, and the American university would be changed forever. Enrollments at colleges and universities grew from 3 million in 1957 to 11 million in 1975.[7]

The aging baby boomers have affected each decade, as shown in Figure 2.2. In 1960, there was an increase of more than 10 million five- to thirteen-year-olds compared with 1950. Ten years later, in 1970, there were two age groups that had grown substantially—the five- to thirteen-year-olds, by almost 4 million, and the fourteen- to twenty-four-year-olds, by more than 13 million. In 1980, the baby boom had aged by ten years; there were 84 million fourteen- to thirty-four-year-olds, an increase of 18 million over 1970. In contrast, the younger age group, the five- to thirteen-year-olds, decreased in 1980 by almost 6 million. In 1990, there were almost 82 million baby boomers aged twenty-five to forty-four.

Just as schools were inundated during the baby boomers' early years, the sectors of American life affected by young adults were eventually overwhelmed by their presence. Growing numbers of people needed to be housed, fed, clothed, employed, ministered to by health and mental health systems, dealt with by the criminal justice system, and for those in poverty, assisted by the social safety net. Given this population growth, the fact that homelessness began to increase by the late 1970s and early 1980s is not surprising, particularly when the term "homelessness" is used as a euphemism for all the ills discussed in Chapter 1. There were simply enormously greater numbers of Americans reaching young adulthood, the age at which people leave their parents' homes, look for jobs, and sometimes become addicted to drugs and alcohol, experience the onset of serious mental illness, and become engaged in criminal activity.

In 1980, the boomers born in 1946 had just turned thirty-four, not coincidentally about the average age reported for the homeless population in the United States in most studies.[8] In each of the eleven succeeding years, the total number of thirty-four-year-olds in the United States has increased. The Urban Institute's 1987 national survey of the homeless indicated that the vast majority of homeless adults were between the ages of eighteen and forty.[9] In 1987, baby boomers ranged in age from twenty-three to forty-one, an almost identical age grouping.

A Generation of Change

The baby boom was more than just a numerical population explosion. As they matured, the boomers were an integral part of the many social upheavals of the 1960s and the 1970s, and many experimented with counterculture life-styles that would eventually lead some into homelessness as the counterculture disappeared in the early 1980s. A full understanding of homelessness today is incomplete without an examination of the social experiences of the

34

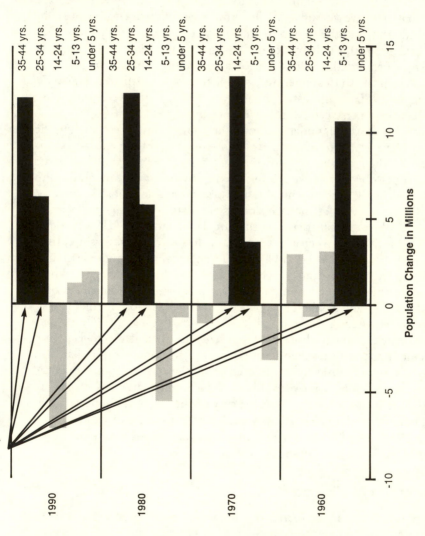

FIGURE 2.2 Population Change by Age Cohort, 1960–1990
Source: U.S. Bureau of the Census, *Current Population Reports*, P-25, no. 1018 (Washington, D.C.: U.S. Government Printing Office, 1989). Table F; U.S. Bureau of the Census, *1950 Census of Population*, Vol. 2 (Washington, D.C.: U.S. Government Printing Office, 1953), Table 94.

baby boom era—an examination that is all too frequently missing in analyses of homelessness.

The social experiences of the baby boom had an unsurpassed influence on society not only because of their sheer numbers but also because of the changes in the ways information was transmitted during their formative years. Television had become the ubiquitous medium of mass communication and, according to baby boom chronicler Landon Jones, "by the time an average child of the baby boom reached the age of 18, he or she would have been under television's hypnotic influence an average of four hours a day for sixteen years. The total of roughly 24,000 hours—one-quarter of a person's waking life—is more than children spend in classrooms or with their parents."[10] Television not only transmitted information and values, it also had the unifying effect of exposing everyone simultaneously to the same events. At the same time, radio, seeking a comeback from its near extinction at the hands of television, discovered that young teens could be mesmerized for hours by radio broadcasts of rock and roll music, and radio "played an important part in extending the peer group, certifying rock lovers as members of a huge subsociety."[11] According to one historian, "for those of us who were ten or twelve when Elvis Presley came along, it was rock 'n' roll that named us a generation."[12]

The transforming messages were many. On the lighter side, baby boomers enjoyed the Mickey Mouse Club, Dick Clark and the American Bandstand, Hula Hoops, Barbie dolls, and the Beatles. On the serious side, they lived through events such as the Cuban missile crisis, President John F. Kennedy's assassination, the civil rights struggles, Martin Luther King's murder and the riots that followed, and, of course, the first "living-room war" in Vietnam. Furthermore, the baby boomers presented the greatest market in history for producers of goods—imagine the necessary explosion in the diaper industry—and they became the targets of strategic advertising campaigns designed to capture their attention and their parents' dollars. They learned that they were powerful, that everyone from parents to teachers, from advertisers to producers catered to their every need and wish, and that their generation controlled and drove both the popular culture and the U.S. economy.

They learned other things as well. Mass production was industry's answer to meeting the needs of a society with huge appetites for the good things of middle-class life—washing machines, refrigerators, Levittown bungalows. For the first wave of boomers, the "leading edge," conformity was the rule: Malvina Reynolds's "little boxes made of ticky-tacky," "Leave It to Beaver" standardized families, and Doris Day behavioral norms. Then, with the launch of Sputnik in 1957, families learned that, despite all the new school buildings and almost universal graduation from high school (a phenomenon unheard of in previous generations), the United States was losing the Cold

War. The U-2 incident, the Cuban missile crisis, and the Bay of Pigs fiasco conveyed the message that the world was a very dangerous place—a fear that was exacerbated on a personal level by regular bomb drills where children cowered under school desks and in hallways awaiting nuclear annihilation.

The political assassinations of the 1960s, the riots, Vietnam, and finally Watergate convinced the boomers as well as their elders that there were serious tears in the fabric of American society. For the baby boom generation, the fear of being drafted was unrelenting, even though only 6 percent of the baby boomers actually served in Vietnam.[13] Hundreds of thousands of youth engaged in antiwar protests, marches, and political activism opposing what many believed was an unjust war. Throughout the nation, boomers were grasping at ingenious and sometimes lawless schemes to evade the draft.

Then, as their older baby boom siblings began to exhaust the available housing supply and job openings, the younger boomers, "the trailing edge," realized they would have to compete with their seniors as well as their peers for opportunities that were becoming less and less plentiful. Raised by doting parents to live in a world of opportunity, cooperation, and reason, the younger baby boomers had to face disappointment, disillusionment, cynicism, frustration, and fierce competition.

On the one hand, conformity, competition, and crowding led to feelings of alienation—from parents, from society, from helping systems, and from the political process.[14] On the other hand, paradoxically, baby boomers, raised in the affluent 1950s and 1960s, had developed a sense that they were entitled to a good life—good education, good jobs, good housing, and protection from want and need. They developed what Landon Jones called "'the psychology of entitlement.' What other generations have thought were *privileges,* the baby boomers thought were *rights*" (emphasis in original).[15] Because of their obsession with these rights, observers and social historians suggest, the boomers moved from the conformist "We Generation" to the "Me Generation." The boomers of the Me Generation have continued to cut a swathe through contemporary society spending their collective resources to satisfy their every desire and using their political influence to change America into the kind of benevolent society they were promised.

Born into an atmosphere of optimism conveyed by their parents, the baby boomers were confronted by a reality of war, deceit, shortage, competition, racial unrest, violence, and fear. They questioned the values and life-styles of their parents; they rejected existing institutions; and starting in the mid-1960s, this same group that had swayed huge markets in gadgets and toys, had supported the birth of rock and roll, and had overwhelmed America in so many ways decided to take matters into its own hands.

The Emergence of the Counterculture

*I am an orphan of America ... I live in Woodstock Nation ... a nation of
alienated young people. . . . My age is 33. I am a child of the '60s.*[16]
                                                                    —Abbie Hoffman

Take matters into their own hands they did; the baby boomers of the 1960s
created a culture that affected all aspects of society, even for those who did
not directly participate. Starting with the sit-ins and the people's park in
Berkeley, followed by a cascade of happenings that included Professor Timothy
Leary's admonition to turn on and tune out with LSD, the 1967 summer of
love, flower children in Haight-Asbury, be-ins, love beads, tie-dyed clothes,
the take-over of Columbia University, teach-ins, antiwar protests, and peace
marches, all immortalized in the popular musical *Hair,* the boomers "dismissed the Protestant Ethic of their parents—hard work, competition, and
material success—[and moved] into tepees and adobe huts and [gave] their
children names like Morning Star. Their friends were their 'brothers' and
'sisters' and all part of the tribe."[17] In 1969, some 400,000 strong, they
arrived at Woodstock, the ultimate be-in, where they openly and defiantly
used drugs, had sex, and produced "400 LSD freak-outs, three deaths, and
two births."[18] Woodstock, for many, came to symbolize the power of the
baby boom. As Arlo Guthrie announced to the world from the Woodstock
stage, this throng of boomers had closed down an interstate highway.
Having done that, they could go on to stop the war and change the world.

   The counterculture was in full swing, and drugs were an important part of
its new ethic. Drug use symbolized rejection of their parents' use of alcohol
as a social medium, open defiance of society's laws, and the hedonism
expressed in the new credo: "If it feels good, do it." By the end of the 1960s,
an estimated 8 million young people were using marijuana, and by 1977,
more than two-thirds of all college students were getting high.[19] It might
have started out as a full-time party; however, like the downward spiral of
alcoholism, drugs were devastating for this generation.

> Too many kids were taking off on trips and not coming back. . . . They disap-
> peared into a deepening wilderness of drug use—acid, hash, peyote, angel dust,
> PCP—and only occasionally reappeared to tell us of the wonderful things they
> found there. Others lost their inner maps; either they never returned at all or, if
> they did, they might as well have not been there. Every baby boomer has a
> friend or two from school who did not make it back and wound up dead or
> effectively lobotomized by drugs.[20]

This youth movement combined radical politics, adolescent rebellion,
experimentation, and a frantic search for a new identity. In the late 1960s
and the 1970s, hippies, yippies, and flower children, some of whom were

returned Vietnam veterans, lived in parks, communes, and often under the stars. They were frequently on the move in *Easy Rider* style, knowing they could always find a place to "crash," where others from their generation would give them shelter. If today's term had been used then, these young people would have constituted a major part of that period's homeless population.

Then, in the late 1970s and the early 1980s, the baby boomers started turning thirty. For most, their "prolonged adolescence"[21] ended and they began to marry, get jobs, settle down, and start families. As the counterculture began to disappear, however, not all of its members were able to let go of their alternative life-styles, their drugs, and their wanderings; these are among today's homeless. The counterculture, having changed the way much of society looked and acted, was disappearing, and the most disillusioned, most troubled, most traumatized, and most mentally and emotionally disturbed of the baby boomers gradually found themselves exposed, no longer able to hide among their peers.

In the media and other forums, it is often reported that today's homeless people are different from the typical "skid row bum," the white male wino of years past. The homeless of the 1980s are younger and better educated than those of decades past and include more women and minorities. These additions to the ranks of the homeless include two identifiable groups. First, many are baby boomers who "lost their inner maps" or who are mentally ill, often dually diagnosed as showing symptoms of mental illness and alcohol and drug abuse. Second, many are members of the impoverished underclass, single men and women as well as single-parent families. In the remainder of this chapter we examine the first group; homelessness and the underclass is the topic of Chapter 3.

Despite differences between these two groups, they share many characteristics of their generation. They grew up in a crowded society but nevertheless developed a sense that they were special and that, if they had needs, society, through programs emanating from the Great Society and the War on Poverty, had a responsibility to address those needs. They participated in the evolution of the counterculture and the drug culture that permitted, in fact encouraged, alternative and deviant life-styles including remaining single, coupling, having children outside of marriage, living and traveling in communal groups, using drugs, romanticizing psychedelic or "out-of-body" experiences, and just being different—in clothing, in hairstyles, in naming their children, and in rejecting the values of their parents' generation.

Chronically Mentally Ill Young Adults

Although it is difficult to estimate the precise number of mentally ill young adults,[22] researchers agree that this is one of the fastest-growing segments of the disabled population in the United States. The increase is due to the simple fact that aging baby boomers have now entered the age range, from eighteen to forty-four, when the onset of schizophrenia and other serious and chronic mental illness is most prevalent.[23] Nevertheless, by combining recently published data about the prevalence of mental illness in the United States and census information, it is possible to estimate their numbers.[24] Since 1964, when the first baby boomers reached the age of eighteen, the U.S. adult population has increased exponentially. The greatest increase added more than 20 million people to the ranks of those at risk between 1970 and 1980, the same years during which homelessness began to come to national attention. A 1990 study of mental illness in the United States estimated that some 22 percent of the population would suffer from some form of mental illness, excluding alcohol and drug abuse, during their lifetime and that 1.5 percent of the population would suffer from schizophrenia, the most severe and disabling mental illness.[25] By applying these findings to the increases in the at-risk population, we calculate that between 1970 and 1990 there may have been an increase of some 8 million people suffering from some form of mental illness, including an increase of up to 500,000 schizophrenics.

An increase of this magnitude in the number of people suffering from mental illness, by itself, would have severely taxed the existing system of mental hospitals and treatment facilities for the mentally ill. However, not only did the mental hospitals not expand to meet the growing needs, they actually did the opposite. Just as the first baby boomers began to enter their teens, public, inpatient mental health treatment facilities were being systematically decimated. Between 1955 and 1985, more than 442,000 beds in state mental hospitals were eliminated—80 percent of the 552,150 beds occupied in 1955.[26] It has become conventional wisdom that deinstitutionalization led to increasing homelessness in the 1980s; however, what is even more important for our consideration is that, just as the huge at-risk cohort of baby boomers reached the age for onset of mental illness, most of the inpatient facilities for treating mental illness had already been closed. For the exceptionally large numbers of baby boomers with psychiatric problems such facilities have never been available *at all*. As one writer has said, "They are a new generation of mental patients, a generation that, in the optimism of the 1960s, was to be the beneficiary of nontraditional, noninstitutional, and nonrestrictive care."[27]

The Dually Diagnosed:
A Major New Problem

The counterculture, with its widespread tolerance for alcohol and drug abuse, its encouragement of bizarre behavior, and its norm of mobility within and between communities, had a profound effect on this new generation of mentally ill young people. Initially, in the 1970s, these troubled baby boomers were able to blend into the counterculture, even though they were "judged by other street people to be delusionary, unpredictable, and unreliable—in the lexicon of the street: 'burned out,' 'fried,' or 'spaced.'"[28] But as the counterculture disappeared during the 1980s, they lost their "cover" and became part of the visible new homeless.[29]

> *Paul was wired when he came to the day shelter. He had just been released from the city's twenty-eight-day inpatient addictions program. Even though the year was 1988, his outfit was reminiscent of the 1960s: headband, beads, tie-dyed shirt and all. His curly red hair was tied in a ponytail and looked badly in need of washing. He was thirty-five years old, a college dropout who had started using drugs (LSD, marijuana, and later cocaine) when he was in high school. He spent some of his time in Vermont and some in Colorado, where he had loose associations with friends and girlfriends, one of whom was the mother of his six-year-old daughter. He talked about the winter when he slept in Chicago's train station and how paranoid he was during that period—sure the commuters were government agents ready to imprison him for his political ideas. He had come to Washington to participate in a political demonstration, "freaked out," and was arrested, either for his strange behavior or for the bad stuff he was on—he didn't know which. Offered drug treatment by the judge, Paul eagerly enrolled rather than go to jail. When he was released he was frantic. He still craved cocaine, but he knew he needed to stay away from the drugs in the streets and in shelters. He objected to any suggestion that he might consult the local mental health center. "I'm not crazy," he said, "I just need a place to stay." He had no money and nowhere to go; he became homeless.*

The baby boomers experienced mental illness in very different ways from previous generations. Viewed through the lens of the "antipsychiatry" movement, which suggested that there was no such ailment as mental illness,[30] many baby boomers saw treatment for mental illness as an attempt by a repressive government and society to subdue people who had a higher consciousness than others and a greater ability to act in response to their natural impulses. Books and movies like Ken Kesey's 1962 book *One Flew over the Cuckoo's Nest* and Philippe de Broca's 1966 film *The King of Hearts* promoted the antipsychiatry notion that psychotic behaviors were actually a "sane" response to the Establishment, whose role it was to turn everyone, cookie-cutter style, into conformist replicas of the most mundane and passive elements of society. Consequently, chronically mentally ill baby boomers tend not to define themselves as mentally ill or as patients, preferring to view themselves as victims of a repressive society and often believing that psychotic episodes are the proverbial "bad trip."[31]

Simultaneously, ideas of self-determination and participatory democracy molded the patients' rights movement in the image of the civil rights and welfare rights movements. As we will explore more fully in Chapter 9, several tenets of the patients' rights movement—such as the right to treatment in the least restrictive environment and the right to refuse treatment altogether— have had the effect of denying to many of this very large cohort of mentally ill boomers exactly the kinds of psychiatric treatments that were being developed to permit treatment outside of institutional settings.[32] Lacking treatment, either because of their own refusal to seek or accept it or because of their inability or reluctance to follow medication regimens, many of these young mentally ill patients use drugs or alcohol as a way of self-medicating to help them cope with hallucinations and alleviate the anxiety and stress associated with their mental illness. Substance abuse also provides them an opportunity to participate in the continuing drug subculture of their age mates, which in turn helps them to see themselves as normal and to deny their illness.[33]

Stuart R. Schwartz and Stephen M. Goldfinger presented a case report on an individual who represents a "prototype of the new chronic patient," one who is bitter and angry and who feels "that the mental health system can't help him":[34]

> Mr. R is a 27-year-old white male who was brought into the psychiatric emergency services by the police after he was found wandering in traffic. Police said he appeared intoxicated and angry, yelling at them to mind their own business. His angry behavior persisted at the emergency services. . . . He has been seen eight times and hospitalized three times during the last year. . . . During several visits he was intoxicated on alcohol, marijuana, or both; on one occasion he was flagrantly delusional following ingestion of PCP. After three of [his] more serious suicide gestures . . . he was referred to a day care program but dropped out after three days "Because I don't belong with those crazies." . . . After two visits [to the day care program] he began missing scheduled appointments and dropping in at odd times. When his therapist was unable to see him during one of these drop-in visits, he screamed at the secretary that no one really cared, knocked over a vase, and walked out.

Dual Diagnosis and Homelessness

Alcohol and drug abuse combined with mental illness creates a matrix of problems that often includes homelessness; 10 to 20 percent of the nation's homeless are dually diagnosed.[35] Described by clinicians as being in constant crisis, the dually diagnosed are extremely disorganized.[36] They experience difficulty maintaining simple daily living routines, including maintaining regular meals, managing money, sustaining regular activities, keeping appointments, maintaining personal hygiene, and maintaining social supports. As a result, they have difficulty maintaining stable housing and drift in and out of homelessness, and they tend to be homeless for longer periods of time than other subgroups of homeless people. They are extremely dependent, but not wanting to see themselves as being ill, they deny their dependency, refuse treatment, and run away from intimate relationships, including therapeutic and helping relationships. They are often drifters, moving from community to community or within the community in search of autonomy. They invoke the "geographic cure" as a way of denying their dependency and avoiding the "system" at large and the mental health system in particular. Because of these behavior patterns, the dually diagnosed are unlikely to be employed or employable, and lacking money, they are often unwelcome and frequently evicted by family and friends. The dually diagnosed are more likely to engage in violent and criminal activity than other homeless people. Moreover, the suicide rate for this group is more than three times higher than that of the general population.[37]

The new population of mentally ill young people has presented formidable challenges to psychiatric helping professionals. They often resist treatment and "are as likely to blame mental health professionals as they are to turn to them for help."[38] Often labeled as problem patients who are demanding, manipulative, hostile, and unresponsive to treatment, they "confound all . . . treatment efforts, . . . take emergency workers and your other treatment people and run them in circles for many hours and many days, so that staff reaction to them is basically a lot of anger and frustration."[39]

Substance abuse impedes every aspect of care for the mentally ill, complicating diagnosis, interfering with treatment, and increasing the likelihood of relapse. Misdiagnosis of psychosis induced by substance abuse is not uncommon and can only be verified by observing patients over a period of time. Clinicians report cases where patients' symptoms of severe mental illness have disappeared after the patients have stopped using alcohol or drugs for extended periods of from nine months to a year or more.[40]

There are very few helping programs able to cope with the intertwined symptoms presented by the dually diagnosed. These individuals are difficult to keep in shelters because of their aggressive and sometimes violent behavior; they are difficult to treat in mental health facilities because of their denial and because such facilities often exclude people with alcohol and drug problems; and they are difficult to treat in alcohol and drug treatment programs where their psychotic behavior marks them for exclusion. They are often discharged from all of these settings only to be arrested for aberrant behavior on the streets.

The dually diagnosed are truly system misfits. Because their behavior is so reminiscent of the counterculture, however, many people tend to think of them as "old hippies" and accept their aberrant behaviors as throwbacks to the 1960s—a decade about which many Americans now have exaggerated and romantic ideas. The problem, of course, is that they are more than "old hippies." They are severely troubled people who in former times would have been hospitalized for their mental illness. Now, too often, our society leaves them to their own devices to live in tent cities, in shelters, on city street grates, or to spend time in jails and prisons.

By denying the seriousness of their illness, our society does them no favor. Their extraordinarily high suicide rates corroborate this fact. Those who encourage the belief that they are no different from their peers constantly help set them up for failure. As one group of researchers has written:

> Their persistent lack of success in achieving the goals that are socially appropriate to their age—education, mating, a steady job—does set them apart in their own despairing perception, not as patients or impaired people with special needs, but as social failures. Viewing themselves as "just like anybody else," they have to experience, again and again, the pain of difference, the despair of failure. They take refuge from this perception by acting out, by aggressive outbursts, by taking drugs, by taking to their beds, and by blaming and raging against their parents, their landlords, their therapists, the police, the hospital, and society.[41]

Despite the difficulties involved, there are innovative strategies for providing services specifically designed to help this population. Robert E. Drake and Michael A. Wallach have made a convincing case for providing appropriate treatment early. They reported evidence that, over the course of twenty to thirty years, many severely mentally ill patients will stabilize, improve, and even recover; however, the young mentally ill are significantly at risk for behaviors that could cause their deaths before their illnesses have run their course. As Drake and Wallach wrote, "Since all these problems are related to dual diagnosis, it seems fair to conclude that substance abuse constitutes a major threat to the long-term adjustment of the chronically mentally ill. Yet substance abuse may be the most treatable and controllable of these patients' problems."[42] These innovative strategies are discussed in detail in Chapter 10. As in the case of the other disabling conditions affecting homeless people, this nation must first acknowledge the complex problems of chronic mental illness accompanied by alcoholism and drug abuse before it can develop programs that are of real help.

3

Family Homelessness and the Underclass

By the mid-1980s, not only had the baby boom swelled the ranks of chronically mentally ill young adults, but a new confluence of economic, social, and demographic forces was beginning to shape what has come to be known as America's urban underclass. Whereas the counterculture was primarily a white phenomenon, the emerging underclass was primarily black.[1] Homelessness has become only one of the many problems faced by this large group of very poor and very alienated people.

Poverty and the Underclass

Among the important social achievements of the baby boom era was the success of the civil rights movement and Great Society programs that provided increased opportunities for African American middle- and working-class individuals. Doors to education and training, professional jobs, and housing in middle-class neighborhoods and suburbs, long closed, slowly began to open.

According to William Julius Wilson, noted scholar of the underclass, these very successes had the simultaneous and unintended consequence of dividing the African American community. Many people were able to move out of what had been racially segregated but economically and socially integrated communities where community institutions, churches, social clubs, and extended families served as vehicles for communicating values and mores to all who lived within the community. Those left behind were the poorest, least able members of the community, who now became isolated in economically *and* racially segregated ghettos where few, if any, positive options or role models remained.[2] Neighborhoods that once mixed poverty and deprivation with social and economic vitality are now plagued by the loss of strong community institutions and of viable local economic activity. Whole city blocks are filled with burned-out and boarded-up buildings, many of which are used as crack houses or havens for other illegal activities. Perhaps most destructive, in dilapidated inner-city schools—where teachers are often

44

overwhelmed by students who need special resources that are frequently not available—low expectations lead to miserable student performance, failure, high drop-out rates, and an attenuation of the relationship between education and future opportunity.

These communities suffer from high concentrations of families living in poverty who have established long-term and multigenerational welfare dependency. High crime rates are the norm, as are underground economies fueled by drugs, prostitution, and black markets in goods of all kinds. Most disturbing is the daily body count of young African American men who are victims of drug wars, gang killings, and the hunger for material possessions so perverse that children kill each other over $100 sneakers and $20 drug debts.

The social isolation and poverty of those left behind has been made even more desperate by changes in the national economy. As the U.S. economy changed from an industrial to a service economy, more education and training were required for even entry-level jobs. At the same time, manual labor was being replaced more and more with automation. As Fred R. Harris and Roger W. Wilkins have written:

> If one had to choose the single most potent factor behind the growing misery of the ghetto, it would have to be the momentous economic transformations that have *undermined the manufacturing base* of central city economies. . . . Those very blue-collar jobs upon which poor minorities are most dependent for steady employment and economic sustenance have disappeared by the hundreds of thousands, leaving behind what is for them an economic wasteland (emphasis in original).[3]

As inner cities deteriorated, residents of these wastelands became victims of a nation unable to cope with what appeared to be ever-expanding misery, joblessness, poverty, crime, drugs, alcohol, and connected with all of these, homelessness.

Concomitant with economic stagnation, poverty, and isolation, young people of the ghetto have developed an overwhelming sense of hopelessness. Children are teased unmercifully or physically beaten if they do well in school; it is not "cool" to get good grades. Young women give birth to babies when they themselves are little more than children and are overwhelmed by their responsibilities as mothers—responsibilities for which they are grossly unprepared. They soon lose all sense that their lives can improve and cease to believe that they can escape. Confronted by an unwelcoming work force, young men find that job opportunities are few, and those unskilled jobs that do exist often require inhumane hours and long and expensive bus rides to suburban construction sites. The jobs produce little income, no benefits, and often racial harassment. The alternative is the magnetic world of the drug economy and at the end, for all too many, a bullet or an overcrowded jail cell.

The value of human life takes on a whole different meaning in this environment. Unlike the nation's response to the Great Depression of the 1930s when people virtually stopped having babies, in today's depressed inner cities there is an extraordinary increase in births. Many speculate that, in a society otherwise devoid of fulfillment, young men father children as a way of affirming their manhood and young unmarried women have babies to give them something to love and to produce love in return. Regardless of the underlying reasons, the dramatic increases in teenage births, out-of-wedlock births, and single-parent families are all closely related to the persistent poverty, dependency, and disconnection from mainstream society that define the underclass.

The Underclass and the Baby Boom

A first step in understanding the growth of the underclass requires us to take another look at the baby boom. According to Wilson, "Much of what has gone awry in the inner city is due in part to the sheer increase in the number of young people, especially young minorities."[4] The same bulge that occurred in the general population from 1946 to 1964 occurred in the inner cities among African American women. What is remarkable is that, in contrast to the overall demographic pattern, the dip in African American births in the years immediately after the baby boom was followed by another increase so sharp that current annual African American births are higher than at any point during the baby boom, as shown in Figure 3.1.[5]

Accompanying the increase in black births were two other important phenomena: the rise in the number of single-parent families and the increase in the number of poor families. During the 1980s, single-parent African American families as a percentage of all African American families increased continuously, reaching almost 42 percent in 1983[6] and 51 percent in 1988;[7] many of the births are to teenaged mothers. The relationship between single-parent families and poverty is well established: single-parent households have a median income less than half that of two-parent households, and 64.7 percent of all poor families with children are headed by a single parent, usually a woman. One measure of poverty in America today is that 72.3 percent of African American children are supported by Aid to Families with Dependent Children (AFDC) at some time before their eighteenth birthday.[8] Poverty research during the past fifteen years has produced considerable evidence of long-term intergenerational welfare dependency by women born into single-parent families. Daughters of single mothers are more likely than those with two parents to have children early, including having children out-of-wedlock, to divorce and become single mothers themselves, and to receive welfare.[9]

Compounding the picture are the statistics of crack addiction among pregnant women in U.S. inner cities. According to Elizabeth Graham, New

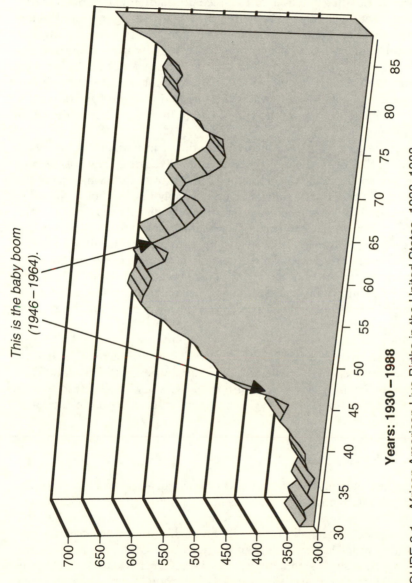

This is the baby boom
(1946 – 1964).

Years: 1930 – 1988

FIGURE 3.1   African American Live Births in the United States, 1930–1988
Source: National Center for Health Statistics, *Vital Statistics of the United States, 1988,* Vol. I, *Natality,* DHHS, Pub. No. (PHS) 90-1100 (Washington, D.C.: U.S. Government Printing Office), 1990, Table 1-1.

York City's assistant health commissioner, cocaine abuse among that city's pregnant women has increased by 3,000 percent since 1985 when crack became available.[10] Researchers have reported that the consequences of crack are "decimating the lives of low-income children and families in the inner cities. Young children are entering the lucrative drug trade and falling prey to its violence. Fragile families that are often held together by only the mother are being destroyed as more and more mothers are lured into addiction."[11] According to a congressional report on troubled children, between 1986 and 1987 there was a 90 percent increase in the number of newborns having drug or alcohol withdrawal symptoms, and in one urban county, 80 percent of all children under the age of one in foster care had a history of drug exposure.[12]

In addition to the violence surrounding the drug trade on the streets is the violence that drug use inflicts on children. Reports of child abuse and neglect have accelerated. So too has the need for foster care, which has risen so dramatically that foster parents are often simply not available; when this happens, hospitals have no choice but to release addicted newborn babies to their addicted mothers. Unfortunately, what has not increased is the number of drug abuse treatment facilities willing to admit pregnant women or women with children. According to estimates compiled by the National Association of State Alcohol and Drug Abuse Directors (NASADAD), of the 250,000 pregnant women nationwide who needed treatment for drug abuse during fiscal year 1989, only 12 percent received it,[13] even though the cost for intensive medical care for a cocaine-exposed newborn is estimated at $100,000.[14]

The picture that emerges is devastating. The rise of births to single or unmarried women and teenagers, particularly poor African American women, is profoundly linked to long-term poverty and to the intricate web of dependence, unemployment, violence, and drug addiction in the inner city.

Family Homelessness

As in the case of drug addiction, those who are advocates for the homeless are wary of discussing the underclass in relationship to homelessness—particularly family homelessness—for fear of losing popular sympathy. This reluctance is understandable, especially given the various negative descriptions of the underclass in the recent literature. Descriptors such as "social pathologies in ghetto communities,"[15] "antisocial behavior,"[16] and "*behavioral* deficiencies"(emphasis in original)[17] are commonplace, and critics object that "underclass is a destructive and misleading label that lumps together different people who have different problems . . . and . . . is the latest of a series of popular labels . . . that focuses on individual characteristics and thereby stigmatizes the poor for their poverty."[18] Many fear that, by discussing the relationship between homelessness and the underclass, they will undercut public sympathy for the homeless in general and for homeless families in particular.

As Jonathan Kozol wrote in his very popular and award-winning book about homeless families, *Rachel and Her Children:*

> Why are they without homes? Unreflective answers might retreat to explanations with which readers are familiar: "family breakdown," "drugs," "culture of poverty," "teen pregnancies," "the underclass," etc. While these are precipitating factors for some people, they are not the cause of homelessness. *The cause of homelessness is the lack of housing* (emphasis in original).[19]

However, Kozol's failure, like that of so many others, to make the connection between substance abuse, marginal living conditions, family disruption, and homelessness will only delay the development of services and programs that truly help very troubled and disadvantaged people. Although the growth of the underclass and the increase in births to unmarried women, many of whom are teenagers when they first give birth or addicted by the powerful lure of crack, are not perfectly correlated with the increase in family homelessness, these phenomena are closely related. The most troubled, dysfunctional, and isolated of these underclass families are among the new homeless.

Disaffiliation
Among Homeless Families

The rapidly growing preponderance of homeless families has received extensive media coverage. Statistically, 10 percent of all homeless households are families, that is, adults, most frequently single women, accompanied by young children.[20] Minority homeless families predominate in inner cities,[21] while white homeless families are more prevalent elsewhere. The average age of mothers in homeless families is twenty-seven, and most lack high-school diplomas, have poor work skills, and are long-term recipients of AFDC, although their rate of participation in federally subsidized benefit programs and AFDC is often lower than that of nonhomeless poor women.[22] The pregnancy rate for homeless mothers is higher—by perhaps as much as three times—than for the general population.[23]

Although homeless families bear a striking resemblance to "underclass" families, membership in the underclass is by no means synonymous with homelessness; there are many more families in the very poor and isolated inner cities of America than there are homeless families. What, then, is the difference between the impoverished families of the underclass and the single women with children who use the shelters or motel rooms set aside to house homeless families? Just as we saw in Chapters 1 and 2, it is the extent of personal social isolation of homeless mothers that distinguishes them from their domiciled underclass counterparts. This same phenomenon of disaffiliation differentiates all homeless people from the domiciled poor. According to David Wood and colleagues, "The dire economic plight of homeless families must be viewed in the context of their social isolation and their more severe legacy of personal distress. . . . Economically, both [homeless mothers and stably housed mothers are] extraordinarily vulnerable, but the homeless [have] distinctive histories of personal and family trauma."[24]

Authors of several major studies of homeless families paint consistent and frightening portraits of the social isolation of homeless mothers—social isolation that results from histories of family violence and disruption and that, in turn, is repeated in the next generation.[25] As many as two-thirds of homeless mothers grow up in broken homes, where alcoholism and drugs often lead to physical and sexual abuse and where family turbulence is common. In addition, there is an "extraordinary over-representation" among the homeless of individuals who as children have been in foster care, another indication of weak family ties.[26] As they grow older, homeless mothers repeat the patterns of their parents, entering into abusive relationships with alcoholic and drug-addicted men who beat them and often abuse and molest their children. According to one study, more than a third of the homeless mothers reported being abused as children and more than 25 percent of them now had "open files" themselves of child abuse and neglect charges.[27]

Josephine had five children. After the birth of the first two, she had moved from her hometown, hoping to start a new life with the children's father. It turned out that nothing changed because they both continued to drink too much and to use drugs. On two different occasions, Josephine almost killed two of her children; she told us that she tried to drown one in a bathtub and seriously cut the other with a kitchen knife. When the authorities declared her an unfit mother, she swore she couldn't remember hurting the children; nevertheless, both of these children were removed to foster care. When Josephine moved back to her hometown, she came to us for employment counseling.

At first, it was not clear whether she had a drinking or drug problem; what was clear was that she would not go for job interviews that were arranged for her. She revealed that she was very much afraid of being rejected, even though the employment counselor was very careful to arrange appropriate opportunities. Gradually, she came to trust us and began to tell her story. Her alcoholic mother had abandoned her as a young child and she was raised alternately by two aunts whose husbands or boyfriends sexually abused her. She was overwhelmed by feelings of shame and guilt and was sure that no one could value her enough to give her a job. Without a job and without a steady male partner, Josephine had meager resources to care for her three remaining children. Josephine had lived in a family shelter for more than two years.

Summarizing the trauma of childhood abuse found among homeless mothers, Ellen Bassuk, an authority on family homelessness, stated, "The resultant chaos profoundly affected the early development of many of these women, particularly those who had lost both parents when they were very young. . . . With such histories of family disruption and instability, it is understandable why some of these women are now having trouble establishing themselves as independent adults."[28] In addition, as a result of this disruption, homeless mothers can count on supportive parents only half as often as poor single mothers who are not homeless, and 50 percent of the mothers in one study could not identify any adult on whom they could call for help.[29]

Another consequence of the "resultant chaos" is a frequent pattern of residential instability. In comparison to poor families who are stably housed, homeless mothers change residence substantially more often and experience cycles of homelessness that include shelters, hotels or motels, doubling up with relatives or friends, and in a few cases, sleeping in cars or on the streets; during the year prior to homelessness, the pattern of instability often worsens.[30] Many homeless mothers have been evicted from their apartments for nonpayment of rent; others have had to leave their living quarters because of the break-up of a domestic relationship, because of physical abuse, or because of family disagreements resulting from overcrowding.[31]

Wanda was mentally retarded and was in a special education program for pregnant teens. Just before she gave birth to her first child, she came to the day center for help finding maternity clothes. The social worker tried to give her much more, including basic education about sex, pregnancy, and childbirth. Wanda became part of the church-based program for women and children. When the baby came, he was baptized at the church, and Wanda and her son were "adopted" by church members who gave freely of their time and energy. With their support, Wanda was reconciled with her sister and was able to move into her sister's small, but clean, apartment. Despite the efforts to teach Wanda about how she became pregnant the first time and to describe how having another child would make her life more difficult, Wanda became pregnant again, still not quite sure how it happened. When her second child was born, her sister told her to leave the apartment, saying it was too small for another baby. The best the social worker could do was to find a family shelter where Wanda could stay.

According to a service provider in Philadelphia, going to a family shelter has become almost a rite of passage for single mothers. They used to go from their mothers' houses to public housing. Now, they seem to see shelters as a way station before getting into public housing.[32] In fact, government housing policies giving preference to families with the severest housing deficits give an advantage to "homeless families" over other families on waiting lists for subsidized housing and may have the unintended consequence of encouraging use of shelters.[33] According to an official of a large public housing authority in the Washington, D.C., area, "It is almost impossible for families who are poor but not homeless, even those who have been on waiting lists for years, to get into public or subsidized housing because of the point system designed by the federal government to give priority to homeless families."[34]

In addition, homeless mothers acknowledge that they tend to have many sexual relationships, especially with alcoholic and drug-addicted men, some of whom are mentally ill and many of whom are unemployed. They also tend to have more children than nonhomeless poor mothers. One 1989 study suggests that pregnant women on welfare are nine times more likely to become homeless than nonpregnant women on welfare.[35] Their multiple partnerships expose them and their children to sexually transmitted diseases—especially, and increasingly, AIDS. Finally, crack addiction has become epidemic among homeless mothers, with some reports indicating that the majority of all sheltered mothers have crack addiction problems;[36] Fischer and Breakey reported that homeless mothers have drug abuse problems four times more often than poor mothers in homes;[37] and the New York City Commission on the Homeless reports that 42 percent of homeless mothers have substance abuse problems or are mentally ill.[38]

Most troubling are the devastating effects of these various factors, including homelessness itself, on the children in homeless families. Most of the children are five years old or younger. In New York City, for example, 75 percent of homeless mothers have at least one child under six and 47 percent have a child under two.[39] Children suffer a variety of serious difficulties: They tend to be shy and withdrawn; they have eating and sleeping problems; they have health problems and are delayed in language, social, and motor development; and they show evidence of depression and anxiety. School-aged homeless children have spotty school attendance, even though most are enrolled in school.[40] According to one study, the vast majority of these school-aged homeless children are either failing in school, are in special classes, or have already repeated a grade.[41] Family violence is a major factor in the emotional lives of homeless children. A California study reports that some 50 percent of homeless mothers who were interviewed said their children have witnessed them being beaten, while almost the same proportion reveal that they themselves abuse their children.[42] Not surprisingly, homeless children tend to be severely withdrawn or intensely aggressive; they are often violent and angry and "act out" to gain attention. A nurse who regularly visited a welfare motel told us about some of the families she saw and about the violence to which children were regularly exposed.

Jamie and Janine were usually hiding behind the bathroom door when she visited the shelter to check on the family. They told her about the man who came to their motel room and how frightened they were when he came. They said their mother acted funny when he came; sometimes she made them stay in the bathroom; sometimes, even when it was cold, they had to stay outside in the parking lot. Sometimes their mother hit them when he was there, and they didn't like that. Once after the man had been there, their baby brother wouldn't wake up and they heard adults saying that the man had killed the baby because the baby had cried too much. When she examined them, the nurse knew that they were afraid she would make them shave their heads like the boy from next door—the one who couldn't go to school because what he had was catching. Jamie and Janine didn't like school; everything the teacher said was very confusing. But they liked school better than the motel room. It was too dark in the room to play, so most of the time they just sat. Not even their mother played with them.

As would be expected, homeless children suffer more frequent and more serious bouts of illness than other children, including frequent colds, head lice, respiratory disorders, and childhood diseases.[43] Unfortunately, homeless children rarely receive either the medical attention they need or the inoculations that could prevent serious illness.

Another frequent phenomenon related to family homelessness is drug addiction among the children, often, as we reported above, starting at birth. In studies of homeless children, drug abuse is found to start at an early age and to increase as the children get older. A congressional report found that:

> Alcohol and drug abuse are appearing very early. We're seeing nine- and ten-year-old kids who are heavy drinkers and are beginning to abuse crack. These kids are abusing everything that's on the street. . . . [T]hey're grabbing at drugs that have as a direct toxic effect, hyperactivity and violence. . . . They need treatment.[44]

Despite all the problems that homeless children suffer and their mothers' inability to provide adequate care and support, the mothers are wary of seeking help, especially for substance abuse and domestic violence, for fear that their children will be taken away and placed in foster care. Substance abuse treatment programs designed to keep mothers and children together, even during treatment, are needed, as are significant improvements in foster care systems. Separation from parents under traumatic circumstances results in fragile psychological development and problems in making the transition from childhood to self-sufficient adulthood;[45] moreover, as we noted above, histories of having been in foster care are common among the homeless—children in foster care are more likely than other children to become homeless as adults.[46]

Despite the overwhelming evidence linking homeless families to the pathologies of the underclass, it would be a mistake to conclude that all homeless families are impoverished or are members of the black urban underclass. Some are white, some are rural, some come from the ranks of the chronically mentally ill;[47] in one study, some 40 percent of homeless women in shelters were battered wives, many of them from the middle class.[48] Nevertheless, the interrelated problems of homelessness and the underclass cannot be overstated.

Denial and the Underclass

Wilson suggested that the problems of the underclass have been largely ignored "because many of those who represent traditional liberal views on social issues have been reluctant to discuss openly, or in some instances, even to acknowledge the sharp increase in social pathologies in ghetto communities."[49] Forewarned by the furor in response to the highly controversial 1965 Moynihan report on the disintegration of the black family, policymakers who could have focused on ways of addressing the emerging problems of the underclass chose instead to avoid such troubling and divisive issues. Similarly, in the 1980s, when homelessness among families became an important item on the national agenda, policymakers and others continued to avoid making the connection between these families and the underclass.

The consequences of understating the matrix of profound problems confronting homeless families, particularly those from the underclass, are disastrous for those families. The overly optimistic belief that homeless families are "temporarily down on their luck" leads to inappropriate placement in independent housing (or transitional housing with minimal services), which all too often results in total failure and the return of these families to shelters in worse condition than before. The New York City Commission on the Homeless reports that "placing thousands of homeless families, many of whom had only recently entered the shelter system, into permanent housing appears to have contributed to an enormous surge of families [re]entering the system in the latter part of 1990."[50]

More disturbing, the staff in most shelters and not-for-profit transitional housing programs are not prepared to work with very disturbed families, especially those with addiction problems, and many such facilities establish careful screening procedures that exclude such families. By perpetuating the belief that homeless families are just ordinary people, we fail to create appropriate services staffed with people who have sufficient training and expertise to give the kind of help that is needed. Instead, our denial has the effect of leaving the most needy and desperate mothers and children with little or no help at all.

The Homeless of the 1980s

The "new homeless," the homeless of the 1980s, are in fact different from the typical white male "skid row bums" of years past. They are the baby boomers—those who "lost their inner maps" to drugs in the 1960s and who suffer from serious and persistent mental illness—and they are members of the urban underclass, who like their domiciled counterparts live in abandoned inner-city neighborhoods where crime, violence, crack, and extreme poverty appear to erect impenetrable barriers to a better life, but who also have experienced abandonment, terror, and violence in their personal lives. They are "battered wives" and "throwaway" children of all races and classes whose worlds have been filled with alcohol, drugs, and the violence that is so connected to these substances. And, because of the baby boom, there are great numbers of them.

As America has confronted the increase in the "new homeless," its public and private institutions have tried to respond to the perceived needs of the homeless with shelters, soup kitchens, emergency and transitional housing, and "ambulance services," as we will show in Chapter 5. The response, however, has been enveloped in denial—denial of the real problems confronting the homeless, denial that ultimately exposes them to continued poverty, illness, imprisonment, and sometimes early death.

4

A Homeless Man's Story

This is the story of a man we call Franklin. We first met him in 1987 when he came to our center asking for groceries. Franklin told us he was nearly forty years old and unemployed. Impressed with him, we hired him as a part-time worker. When he started working for us, we were not aware that he was living at the city-run Pierce shelter in Washington, D.C. He told us only after he had left the shelter to live either with his mother or in an abandoned house. Eventually, Franklin saved enough money to rent a room in a boarding house, but even though he worked at two low-paying, part-time jobs, he found it difficult to accumulate sufficient funds to make a rent deposit on an apartment and to pay child support for his eleven-year-old son. In the meantime, the boy lived with his maternal grandmother and Franklin spent as much time with him as he could. Franklin's dream was to rent an apartment for himself and his son.

In the spring of 1989, Franklin agreed to tell us about life as a homeless man as a basis for this chapter. What follows are Franklin's words, which we taped during six hours of interviews with him.[1] The places described here are in Washington, but conditions are comparable to other cities.

There Wasn't Always a Place
I Could Go to Lay Myself Down

People would always say, "If you pay, you can stay," but I really couldn't pay rent anywhere. I was going through hard times at home with my family. It was crowded there, my mother and I were on bad terms, and she was telling me that I had to move. Sometimes I would go back to the garage where I had my clothes. There was a car back there, and sometimes I would end up sleeping on top of the car or inside the car whenever I could get into it without causing a disturbance. At one time, I was staying in the basement in my aunt's house, but I got into an argument with one of my cousins, and my aunt said, "Well, you will have to leave." Or, I had a cousin who had an apartment, and I would go there, but he would cause so much confusion until it was best to just go back to the streets. There wasn't always a place I could go to lay myself down just to get some rest.

I started sleeping in the neighborhood park because it was warm, rather than going to a shelter because I knew basically how they were. I would get a blanket and I would just camp out there. A lot of guys would hang out there during the summer listening to music, riding bikes, throwing Frisbees. Then at night, they would plug the TVs and radios up to the [electrical] box to save the batteries until the park police would come by and put a lock on the box. Then guys would break it open and plug their stuff back up again. I kind of, like, fitted in with them off and on for a month, a month and a half.

In the park, you got a lot of guys, gay guys, that come around and try to fondle you if they caught you laying there. So I said, "Well, I'd better try another alternative—get out of the park and just try a shelter." I didn't like it, but, you know, it was a bed. At first, I ended up on the streets for a couple of nights. As it started getting colder, I ended up going to the shelter because I just didn't have any particular where to go.

I Felt Like My Pride
Had Been Stepped On

I went to the Pierce shelter because it was in the neighborhood and within walking distance from the jurisdiction that I would normally be in. I didn't have to worry about bus fare or anything like that, and I basically knew what time the guys lined up from walking past there before I became homeless. I said to myself, "I hope I will never end up in this situation." And it just so happened, one of those nights I did.

The first time I felt like this is not me. I felt like less than a man, that something was wrong, that it just wasn't supposed to be this way. In other words, I felt like my pride had been stepped on. But then, I had to push my pride aside and say, "Well, you are either going to be on the streets or in here," so I had to take it on the chin and stand in line.

Sometimes there were fifty or sixty guys in line at one given time, and the line would wrap around the building. There was jostling in the line and people got in fights. A lot of the guys were very hostile because they were drug addicts and alcoholics. By the time they got to the shelter, they would be drunk, rowdy, fussing. They would make it hard for a guy who was just standing there trying to get inside. Tempers would flare and the security guards were armed—they were just waiting to shoot somebody. I've seen guys get rassled around with pistols at their heads. The guards would say, "Don't nobody move," and he's got this gun on everybody. I've seen old guys that really couldn't help themselves get knocked down by one of the security guards, and it didn't make sense. They really treat you rough down there. So I made up my mind that there weren't going to be too many nights that I was going to be coming down there, just the nights that I had to get out of the cold.

Hey, You're in My Bed

They would let in groups of fives. They would say "Five more, five more." Once you got inside, they had a guy sitting at a desk who would take your name, date of birth, social security number and ask you if you had been there before. I never could understand why they would ask the same questions every night, even if a guy would see you there five or six nights a week. "Have you been here before?" You would say, "You just saw me last night," and they might say, "I can't remember everybody coming in here. Just give me your name and address and don't give me no crap or else you're going back outside." So you would say, "Yes sir, my name is so and so, my social security number, my date of birth, and yes, I did stay here last night." They'd say, "Okay, next."

To get a really good bed, you'd have to be there by six o'clock. After 8:30 or 9:00, you were almost certain you could get into the shelter, but you wouldn't get a bed. They wouldn't turn you away. They would tell you that it was crowded, that they didn't have any more beds, but that if you wanted to take a chair, you could, or if you wanted to sleep on the floor, you could. A couple of times, a guy would come in with his buddy, and he couldn't get a bed and he didn't want to sleep in the chair. He'd say, "Man, look. You sleep down at the bottom and I'll sleep up at the top." They'd end up sleeping in the same bed together. Sometimes, you might see three guys in one small bed. They were tight.

Some guys would come there early enough to get in and they would tell a guy, "Look, I got somewhere to go. I'll be back." The other guy would say, "As long as you're back in before eleven, I'll hold your bed for you." You had guys that had lived there for five years, and they were regulars. Some of the regulars would get the same bed every night, regardless of whether they got there on time, even though you're the next guy in line for that particular bed. If you wanted one of their beds, you would end up getting in an argument—"Man, this is my spot," or "Hey, you're in my bed"—and you would say, "Look, you weren't here," and that would cause a fight. Or I would say, "Man, that's ridiculous. I'm here and I need a bed, and I'm trying to go to sleep. So and so will just have to get another bed." That's how the system worked. So, a lot of time, I would say, "Well, hey." I would just walk the streets half the night until daybreak. You have to go through a lot of flack until you got tight with the guys and they started calling you on a first-name basis, then you were in. Until then, you just had to put up with the crap.

Some Real Treacherous People

There was no age limit for the guys they took, and I've seen guys come in as young as fifteen or as old as seventy. Some guys were really intelligent, some very illiterate. You had some real nice people, and you had some real treacherous people in there. We had everything from murderers, thieves, to guys that had committed all kinds of crimes. You would never know until you actually overheard someone or got into a conversation with one of them. There were brilliant, intelligent guys there, guys that had degrees and they had been married, had families; they were down on their luck. I saw guys with briefcases, books, and they were still going to school. Some held jobs. But for the most part, guys there were illiterate, couldn't even read the newspaper.

Most of the guys there really looked like someone who pretty much spent time standing on the corner. They didn't take time to shave. Maybe they had a skullcap or something like that pulled down over their face. They didn't take a lot of care about their overall appearance. They never took the time to even bother to wash their jeans.

There were a few handicapped guys there. If there were any types of barriers there, they would suffer because the shelter provided nothing in terms of helping these guys get around. They didn't have wheelchairs, lifts, or ramps; the poor guy might be in a wheelchair or had one leg and he pretty much had to get along on his own with crutches or canes or walking sticks.

Soup or Beans

Once you got up there and got your property secured, if you could get it secured, you would go downstairs and get a meal. A lot of guys would try to get a meal first, but you couldn't do that. You had to go check into your bed, because if you came back upstairs after eating and your bed space was gone, that was your loss. You got a meal, but then you haven't any place to sleep.

If you didn't leave anything on your bed when you went to eat, that was grounds for somebody to come in and say, "Well, he's not here." So they would be laying on your bed, even though you had been assigned that bed. Sometimes I would leave a newspaper or a blanket, if I found one. If I had a backpack with my stuff in it, I would wrap my stuff up in my blanket and put it underneath the mattress. Most of the time, I would go in with a guy that I knew, and I would say, "Look, you stay up here and watch the beds, and I'm going to eat." So we had a little buddy system.

Once you got your bed, you go downstairs to the little cafeteria that would seat about twenty to thirty people at a time. Sometimes, you might get homemade spaghetti or chicken or some sort of piece of meat, but for the most part, it would be soup or beans. It was edible and nutritional. We all ate in shifts. Most guys would try to get to the shelter early because you could get in, get your bed, and get downstairs, and that meant you probably got a better proportion of whatever they were serving. It was first come, first served. A lot of guys didn't eat, because the food was gone. Some guys just don't bother eating, "I'll pass, I'm tired. I just want to lie down." And they would do that. But for the most part, guys would be so hungry that their main objective was getting something to eat as well as getting some sleep. Sometimes people try to get fed twice.[2]

If You Rolled Over, You Might Be in the Next Guy's Bed

Pierce used to be an elementary school. They had three floors that they would bed you down on. I think there were possibly five to six classrooms on each floor, and they used every one of those rooms on each floor for beds and even the hallways. Where they couldn't get beds, they would have mattresses piled up on top of each other where you could take one. I would say there were anywhere from twenty to thirty beds in each room. You would always like to be in the middle, because those beds were a little wider than the other ones. The majority of them were like little bunk beds, like little cots. You could touch the next bed easily. If you rolled over, you might be in the next guy's bed. It was real tight space.

For the most part, when you went in, there would be a bed with a blanket or a sheet, not both. In some cases, there wasn't a blanket or a sheet. If there was neither, you tried to find one or you would ask the monitor, "Is it possible for me to get a blanket or a sheet?" Nine times out of ten they would tell you, "What's there is there." Sometimes, you were lucky enough to go into another room before it got filled and find a blanket that was on another bed. A lot of guys would take the blanket from the night before, fold it, and stick it underneath the mattress. If they got that same bed the next night, nine times out of ten that blanket would be there, because most guys weren't smart enough to look underneath the bed.

There Was Blood on the Sheets

After you go to your bed, you dust it off, spray it. Most of the guys brought some kind of spray, because there's lice, crabs, bedbugs everywhere. They used newspapers to wipe the mattress down. The first time I was there, I couldn't understand what was going on. Guys would be flipping this mattress over and wiping it down for half an hour. Then, it dawned on me, "There's a lot of bugs in here." One morning, I woke up and I was scratching, and I had to go down to D.C. General to get some stuff to get the body lice off my body. You put it on and kept it on for about ten minutes and really washed it out with soap; then you had to take a comb and just comb the lice out. It worked pretty good, because you could see them falling off you. The stuff was good, but it smelled horrible. After that, I would sleep in my clothes, like long johns or sweat pants. If you just slept in your underwear, you would almost be certain to wake up scratching.

I carried the stuff with me every time I went in there. You could also put it on the bed, because it would kill lice instantly. I always carried my newspaper and wiped the mattress down. They wouldn't change the sheets or the blankets. They wouldn't wash them. If you went in there and you got a blanket, it was probably a blanket of somebody that was so filthy that after you put it on, you're going to wake up with a rash or something—it's pretty unsanitary in those places. There was blood on the sheets. If it were a white sheet, it would be filthy. You might see some blood stains that came from an infection or something like that where a guy would take the sheet and just wipe the blood away—that's common. You always got a sheet that someone had slept on, wrinkled, soiled some kind of way. The only thing you could do was to shake it out and turn it over. Some guys would try to bring a blanket of their own in there; I've done that before.

In most cases, you needed a blanket to stay warm, because it got real cold if you weren't by a radiator. But sometimes, it would be so hot by the radiator guys would try to open the window; if it was stuck, they would just break the window to have some ventilation. There were a lot of broken window panes in some rooms. In some cases, there might be a pane broken out in each window all the way around the room, and they might have a piece of cardboard stuck there.

Whoosh, Right out the Window

There was only one bathroom for the whole place, downstairs in the basement, next to the little cafeteria where you eat at. It was just one bathroom for all these guys. There were six urinals on each side and five stalls which were always full of defecation, which made it virtually impossible for you to sit down. You got guys that had lice, crabs, so you didn't want to use it anyway. They had a shower, but a lot of times it would be cold water. You had a lot of gay guys in there, so that was a problem—you stand in the shower, and a guy would just stand there watching you all the time, and you are trying to figure out what type of time he's on.

Pierce was a place that I never took a bath or showered, because the bathroom was so filthy. I always put newspapers or something down on the floor so I could stand outside the bathroom where there was a sink. I would wash my face and maybe under my arms and brush my teeth there. And if I had to do anything else, I would go someplace else, like McDonald's or a gas station, or go down to the hospital and take care of all my hygiene problems.

If you got up in the middle of the night and had to go downstairs, you better take all your property with you because if your buddy's not awake, it's going to be gone when you get back. So this means you had to wake up, put your shoes on, then grab your bag, your blanket, go downstairs, then come back upstairs. You might tell the guy that was monitoring the floor, "Hey, Mike, I'm going to the bathroom and I'll be right back. Can you see that nobody gets my bed?" "Well, I can't be responsible." When you get back, somebody would be in your bed, and you'd say, "Hey, Chief, this is my bed." "Your name ain't on this bed. I don't see no property here." So that causes static.

Sometimes, when guys upstairs had to go to the bathroom, they would stand up, open the window and say, "I'm not goin' downstairs" and then whoosh, right out the window. "It's going to hit the ground anyway." Or they get a cup and go in the cup and throw it out the window. It was pretty rough.

You Act Up and We'll Put You Outta Here

After the security guards got everybody in and bedded down, they would be making noise all night long, keeping us from getting sleep as much as the guys on the inside. Some of these guys would bring portable TVs, and they were out in the hall just having a ball. If you say something about it, we don't count; they're out there trying to make their eight hours. "Go to sleep. You act up and we'll put you outta here." They have that authority. If someone got out of hand, the security at the shelter would call Metropolitan [the police].

Employees of the shelter didn't care about the guys. "Ah, it's so and so. You, over there, I know where you're at. Get outta my face." That's the kind of attitude they carried. The gay guys and some older guys were the ones that really caught it, because no one seemed to care for them. You would be saying to yourself, "You're going to get old one day. Do you want somebody treating you like that? Who are you? Who died and left you in charge?" But you have to go through stuff like that.

Shelter was like prison. You had security—the security guards were armed with .38 Smith and Wessons, nightsticks, and handcuffs—and they would basically control everything. They told you what to do, how to do it, because if you got out of hand, they would have the authority to lock you up or put you out of the shelter, and you didn't want to get put out on a cold night. A lot of the men that were in there were on escape or fresh out of jail. So that was the attitude and the mentality of the shelter. The atmosphere was like being locked up, because they ran it the same way.

This Ain't No Hotel

Mostly, it was chaos, because everybody had full stomachs and were still high off whatever they had, so everybody wants to talk and yell and scream all night long. "Hey, what's happening? What's up, doc?" It was really like a convention, just sitting around and laughing and joking. And guys are coming in with stereos and rowdy radios and playing them all loud, and that wasn't allowed. Also, some of them would have a boom box, and they would blast that until the lights went out. It was like that every night. You go out and say, "Hey, security, can you come in and tell this guy to turn the radio down?" and then you would be called a snitcher and a fight might break out. So they end up moving you to another floor. Or you would say, "Be quiet so I can get some sleep." "So what, man, this ain't no hotel. Go somewhere else." And this went on every night.

There was a policy about lights out—nine o'clock. Between nine and ten, they would say, "All right, quiet down." Then they would close the doors and turn the lights out. That meant that if you had a radio on, you had to turn it off. You could be reading a book and the book might be interesting, and all of a sudden it would be lights out and there was nothing you could do about it. A lot of times, once the lights went out, somebody would get up and cut them back on, being funny. That would wake up everybody.

I would say about half the guys in the rooms and the hallways were high on something. A lot of them would wait until the lights went out and, if they had anything that they had snuck in, like wine or weed, they fired it up right there and smoked it. That kind of thing happened almost every night. They had a little system where one guy would sneak the wine in, one guy would sneak the weed in, and they would all try to get a bed in the same corner together, and then there would be a little party. Some guys that came in were tired, and they would try to get some sleep; but there would always be one bunch of guys on each floor that would always keep the confusion going.

Other guys would sneak stuff in just so they could have something to sleep off of, like the end of a bottle—it might be vodka, wine. If they caught you trying to sneak a bottle in, they would give you a choice, "Pour it out and you can stay or you can take it and leave." The guard would say, "I know you got that bottle in your pocket." "Man, I ain't got nothing." They go through this thing, and all of a sudden the guard says, "What you wanna do?" A lot of guys would say, "Look, man. I got to have that. I'm leaving." So they take their bottle and leave, even though it's pretty cold out there; and they were not allowed back in that night.

A lot of guys were on heroin. If they could get what they called their "works," their needles and stuff, they would sneak them in and they would go down to the bathroom to get water to melt the stuff down. Then they had to get the little tops to draw it up into the syringe. They would shoot the stuff, and then you would find hypodermic needles all around the floor. You knew they weren't IV needles for diabetics, so you just put one and one together, and you know that they're doing it all down there. I never saw a guy shooting up in the rooms upstairs, but you might go into a stall in the bathroom, if you thought it was clean, and a guy might be sitting on the stool, taking his arm.

AIDS was an issue at the shelter. The guys would bring it up. The monitors would mention it because they were fully aware that a lot of the guys were drug abusers. They had literature about AIDS that they would post on the walls about bleach. And they'd be telling the guys what they were up against in terms of sharing needles.

Usually, because of all the chaos, I got to sleep about one. At five o'clock they were waking you up, so I got sound sleep for three to four hours. A lot of guys probably got more because their whole objective was to come in there and go straight to sleep as soon as the lights went out, regardless of what was going on. If a guy was ripped on something, it was automatic that he got more sleep. I felt if I got some rest and I laid my head down somewhere where I felt halfway safe, I could get up and make it the next day.

These Guys Needed Treatment

There were some mentally ill guys, really crazy. Some guys would holler in their sleep, and some guys didn't communicate—they didn't respond to anything. Guys would talk to themselves and would think that they were animals, things of that nature, so you knew right away that something was wrong with them. There was one guy in particular. Every night, this guy would come there with a stack of books. He was always dirty, from head to toe. He never bathed, he never did anything. Every night he would just come in and talk to himself. You would find some guys who would just sit up and beat their heads on the walls.

I guess they were guys who just had nowhere else to go other than the shelter, and people just didn't detect the fact that these guys needed treatment. Every night, whatever floor you were on, there would always be some guy in there that had something wrong with him that was noticeable. You might have two or three in one room, two or three on the same floor. Sometimes, they became disoriented where the guards would have to call the police or paramedics and just get them out one way or the other. I don't know if they got sent off to St. E's [St. Elizabeth's, a mental hospital], but somebody would come, and they would eventually leave. We had a lot of people in there that had been released from St. Elizabeth's before time; a lot of them ended up there at the shelter. Guys were in there that shouldn't have been in there, but they had no place else to go.

Also, guys used to get physically ill in the night, usually seizures from drinking, and they'd go into convulsions. Guys would say, "What's wrong with him? He's laying on the floor, going crazy." Others would say, "Hey, there ain't nothing wrong with him; he's just flipping out." They would just leave him alone. But, I've seen it happen before, so I could identify with it.

"The guy's having a seizure. Go over and tell the guard that the guy's having a seizure. Get the paramedics." The paramedics and ambulances would come roughly two or three times a night.

We Got Our Man

If guys had committed a crime, the shelter was an easy place for them to go. They would run to the shelter, and once you thought everything was quiet, the police would end up coming in and cutting the lights on, shining a light in your face. "We got our man." I've seen them take a lot of guys out of there. Guys had just snatched a pocketbook and had come right in there with the pocketbook and the money. If it had happened in the area, it would just be a matter of time. The first thing the cops would do, they would check all the shelters. A lot of guys were parole violators, or they had just committed crimes earlier in the day. It was easy for those guys to just go into a shelter.

I've always wondered whether they took the information about social security numbers to enter into a computer to cross check. I think a lot of times the cops identified somebody that had done something through their social security number. They could just run down this sheet and say, "Oh, yeah. He's in room 36."

In terms of weapons, it was not so much guns but knives. Guys would pick up knives and play with them at night—homemade weapons, shanks, knives. I never saw any knife fights, per se. I heard that people had gotten stabbed, but I've never known anyone that got shot. Somebody gets stabbed or cut just once, and they sleep with a shank in case something comes up. That was their penitentiary mentality, you know. A guy would get any type of sharp metal object, file it down, and you could strap it together with a piece of wood.

A lot of the guys were on the run, hiding out in these shelters. They would give aliases, but you could tell where they were from. At night they would sit around and tell you. "Well, yeah, man. I was with the Crips in California, man. I killed so and so, you know what I mean?" Your ears are always open, and you look over and you say, "Yeah. Get the make on this guy." And this guy's saying, "Yeah, man. I'm from Chicago. They got a contract out on me and I can't never go back to Chicago." It was common every night that they would tell their stories: "I can't never go back to Chicago"; "I can't never go back to California." From coast to coast, you've guys who've done stuff and run off and hid. On any given night, I would say, roughly 30 percent of the guys were from out of town and 70 percent were probably from around the D.C. metropolitan area, maybe two or three guys were from the neighborhood. Some of the guys would even go there because their parents were threatening to put them in detoxification.

If You Carried Yourself Like a Man, You Would Survive

There were a lot of advantage-takers in there, guys that take cigarettes from other guys, or take your money, or something that they saw like a jacket or whatever you had—your watch, your ring. There'd be guys who'd be weak, who wouldn't try to speak up and wouldn't try to defend themselves or wouldn't try to get some help or tell anybody; the advantage-takers would just prey on these guys. It's sort of like in the penitentiary—you go to jail, a guy's weak, you might get some guy to do your laundry for you, and there's nothing the guy can say. Guys would say, "Yeah, well I got one here." They were targeted for sexual harassment, and they would get things taken from them. As for the others, they would stand up for themselves, "Hey, man, why don't you take your noise somewhere else?"

One time they stole a kit with the shaving cream that I had gotten from down at the Salvation Army. That was about it, so I didn't do too bad. I always tried to find somebody outside in the yard before I went inside. It was regular that I would run into a guy that I knew, that I went to school with. He and I would always manage to get in line together. It made it easier in the shelter, so guys didn't rip off your things. If you had a buddy sleeping in the next bed, you could carry on a conversation, until you both just dropped off. You'd try to listen as long as you could, just to bide time, and eventually everybody else would doze off so you'd know you were pretty much the last one to go to sleep. That way, your property was safe, unless somebody starts wandering in during the night. It was common for somebody to get up and try to find something that didn't belong to him.

A lot of guys slept with their backpacks under their heads. It's the conditions of the shelter, the guys waiting for you to go to sleep so they could take something of value or take your blanket. If you stay awake longer than the rest of them, you were pretty much safe. I felt sorry for the older guys that ended up on the floor with the younger guys, because they would take advantage of them. They would take their canes, crutches, anything. That's the kind of attitude that they had; it was pretty rough. You turn your back, and your things are gone. Then, you wake up in the morning, your jacket's gone, and your boots are gone. It might be 32 degrees outside, and they might be the only pair of shoes you had, and they're gone. Somebody says, "He ain't going to miss 'em." They take your boots and anything else. That was one of the biggest problems at the shelter, thievery.

When I got my first or second paycheck from the church, I ended up buying a pair of shoes. I went to the shelter one night and a guy looked down at my feet and said, "You're doing pretty good, aren't you?" And I said, "Well, I got paid." Then I said to myself, "I don't suppose I better wear these in here," so I stuck them in my bag and wore my tennis shoes.

Some guys pretended to be really stupid. "Hey, man. You're a crazy duck." Guys see that, and they don't mess with him. "I ain't to be messed with. I'm good and stupid, so don't bother me." All his property was right there, and you wake up in the morning and everything is there, because that's the mentality he gave up in there. If he catches you, man, he's going to hurt you. I was afraid once. This big guy came in there and he was all twisted up, and he said something about my bag. I said, "Man, this is not your bag, and I'm not moving." I was afraid, but I had to maintain my manhood or they would automatically take advantage of you. For the most part, if you carried yourself like a man, you would survive.

Other than that, the only other time that I felt threatened was when a guy approached me for sex. And I said, "Man, look, it's not that type of party." There was a lot of homosexuality in there. Another time, a guy just got in bed with another guy and started having sex with him. There was this one guy in particular who would come there just for that particular reason. They knew this guy was gay; they would put him on one floor and he would go to another floor and then he would work the bathroom, anywhere where he thought he could approach you. It would always be the same guy, but there was more than just one guy in there. Then guys would be in there masturbating once the lights went out. The guards couldn't catch everybody. My gosh, it was open with that; there'd be two, three guys like in the same bed. "Hey, man, why don't you put your blanket over you or something if you want to do that?" It was wild. So there were all types, I mean all walks of life in there; the good, the bad, the ugly, you name it, and they were there.

Someone Started Rattling Your Bed with a Stick

When I was at the shelter, I always tried to wake up about 4:30 or a quarter of, because I knew that by five o'clock they would put the lights on. If you were sleeping and someone started rattling your bed with a stick, you might jump up swinging or something. To avoid that, I tried to be up and out of there. Also, I wanted to get a jump on the hot water at the little sink downstairs. I would wash up real good, and then I was out of there. There were no meals in the morning. All they would do is tell you, "It's time to go." The guards would go out and come back with a nightstick and start banging on the bed. If that didn't work, they would snatch you up out of the bed. If guys are drunk or in a stupor, the guards would just drag them out in the mornings. For some of the real old guys that are really bad off, if it was really cold, they would let them stay in all day long. But if you're young and able-bodied, you're getting out of there. You could come back that evening, but you couldn't stay there during the day, you couldn't hang around.

When you're at 2nd and D,[3] you could stay there all day long. You don't have to leave out of there at all. Guys were always talking about 2nd and D. I don't know what the requirements were to get in there, but once you got there, those guys pretty much could do anything. You could go there, stay there all day long, go into the day room and drink, gamble, get high, you could purchase your drugs there, and the guards would act like they never saw it. Guys said that you can go down and see a guy sitting there smoking coke in broad daylight and they didn't try to hide it. The only thing these guys would go out for was to get some air or to try to bum some money. A lot of guys there were running from the law for crimes they committed in other cities. So you had everybody from drug pushers to murderers to any kind of escaped cons that had jumped bail staying down there. A lot of guys that had gotten out of jail and didn't have any place to go would go straight down there.

I thought about going to 2nd and D a couple of times, and then I started hearing stories, and I decided I didn't really want to go there—Pierce is bad enough. Pierce was like a jail because of the way it was run, but 2nd and D was worse because most of the guys that came from penitentiary ended up there. Their mentality never changed, so they carried the same attitude in the shelter that they carried in jail—the homosexuality, the whole bit. Something could happen to you there, and nobody would ever know. I heard stories about people getting killed there. So I told myself that I'm not going there; you set your life on the line there. At Pierce, you could feel your way around and get by.

As It Got Close to Six O'Clock, I Was Pretty Much Safe

Starting around four o'clock, you could almost always hear the Tracy Labor guys coming in and saying, "Anybody come and work?" That's pretty much your alarm. Guys would say, "I got till six, I'm not getting up yet." Tracy Labor was mostly construction. Sometimes, you might get an inside job in a hospital, folding sheets or work[ing] in the laundry. I never went out, because they would tell you that you would get paid five dollars an hour, and you'd actually get paid three or four. It was cheap labor in a labor pool. You would get your money at the end of the day, but if you lost the ticket that they gave you, then you didn't get a check. Then, you would be stranded way out somewhere in Reston, Virginia, and couldn't get back to the District.

They wake you up at five and you've got to be out at six o'clock. It's five o'clock in the morning, and it's dark and it's cold. That woke me up in a hurry, but it was pretty hard, too. Once you roll out, you knew you had to go somewhere until McDonald's opened at six. So I started walking around to warm the muscles up. I might go over to my stepfather. He was always up at 4:30, so I could always go there. For him, it was no problem, because he and I got along. It was my mother I had the problem with. So I knocked on the door, and he would get the coffee on and give me a cup. I would go get the paper and head toward McDonald's. That was like a custom. I planned each move that I made in terms of my time. As it got close to six o'clock, I was pretty much safe.

By six o'clock, you can go to any hospital which has a bathroom and wash up or you could go to McDonald's and use the bathroom and wash up. A lot of guys would go to D.C. General Hospital—it was within walking distance. For those who had bus tokens or bus transfers and could get around, they would go to the Harrington Hotel or Union Station. Places like that were pretty much wide open spaces in terms of washing areas. Guys like to go somewhere where they weren't much noticed, like in a bus station or train station where people always go all alone and do things like that. If you went to McDonald's and a guy came in and caught you, they could set on you for loitering, especially if you had the lock on the door.

If I had some change, I would go to McDonald's, get a cup of coffee because they had refills. If I had enough change, I would buy a biscuit or egg sandwich or something like that and then I would get my day started, look at the classifieds and start looking for jobs, and read the paper for maybe twenty minutes, something like that. By that time, the buses are running and, if you didn't have money, you could go to a subway stop and find a transfer. That's how you traveled, unless you had money to travel with.

You Just Got Change from That Hamburger

Guys did several things to hustle money. Most of them would panhandle. They'd go to Union Station and beg for money or they would stand on any corner where a subway was and beg for money. Some guys I know would go to Union Station, get one of those carts, and put it back on the rack and a quarter comes back. So you get about ten of those under you and you got drinking money, something to eat with. There used to be a guy near Union Station; he really got a lot of people. He would walk up to you with a Maryland driver's license, saying he was stranded up here in D.C. from Annapolis. And people would go for it. And they would go into their pockets because he showed them this Maryland driver's permit. That was a great scam.

Then you've got guys that have cups. I've seen one lady that would come to McDonald's and just stand there in front of the counter with her cup. Not only would she ask you for money, she would practically harass you. "Do you have any change?" "No." "Well, you just got change from that hamburger," and she would create a real mess. You would say, "Would you get this woman out of here?" She's standing there with a cup full of money, I mean she's got dollar bills over here, change over there, and she's got a cup in front of you.

Then you got people with the signs. I've seen the guys that all they do is sit there with the sign and just say they want you to read the sign, and at the end they just got a prayer or "God bless you." And I've seen another guy who carries a thing like when you go in a gas station and he washes dirty windshields. A lot of people do windshields for a dollar or two.

My Check Comes
on the First of the Month

Or some guys would tell me, "You get in the shelter here, you can go to public assistance and they will give you a check." The shelter is a place to stay rent free. "My check comes on the first of the month, my [food] stamps come after that." Sometimes, the checks would come to the shelter or some of the guys would have them come to a place like SOME [So Others Might Eat, a nonprofit agency in Washington]. All their personal mail would come to SOME. They were pretty smart; they would get their mail at SOME and they cash their check and blow their money and come right back and wait for the next check to come. These are stories that I heard, and there are guys that I know have done that.

See, a lot of them had their schedules already set. "I get up from here, I head for SOME for breakfast. From SOME I go to this place for lunch. After I eat lunch I'm going to the park, and drink my wine. By that time, it's five o'clock and I'm back at the shelter." That's how their day was planned. They went from one place to another where they could always get something, so there was never a need for them to seek employment or anything of that nature. They got the best of both worlds.

Certain guys don't want to go anywhere. Old guys that are on crutches or canes couldn't go anywhere; they would lay around on the ground all day long with a piece of cardboard just drinking, sometimes just drinking themselves into a coma. They didn't go out to hustle money. They could count on folks bringing something back. It's cold, and they figure, "We drink this, this will keep us warm." I guess a lot of them weren't aware of the fact that they were really killing themselves. From the accounts that I read in the paper, I would try to explain to them, "That's not helping you, right?" "Aw, what do you know?"

Depending on what areas you were traveling in, there'd be guys selling drugs. Some guys would go out with someone they knew who was dealing drugs; they would go to a drug area and sell dope all day long, make five dollars off of each bag that they sold. One guy I knew used to run a barber shop that was near a drug strip. You might go in there just to hang out and they were trading drugs for haircuts; you see a lot of money pass hands.

Hanging Around

When I wasn't working, I kind of palled around with guys that were drinking or getting high. If you hung on the corner, you end up drinking wine, vodka, whatever the guys have to offer. I wasn't so much of a drinker, but being in that environment you kind of like go with the flow. You say, "Well, what the heck." Other than that, I was trying to get money for traveling the next day or to go to the laundromat to wash up the clothes. I might be out there panhandling myself. Some days, I spent half of the day hanging around guys that were drinking, smoking, shooting craps on the corner, peddling drugs, or just chatting with the ladies that might come by. Other than that, you could go to the rec center, play ping pong, shoot pool, and play basketball in the indoor gym. Whenever the pool opened up at the E Street Market you go to the pool, anything like that to keep your mind occupied. So I used to do that or go to Lincoln Park, try to get a blanket or a radio, and just chill out.

If it was real cold or it was raining, I knew I could go over to the house of people I knew, sit around, and they might offer me something to eat, or you might go to listen to the radio, to some music. Quite a few times, I went down and called somebody at a government office that I knew from when I was working for the government. You go down and kill time and see if they had heard anything in terms of jobs. I had a network of friends and I could go visit them. I kept a phone book. I could always call and say, "Hey, what're you doing? I'm comin' down that way." I would usually try to keep some change for phones, and if you don't have carfare you could always get a transfer at any subway station. Then, just catch the bus and get right on downtown somewhere. For those guys who didn't have a network of friends like me, most of them would just hang around in the neighborhood, and it would be the same old thing every day. You get up, you come out, you try to panhandle for some change to get a drink, and that's what you did all day long.

You see guys that you knew and you say, "Like, man, it's been a little rough. Can you help with a buck?" Some guys would say, "Well here, man, you don't owe me this." Sometimes you might net five or ten dollars. You would take that five or ten, and this would last me a couple of days; that way, I won't have to get back out there tomorrow. I knew a couple of guys who were working, and I could go to them and say, "I'm in a bind, can you let me have something until things go better?" and they would. By the time I got on my feet, I would go back and say thanks. They would say, "Ah, man, I knew you would turn around, and what are friends for?" In between, for the most part of it, you had to be out there with the rest of them, panhandling.

Then there was this Kentucky Fried Chicken right on the corner of Pennsylvania Avenue. I got to know the manager in there. He would let me sweep the area down, and then sometimes after that he would give me a box of chicken, a few biscuits, and a soda. A couple of times, he's given me money for it. So I got in the habit of going around there every day to see if I could get five or ten dollars from doing that. That was my traveling money. The other days, I would go to the library, or downtown, or to my mother's house to see if I had any mail, or to the employment office to see if they had anything like training programs open or any type of job. You could kill time like that. Especially if it was cold, you just wanted to have somewhere to go.

Usually, I ate at Kentucky Fried or McDonald's. I never went to SOME because I didn't know about those places until I'd heard about them at the shelter. The only place that I knew of was the church which is right on the corner of 14th and C, which is a block and a half from my mother's house, and I knew that they would feed you on Saturdays. So I would go around there on Saturdays and you know you could get a hot meal between ten and twelve. Other than that, if I wasn't getting something from the Kentucky Fried or the McDonald's, if you knew somebody, you could say, "Let's put in and get some lunch meat and a loaf of bread and make a couple of sandwiches." You just save some change and end up getting some sardines and crackers or anything just to put something on your stomach.

For the most part, if guys got change, they weren't thinking about eating because they were too busy drinking. They spent the majority of the day getting their money together. I would see so much wine and vodka from these guys because that is basically what they did. This is all they did. Except for some guys who were hard-core on heroin. Most of them would use the money between drinks and drugs, because you were always going to get something to eat free.

Drowning in My Own Sorrow

I started saying to myself, "You actually live in a shelter." I was in bad shape. I didn't think I could be repaired, that's how bad I was. My mother and I were on real bad terms. A couple of times I did drink, and I ended up laying on a sidewalk, just kind of drowning in my own sorrow. I ended up losing a very valuable watch that I bought in '69 and a ring that went with it. It had a black face. I was laying in a corner, zonked out, and a guy just took it off my wrist. It was a good watch. That kind of woke me up to a lot of things. I guess that goes with the territory. When you go to the shelter, it's not too much better. I just went from the streets to the shelter.

There aren't any pleasant memories I have about the shelter. It got harder and harder to push myself to go there. But you would say, "Well, if I could only go in there and get some sleep, because I'm dog tired and I ran all day long trying to do this and trying to do that." You think, if you could just go to the shelter and get a bed and get halfway comfortable, then make it through the night, then you were okay.

But, you become like a lot of them are, institutionalized; that's where they want to be. They've got three hots and a cot. That's one of the problems. They make it so easy for these guys not to be self-sufficient. You may appropriate funds for a guy to become sufficient, but they'll be saying "Just give me the wine, you know. Its easier this way, man." A lot of those guys have given up. I can't live like that. I started thinking, "There's got to be a better way."

5

America's Response: Part of the Problem

Franklin tells a grim tale of homelessness in the 1980s. Conditions in today's public shelters for the homeless are filthy, violent, and dehumanizing. Large numbers of people are crowded into limited spaces where substance abuse, mental illness, theft, harassment, sexual attack, and disease are so pervasive that survival is at issue, and many homeless individuals, especially women, fear to use shelters.[1] Those who do use them often become, in Franklin's words, "institutionalized." Some of the "regulars" who have come to rely on the "three hots and a cot" have lived in shelters for five or more years.[2]

Franklin's personal account of homelessness, while limited to his experiences in a single Washington, D.C., shelter, summarizes the multiple human tragedies we described in the first three chapters of this book. Franklin testified that it was the deterioration of his relationships with his family that finally forced him into homelessness; he also suggested that his ability to maintain even fragile connections with friends distinguished him from many of the other homeless men whose only networks were the bottle gangs on the corner. The homosexual behavior and intravenous drug use Franklin observed makes exposure to AIDS among the homeless a constant reality, and its incidence is rising rapidly. Even Franklin could see that the mentally ill people at the shelter had been released from St. Elizabeth's Hospital "before time," that is, before they were ready to live outside a treatment facility for the mentally ill. Nevertheless, they ended up on the streets and in shelters because "they just had nowhere else to go" and because "people just didn't detect the fact that [they] needed treatment." Finally, his description—in all its ugly detail—provides a vivid picture of the unsanitary conditions endemic to facilities that do nothing more than warehouse people who are seriously impaired and where there is little attempt to provide the help they so desperately need.

Shelters Fail the Homeless

Franklin's account presents in microcosm the most serious and pervasive failings of America's primary response to the homeless. Merely providing

74

shelter ignores the realities of homelessness. Instead of confronting the troubling realities of addictions and mental illness, our society has doubly victimized the homeless by its obstinate denial. Obsessed by their fear of blaming the victim, advocates for the homeless and policymakers talk about low-cost housing, call them poor and hungry, and shelter and feed them in places that don't even pretend to deal with their very real problems. Like Pierce, a men's shelter in New York City in the 1980s was described as resembling a nineteenth-century insane asylum: "A large room off the lobby is filled with over 100 men. Some lie curled up on the dirty floor; a few are in various stages of undress; others gesture wildly in the air talking to themselves. Some just sit staring into space. The stench of urine and unwashed bodies is strong."[3]

It is hard to imagine that anyone who knows what most homeless shelters are like would want to create more of them, yet shelters for the homeless multiplied exponentially during the 1980s, tripling in number every four years. In 1988 there were 5,400 shelters nationwide with 275,000 beds, almost three times as many as in 1984 when the U.S. Department of Housing and Urban Development (HUD) first commissioned a nationwide survey of services for the homeless, and six times as many as in 1980.[4] By 1988, as a nation we were spending $1.6 billion a year for emergency shelters, two-thirds from public, governmental sources and one-third from private sources—more than five times the amount spent in 1984.[5] During the same four-year period, private, not-for-profit organizations—most affiliated with religious groups—doubled their financial support for emergency shelters and tripled the number of volunteer hours committed to helping. In 1988, some 30 million hours were contributed by 80,000 volunteers to operate about 90 percent of all shelters (80 percent of all shelter beds), frequently by contracting with government agencies to provide services.[6]

Despite the growing number of shelters, expanded funding, and increasing human resources, most shelters do not provide rehabilitative services such as substance abuse treatment and mental health care, and few earmarked federal funds are available to support such services.[7] Overall, in 1988 only 32 percent of the facilities provided substance abuse services; those that did mostly offered Alcoholics Anonymous (AA) meetings or made referrals to services elsewhere. Only 21 percent offered mental health services of any kind, and those that did usually only provided referrals.[8] Research shows that homeless individuals are not very likely to keep referral appointments or to be able to negotiate often arcane and geographically dispersed social service bureaucracies without considerable assistance; thus, even the efforts that do exist fail to provide much help.[9] This staggeringly inadequate response to the needs of the homeless is intentional: In 1988, only 23 percent of service providers interviewed nationwide reported that rehabilitating clients to help break the cycle of homelessness is their goal; the vast majority are not committed to providing rehabilitative services. Many want to give the homeless a sense of "human dignity" or want to fulfill their own religious convictions to help their "brothers and sisters."[10]

> *We were on a site visit in the West and walked into a spacious day shelter. It was filled with Native Americans, women with children, men in cowboy hats, and Hispanics. Many were drunk; some were obviously drugged into some far-off oblivion. Many had just come from one of the overnight shelters in the area and they were going to spend their day here. There were showers, a small first-aid station, a reception desk, and a place to pick up mail. There was a room filled with the discarded belongings of those who had passed through but had never returned. The shelter staff "purged" this storage room every several months and recycled the clothing and other usable belongings to others. The minister in charge told us with pride about his day center and the compassion shown by the many church volunteers who were trained not to change lives but to distribute clothing, smiles, and love. He showed us his greatest achievement with pleasure—he had designated a special place on the wall where brass plaques commemorated former shelter guests. He was proud to be providing the ultimate service for the homeless—he prayed for them when they died.*

Exclusionary Rules

> *i never thought i'd see children on my street*
>   *going hungry*
>
> *or four men freezing to death after being turned away from*
> *a shelter for homeless people so like what happened God?*
> *didn't those four men rate that night? did being drunk*
>   *make them disposable?*[11]

—Pam Wynn

Not only do emergency shelters fail to be proactive in providing services, but many actually have rules and admission criteria that intentionally exclude those who are most disabled and in need of crisis care. According to various studies, including national surveys, many homeless shelters refuse to admit homeless people who show signs of excessive drinking or drug use or who are hallucinating or acting in bizarre or violent ways.[12] In a study of the homeless in Washington, D.C., some 68 percent of the people living on the streets had tried to get into shelters, but a majority of them had been refused admission because they failed to meet admission standards; the others had not even tried to get in.[13] The dually diagnosed are at particular risk of being excluded from shelters because they tend to have even higher levels of psychiatric symptoms and exhibit more bizarre and disruptive behavior than other homeless people.[14] The homeless who live on the streets, sleeping on heating grates, under bridges, in doorways, alleys, or abandoned buildings, are more seriously disabled by mental illness, alcoholism, and drugs than those who stay at shelters and use soup kitchens; they have also been homeless longer and have been unemployed or unemployable for longer periods of time.[15]

> *The speaker, who volunteered every week at a women's shelter, had been invited to speak at a church forum on homelessness. She described Ruth, an elderly woman who was a "regular guest" at the shelter. The description brought to mind the prototypic "bag lady," with layers of dirty clothing, matted hair, and parcels of personal belongings. During the coldest part of the winter, Ruth started acting strangely and attacked several other "guests" at the shelter whom she said were "wolves trying to attack her." The shelter staff agreed that Ruth was no longer welcome and, because she had become so aggressive, they recommended that other shelters in the area similarly deny her admission. The speaker reported that Ruth, "a real terror and a threat to the very survival of the shelter," ended up spending her nights in a local movie theater. A member of the audience asked, "Is a movie theater really the best place for a mentally ill woman? Shouldn't we be able to offer her treatment and take care of her?" The speaker responded, "I never thought of it that way."*

Despite the massive increases in shelters and funding, the existing institutions are still doing very little for a sizable portion of the most disabled among the homeless. They continue to lead wretched lives on the streets. It is just this cohort of the homeless population, excluded from shelters or too alienated to use them, who present the ugliest face of homelessness to the American public—a public increasingly unsympathetic to their presence.

Family Shelters Are No Better

Reflecting the growth in the numbers of families among the homeless, the proportion of shelters that house families more than quadrupled between 1984 and 1988; by 1988, 36 percent of all shelters housed families with children.[16] According to annual reports by the U.S. Conference of Mayors, the need for family shelters on a national level increases every year; during 1991, it increased by an average of 17 percent.[17] Just as in the case of adult shelters, family shelters are squalid places with few if any services for adults or amenities for children. According to 1988 congressional testimony, New York City welfare hotels for homeless families had "rooms with inadequate heat and hot water; bathrooms that lack privacy and are frequently inoperable; single rooms with one or two beds, even for families with several children; filthy, vermin-infested mattresses; no pillows, sheets, blankets, or towels; no cribs for infants; windows without guards; and doors with broken locks."[18] In New York City in 1991, about 1,000 families were sheltered in hotels at a cost to the city of almost $53,000 per year per family. In its stinging review of the shelter system, the New York City Commission on the Homeless stated that "[it] flat out does not work."[19]

Conditions in Washington, D.C., are no better, despite the expenditure of approximately $40 million in federal and city funds for homeless services in 1990. That year the city provided shelter for approximately 5,000 men, women, and children every night, including 500 families and 3,000 single adults;[20] many families were housed in motels operated for profit by contractors who received as much as $3,000 or more per month for each room.

> *The voters of Washington, D.C., had passed an ordinance in 1984 requiring the city to provide emergency shelter to all who requested it, including families. With few municipal facilities available, families were placed at the Capitol City Motor Inn, an old motel on the industrial route into the city. At the height of its occupancy, some 900 people, including almost 700 children, were housed in what was to become an infamous place. Since there was no place to eat, everyone was bused to another "shelter" for meals—a chaotic and stressful event, particularly on wet and cold winter days. With nothing else to do, children played "chicken" with trains that passed on the railroad tracks behind the building. Rooms were crowded, and fire marshals regularly cited the city for the code violations, including the practice of leaving babies unattended in motel rooms. Children died in this "shelter"; on one occasion, killed by their drug-addicted father. Alcohol and drugs were everywhere, as were the big cars of the dealers who supplied the residents with everything from heroin to crack. The one professional person who staffed this facility reported that 85 percent of the mothers were on crack.*

The Capitol City Motor Inn, the largest of the family shelters in Washington, D.C., was finally closed after years of lawsuits and political pressure from all sides; on the one hand, advocates wanted families moved from shabby and dangerously crowded accommodations to transitional or permanent housing, and on the other hand, detractors wanted the city to stop paying up to $3,000 or more a month per family for shelter. Despite the closing of the Capitol City Motor Inn as a shelter for homeless families, in September 1991 close to 700 homeless families, a record number, were still being sheltered by the District of Columbia, many in other motels not unlike the Capitol City.

According to optimistic speculation, "Motels and hotels for sheltering the homeless at the expense of the public and for the benefit of private profit were being phased out by the late 1980s and early 1990s. . . . [T]he more typical shelters for the homeless have [become] the residential facilities, supported, organized and administered by not-for-profit entities."[21] To the extent that this is true, however, the most disabled of the homeless, including families where crack addiction is a serious problem, are likely to be excluded from these "residential facilities."

The Grate Patrols
and Other Band-Aid Services

Church groups, school groups, and voluntary organizations of every kind have tried to respond to the growing tragedy on the streets and have been enterprising in finding ways to help the homeless. One of the most popular is to run a soup kitchen; some 321,000 meals per day were served in soup kitchens located in churches, storefronts, and shelters in 1987.[22] Throughout the country, volunteers also deliver hot food, sandwiches, blankets, and socks to homeless men and women who live on the streets in downtown neighborhoods. In one community, 65 percent of residents interviewed indicated that they had "personally done something to help the homeless (usually by donating money, food, or clothing to charities or directly to homeless persons)."[23] These haphazard systems for helping the homeless are so convoluted that even the homeless are sometimes distressed by them. When the early winter cold snap of 1991 prompted a city-wide blanket distribution to people on the streets of Washington, D.C., homeless individuals sleeping in the Greyhound bus station refused the offered blankets for fear of being identified as homeless and being ejected.

Food pantries distribute bags of canned food, other nonperishable food, and personal hygiene items, including diapers and baby products, and distribution centers provide clothing, shoes, and blankets. Some programs have facilities where homeless people can shower, bathe, and do laundry; a few offer money to the poor for paying overdue utility bills or back rent; and some have either volunteer or paid counselors who try to help people in crisis—by talking to them, praying with them, or helping them find food and shelter. In a few cities, in an effort to cope with aggressive and intrusive panhandling, lists of these services are distributed so that citizens, confused about a proper response, can hand out these information cards instead of money.

These various helping programs, which on the surface seem so sensible and responsive, are nothing more than Band-Aids that have little or no long-term benefit.[24] The homeless receive another meal or a place to sleep for the night, or a family is given one more check for another month's rent, but the underlying problems continue to go unaddressed. In fact, by not confronting the problems of alcoholism, drug addiction, and mental illness, these services fail to create incentives for the homeless to break the cycle of dependency. At their worst, these services enable the homeless to continue their dysfunctional behavior. In some cases, homeless people are perfectly willing to take advantage of naive generosity; manipulation and exploitation of do-gooding is simply a logical extension of the system our society has created.

Mr. McPherson, often drunk, came once a month on his self-assigned day to collect his bag of nutritionally balanced groceries. The church-based organization had run a food pantry in the neighborhood for many years and the rules were well known: only one bag per person per month. The food was regularly collected at area churches and was intended as an emergency supply to tide people over during the last days of the month when food stamps had run out. Many people, however, came to collect their once-a-month supply at the beginning of the month—or, like Mr. McPherson, on exactly the same day every month. As the summer approached and our food supply ran low, we tried to understand the patterns of need that were driving the food distribution. We discovered that Mr. McPherson used the same address as five other men who also had "regular" days, staggered throughout the month, when they collected their emergency food. In a moment of unguarded candor, Mr. McPherson told us that he and his "roommates" lived in an abandoned building in the neighborhood that housed one of the best crack laboratories in town. To our chagrin, we realized that, in the name of the church, we had been feeding the operators of a crack house.

We also learned that, as with food pantries in many other cities, a substantial proportion of the groceries we were distributing found its way to the local black market to generate dollars to pay for drugs and alcohol. Learning about these activities shocked many of our contributors, but we could not easily close the food pantry. The act of donating food was far and away the most popular way to "help the homeless."

If emergency services provide opportunities for the homeless to exploit the system, the expanding system, what Gregg Barak called the "shelter industrial complex" or the "shelterization industry,"[25] also exploits the homeless. The advocates, the sponsors, and the professional and volunteer staff of shelters have become a huge service industry, and now its members have a vested interest in perpetuating their own jobs, income, status, community recognition, and political power and prestige. "As a result," wrote the authors of one analysis, "shelter providers have unwittingly joined with politicians to maintain the status quo" that virtually guarantees the growth of the shelter industry.[26]

One notable exception to the pattern of woefully inadequate emergency services for the homeless is the extraordinary Health Care for the Homeless Project (HCH), originally funded by the Robert Wood Johnson Foundation and the Pew Memorial Trust. HCH began as a demonstration project in nineteen cities across the country and expanded to 109 projects, mostly in urban areas, when federal funding under the Stewart B. McKinney Homeless Assistance Act became available. HCH and similar voluntary clinic programs offer a vast array of medical services in on-site clinics at shelters, missions, soup kitchens, community health centers, and other places where the homeless are found. Although health service programs like HCH have at least recognized the need for serious professional care for the homeless, even these fine programs are limited in what they can do when their patients return to the streets without receiving long-term help for their addictions and chronic health problems.

Transitional Services: Creaming the Homeless

By the mid 1980s, many service providers and program planners had begun to understand that emergency services were creating a new kind of dependency among the homeless. Consequently, they began to develop transitional programs intended to empower the homeless—to eliminate dependency, create self-sufficiency, help people "live with dignity and independence," and "promote the upward mobility of . . . homeless persons or families."[27] In 1991 alone, there was a 70 percent increase in transitional housing units across the country.[28]

A multitude of services is subsumed under the rubric of transitional services. These include such disparate activities as job search seminars, self-esteem and skills building workshops, employment placement and training programs, adopt-a-family projects, short-term assisted housing programs, mentoring and tutoring, adult education, parenting classes, day-care programs, classes in daily living and life skills, budget workshops, and training sessions in political organizing.

Although eliminating dependency and creating self-sufficiency are laudable goals, most transitional programs have not and cannot help the majority of the homeless achieve these goals. It is ludicrous to provide job training and job placement to people who have never worked or who have not had a job for years because of substance abuse, unless the substance abuse problem is addressed first. Similarly, budget workshops for those whose primary interest is hustling money for drugs will accomplish nothing without prior treatment and recovery. So too, short-term transitional housing for the mentally ill that fails to acknowledge treatment needs will almost always assure a return to the streets or shelters.

A 1991 General Accounting Office evaluation of the HUD Supportive Housing Demonstration Program, which focused primarily on transitional short-term housing with typical transitional services, underscores this point. Despite the congressionally mandated requirement that a substantial portion of the almost $350 million in funding for the program be targeted to the homeless mentally ill and substance abusers, the GAO found that many projects tried to screen out clients with these problems. Furthermore, two-thirds of the programs that do offer services for these groups provide them on a referral basis, a method well documented to be ineffective. Finally, the GAO reports that the mentally ill and substance abusers who are permitted to participate are the least likely to successfully complete programs and graduate to independent living. Overall, only 40 percent of the participants in the 534 demonstration projects completed the program; 30 percent were asked to leave and 30 percent left voluntarily before completing the program. Those who were discharged or who left voluntarily did so because of the strict rules regarding substance abuse and curfews.[29]

The Painful Truth

In designing strategies to break the cycle of homelessness and dependency, the creators of these transitional programs—frequently veteran poverty warriors of the 1960s accustomed to thinking of social ills in terms of poverty and disempowerment—made three tragic mistakes in diagnosing the problem of homelessness: They confused homelessness with poverty; they mistook disabling alcoholism, drug addiction, and mental illness for lack of opportunity; and they equated disaffiliation with lack of political power. The underlying problems of homelessness are not poverty, lack of opportunity, or powerlessness, and homelessness is not today's version of the problems of the 1960s. Remedies borrowed from this earlier time simply miss the point; one cannot address the substance abuse and psychiatric illness of the homeless by "empowering" them.[30] To attempt to do so is yet another example of the persistent denial prevalent in society today.

The painful truth, first shared with us by Thomas Nees, long-time director of an inner-city service center for homeless families in Washington, D.C., is that "the homeless population can be divided into three groups: the 10 to 15 percent who are the least dysfunctional, the 70 to 80 percent who have serious problems with alcohol, drugs, and mental illness, and the remaining few who are beyond help."[31] In the absence of sufficient resources to deal with substance abuse and mental illness, Nees suggested that voluntary and church-based organizations focus all their attention on the top 10 to 15 percent. The real meaning of this advice is that 85 to 90 percent of the homeless cannot benefit from most transitional service programs without first participating in appropriate treatment—treatment that is beyond the capability of the vast majority of transitional service providers and unavailable from other public agencies. Thus, transitional programs must "cream" the homeless, using various screening mechanisms to make sure they include only those among the homeless who do not need professional treatment—those who can benefit immediately from the available programs and who will not disrupt the progress of others.[32]

> Our employment services office was originally designed as an adjunct to the emergency services program. When neighborhood residents, both the homeless and those with homes, came for emergency groceries or asked for money to pay back utility bills, they were encouraged to talk to one of the employment counselors about finding work. Volunteers assisted clients in looking through job listings and helped them fill out applications. Although many clients found work, they often lost their

jobs and came back to our offices. We were particularly embarrassed when one of our sponsoring churches complained that we had sent a very drunk individual to a job interview at that church. When we converted the employment services program to a transitional program, we hired an employment professional whose experience included working with the unemployed and hard to employ. She immediately introduced a number of new practices, including screening participants, requiring attendance in a two-week job readiness program, and refusing to send people who were drinking or otherwise incapacitated to job interviews. Because of these new procedures, the more disabled regulars of our employment services office, including all the homeless, stopped coming.

Many service providers, both private and public, feel uncomfortable admitting that as many as 85 to 90 percent of the homeless are not ready to participate in programs intended to lead to self-sufficiency. Therefore, they merely ignore the problems and enroll the homeless in the new programs, usually doing little more than wasting time and resources and promoting yet another alienating failure for the homeless at the hands of the unresponsive "system." By permitting those whose basic problems have been ignored to participate in transitional programs, they have inadvertently concocted another version of the "revolving door"; these clients end up back in the shelters or on the streets.

The failure is compounded when disabled homeless individuals, whose major problems have been ignored in transitional facilities, are expected to move into independent living situations. As the authors of one article reported, for some participants in transitional programs, the anticipation of moving from transitional housing to another setting can "cause much anxiety and apprehension. Individuals who are very close to obtaining housing sometimes abruptly change their minds about a previously agreed-to housing option, or otherwise sabotage a pending housing placement (e.g., by beginning to abuse drugs again)."[33] The situation for homeless families is no better. According to the social worker at a large urban family shelter, for example, more than 50 percent of all families who moved from the shelter into transitional housing returned to the shelter within ninety days; in New York, half of all homeless families placed in permanent housing without screening returned to shelters.[34] Andrew Cuomo, chairman of the New York City Commission on the Homeless, reported in a 1990 interview that at least half the mothers and older children in the transitional housing facilities his organization built in the South Bronx had a drug problem. He said that by placing these families in permanent housing with no prior drug treatment, the city had "built a time bomb."[35]

Case Management:
The New Panacea

Marjorie and her four children had lived in shelters and motels supported by the county for more than three years. With funding from the federal government, the county embarked on an ambitious transitional housing project, contracting with a local developer to make townhouses and apartments available to resettled homeless families. The plans called for social workers to maintain steady contact with the families to insure that they were receiving the various support services they needed. With much hope and excitement Marjorie readied herself and her children for their new life. A local church gathered furniture, pots and pans, and bedding and helped Marjorie move into her three-bedroom home. A month later, Marjorie realized she just couldn't handle the responsibilities of her new life. Marjorie never heard from her social worker, nor did she have any contact with anyone else from the county. She started drinking again, and when she began to rely on her old boyfriend for support, she got pregnant. As her drinking problem worsened, she was unable to control her older children, who started selling drugs in the neighborhood. After only a few months, she was forced to give up her house and move back to a shelter.

Marjorie was abandoned—not on the streets, but in a three-bedroom townhouse that she was totally unprepared to manage without considerable help, which was not provided. Even though she had a "case manager," Marjorie's was just one more transitional family failed by an overloaded system.

Case management has become a recent buzzword, one that has captured the attention of almost everyone involved in providing transitional services to the homeless. Case managers, usually professional social workers, are responsible for assessing the varied needs of a client, developing a plan to address those needs, identifying and procuring the various needed services, monitoring progress, and maintaining an ongoing supportive relationship with the client to insure that he or she continues to utilize the helping services. Many transitional service programs offer case management as a stand-alone service program. However, case management is, in fact, only a process, and only an effective one when case managers are adept at assessment, familiar with the problems of the homeless, have access to professional services, and have caseloads sufficiently small to permit them to meet the enormous demands of seriously troubled people.[36]

Finding appropriate case managers to work with the homeless is not easy. According to the director of an alcohol and drug treatment program in Louisville, Kentucky, "Case management may attract 'missionaries' who want to save the world but kill the patient along the way, and 'rebels' who are so convinced the system is fouled up that [they are] destructive to the clients."[37]

Luke, a case manager with a social work degree, had been working with Mr. Brunswick for some months. He had already helped Mr. Brunswick recapture some $2,500 in veterans' benefits that Luke believed had been intentionally withheld in violation of Mr. Brunswick's rights. They had agreed to a budget so that Mr. Brunswick could pay his rent on time and avoid eviction and more homelessness.

Now Luke was trying to find a legal services attorney to sue Mr. Brunswick's bank. Mr. Brunswick said the bank was conspiring with his brother-in-law by allowing him to use his automatic bank teller card to steal his money. When Luke asked for my help in locating a free legal clinic, I talked to Mr. Brunswick about his situation. Using a simple alcohol assessment test,[38] I soon suspected that he might have a drinking problem. Mr. Brunswick finally admitted that he always discovered that money was missing from his account after one of his frequent alcohol-induced blackouts and, yes, he probably had used the money himself to buy liquor. He had made up the story about the bank and his brother-in-law because he was embarrassed that all his savings were gone and that he now had to ask Luke for money to pay his rent. Luke reported that, even though he usually smelled alcohol when talking with Mr. Brunswick, he had never thought about him being an alcoholic.

Even when case managers accurately assess treatment needs, all too often their only alternative is to place their clients' names on months-long waiting lists for admission to treatment facilities. Regrettably, many programs that pride themselves on having a case management approach are deceiving themselves, their donors, and most important, their clients. As one writer has pointed out, case management is not a "quick fix" because "introducing a separate bureaucratic stratum of case managers will not by itself assure the provision of [effective services] . . . and it may even foster a false sense of security."[39] In fact, in too many cases, inadequately trained case managers are failing to provide hard-to-secure services to more people than they can handle.

Prevention: The Newest Fad

Frustrated by infrequent successes, policymakers have recently developed a new program concept: preventing homelessness among "at risk" populations. Homelessness prevention programs, like transitional programs, include the following array of services: education, mentoring, tutoring, and training programs for children and youth; parenting and adult education programs; home maintenance and budget management programs; anti-drug and alcohol campaigns; and prenatal and infant care and child nutrition programs. These programs are all beginning to flourish in public housing projects and in other places where there are people who are purported to be "at risk" of becoming homeless. For example, a demonstration program included in the 1990 Amendments to the Stewart B. McKinney Homeless Assistance Act, the Gateway Program, calls for education, job training, and various kinds of supportive services for public housing residents.[40]

If many transitional programs screen out the most disabled of the homeless population, prevention programs finish the job—they are the ultimate creaming mechanism. Like transitional programs, prevention programs are targeted to people who are not disaffiliated or disabled by alcoholism, drug addiction, or mental illness and who are therefore not homeless. According to a 1990 government report, "These programs are not intended for the mentally ill or substance abusers who are at risk because their problems go beyond a short term financial crisis. These people require much more in the way of support services, including long-term professional help and drug abuse treatment."[41]

After a full decade of concern for the homeless, the American public seems to be giving up on those who are already homeless. It is as though people have redefined the "few who are beyond help" to include the entire homeless population. Some of these new prevention programs exploit the issue of homelessness to accomplish what many in the public housing arena, including tenant organizations, have wanted for many years—training programs, health clinics, day-care, anti-drug and anti-gang activities, and building improvement projects. Other prevention programs, like the $14 million New Jersey Homelessness Prevention Program, target the "'working poor' who have temporary setbacks that make them unable to meet their housing expenses."[42] These may be good and necessary programs, but they are not programs to help the homeless.

Ten years ago public housing was considered a major part of the solution to the problem of homelessness; what cities had to do, it was thought, was to increase the number of low-income subsidized public housing units. Now, public housing is being viewed as the flip side of the coin, not as housing for the homeless, but as the location of those "at risk" for homelessness. Paradoxically, however, at the same time that these homelessness prevention programs for public housing residents were being developed, policies emanating from the War on Drugs campaign put exactly those individuals who were truly "at risk" of homelessness beyond the reach of the prevention programs. Under the new policies, public housing tenants involved with drugs are subject to eviction. Once evicted from public housing—housing of the last resort—they are likely to become homeless.

Failure to Help the Homeless

For more than a decade, the American public has been bombarded by images of homeless men, women, and children roaming the streets and sleeping in cardboard boxes or in doorways. Whether or not these images are accurate,[43] there has been a nationwide outpouring of compassion, altruism, philanthropy, and charity. We have been called upon "to share our outrage at the very existence of homelessness in this country and to take action. All of us . . . must join in an alliance to solve this problem, united by the conviction that homelessness is unacceptable."[44] Thomas L. Kenyon and Justine Blau's 1991 book *What You Can Do to Help the Homeless* exhorted us to "offer assistance to the homeless—options open to ordinary people with a few minutes or a few dollars to spare. Try just one [activity to help the homeless], and find out how easy it is to help—and how good it makes you feel."[45] These authors further said that there are "numerous ways [we] can ease the plight of the homeless and help make homelessness a thing of the past."[46]

In response, this country has developed a vast system of shelters, soup kitchens, clothes closets, grate patrols, transitional services, and most recently, homelessness prevention programs. Overwhelmed by the hideousness of homelessness, and caught between doing something and nothing at all, most individuals and organizations opt for doing the best they can. These services represent a "can do, feel good" way for most Americans to respond to the tragedy of homelessness, and although they have given people a sense that they have done something, these services have not helped the homeless. Because our society has spent most of its resources, fiscal and human, on trying to alleviate the most immediate symptoms of homelessness—the need for shelter and food—instead of trying to create solutions to the root causes of the symptoms, very little has been done either to ease the plight of the homeless or to make homelessness a thing of the past. Despite all the efforts, homelessness increased during the 1980s and Americans grew weary, angry, and in some cases, bored with the problem.[47] Some have concluded that because nothing to date has worked, the problem of homelessness is insoluble. As columnist William Raspberry wrote in September 1991:

> It once seemed reasonable to me that a lot of the homeless could find work if only they had access to shower facilities, a clean set of clothes and a mailing address. Churches and other organizations started to provide these basics of human dignity, and I'm sure a few once-homeless men and women are now gainfully employed and snug in their modest apartments. Very few. What's more likely is that very little has changed, even for those who found their way to the showers and free clothing centers. . . . Nothing, no matter how promising it seemed at the time, has made any difference. Things keep getting worse. . . . You don't have to be mean-spirited to walk away from social problems. All it takes is the certainty that nothing can be done to solve them.[48]

Why has the American public come to this? People have responded to homelessness in mostly inappropriate ways and now seem to be walking away from the entire problem for many complex reasons, reasons which we will explore in much greater detail in Part Two. Americans seem to hold the naive view that today's homelessness is a new phenomenon, one not connected by historical threads to the age-old problem of people living on the very margins of society. Lacking a historical perspective, this country has repeated many of the mistakes of the past and has added yet another chapter to the seemingly unending process of deciding who are the deserving and who are the undeserving poor. This sorting process, which largely determines which victims of society benefit from its substantial resources and which do not, is always political; the application of this process to the homeless in the 1980s, a decade noted for a dramatic increase in groups claiming victimization, created a political maelstrom. In fact, the politics surrounding homelessness have taken on such a life of their own that much of America's response to the homeless has been driven by political machinations and posturing that have done little to clarify the issue, let alone solve the problem.

The response to any problem is necessarily a function of how the problem is defined. During the decade of the 1980s, in large part because of the politicized nature of the debate, homelessness was defined in so many different ways and attributed to so many different causes that it is a wonder that there was any response at all. But as we have seen, there have been many responses, some laudable, some foolish, most grossly inadequate. Moreover, the public and its policymakers still have not been educated about the real problems of mental illness and addictions that cause the homeless to suffer. In short, misguided ideas about the causes of homelessness have led to America's failure to provide humane emergency care, develop appropriate strategies to solve the complex and pressing problems of the homeless, and help the homeless reenter society.

Only when the American public is able to come to some agreement about this problem and its causes will policymakers and planners be able to respond effectively. In order to do that, we must understand homelessness in the American social experience over time and define its place in the politics of the last quarter of the twentieth century, subjects to which we now turn our attention.

PART TWO

Homelessness
and the American
Social Experience

6

A History of Homelessness

Then from the tents . . . groups of sodden men went out, their clothes slopping rags, their shoes muddy pulp. They splashed out—to the towns, to the country stores, to the relief offices, to beg for food, to cringe and beg for food, to beg for relief, to try to steal, to lie. And under the begging, and under the cringing, a hopeless anger began to smolder. And in the little towns, pity for the sodden men changed to anger, and anger at the hungry people changed to fear of them. . . . [A]nd the comfortable people in tight houses felt pity at first, and then distaste, and finally hatred.[1]

—John Steinbeck

During the past decade, most Americans seemed to believe that homelessness was a new phenomenon caused by the combination of regressive governmental policies and the recession of the early 1980s. The truth is that homelessness is not new, nor are our efforts to respond to it substantially different from those of our forebears. Throughout history, society has been confronted by the problem of people who live on its margins—homeless vagrants and vagabonds, the dependent poor, the unemployed, and the unemployable. Starting in the earliest days of the colonies, Americans have viewed them alternatively as a threat to their young society and its strong work ethic, as heroic rugged individuals forging West to open the frontier, as the shameful derelicts of skid row, and finally, as today's "new homeless." In the past, the public was willing to admit that social isolation, alcoholism, drug abuse, and mental illness were closely associated with homelessness, and from time to time reformers have designed programs intended to address these problems, some punitive, some generous. Today, fearful of blaming the victim, most people prefer to deny these conditions and view homelessness as a single problem: being without a home.

As America has struggled with its attitudes about the homeless and how to help them, endless debates, repeated by each successive generation, have been fueled by the cycle of pity, distaste, fear, anger, and hatred felt by all, rich and poor, when there is impoverishment, homelessness, and destitution in our midst. The questions have ever been the same. Should services provide direct financial assistance or should they provide shelter? Should policies force the homeless into institutions or respect their freedom and right to self-determination? Should the help be compassionate and generous or should it exercise social control by rewarding work and industry while punishing idleness and intemperance? Should assistance be an entitlement paid for by the general public through taxes or should it be available only when it has been earned by work? Should helping the homeless be the responsibility of government or should the primary source of help be private, charitable organizations? The answers to all these questions have always depended on the definition of who is worthy of assistance and who is not.

Outdoor Relief and the Poorhouse

The first American settlers understood the relationship between work, survival, and dependence. The original colonists came from a broad cross section of English society that included many of England's wandering homeless, "vagrants . . . bona fide criminals, lunatics, and misfits of all sorts."[2] In fact, intent on increasing the population of the new colonies, English officials routinely offered criminals the choice of boarding ships headed for America as an alternative to going to prison.[3] Once here, all were expected to join the hard work of building settlements, planting farms, clearing the wilderness, and participating in community life. Those who did not work were viewed with alarm; there was fear that "idleness" or "indolence" would undermine the work ethic, a moral principle embraced throughout the colonies as the means of survival under the austere conditions of early American life. Colonists were extremely wary of the economically dependent because taking care of them put a serious strain on the marginal resources of new communities. In adapting English Poor Laws, laws intended not so much to assist the poor as to control them, the colonists created policies to fit the conditions of America in the seventeenth and eighteenth centuries; in many cases, these were more stringent and more punitive than the English laws from which they were derived.[4]

Four characteristics were central to these early American social welfare policies and are still relevant today. First was the linkage of public assistance to residency, a concept derived from England's Settlement Laws. Although they would care for impoverished neighbors, officials in local communities were extremely wary of providing help to strangers or exiles from other communities, and proof of belonging became a prerequisite for receiving assistance. The connection between residency and public assistance would remain in force until the 1960s when it was successfully challenged in the courts; more than twenty years later, it has reemerged in today's policy debates as state and local governments worry about providing overly generous benefits that may attract the homeless and potential welfare recipients to their jurisdictions.

Second, early policies provided direct cash assistance, a benefit known as "outdoor relief." Those who were eligible for such assistance were usually long-time community residents who had experienced a personal calamity—an injury, a long illness, or the death of the family breadwinner. Because local communities had to levy a special poor tax to provide relief, assistance was neither generous nor frequent. Local officials preferred using alternatives such as "binding out" (indenturing the poor to families needing laborers or servants), "farming out" (requiring men to work for wages that were in turn used for their support), and arrangements similar to modern foster care whereby indigents were placed in homes where they received care or where children were apprenticed to craftsmen to learn trades so that they could become self-supporting.[5] Today's welfare system continues the practice of providing direct assistance in the form of AFDC payments for families, general assistance for individuals, Supplemental Security Income (SSI) for the disabled, and a host of other transfer payments, such as food stamps, Medicare, and Medicaid.

The third practice, borrowed from the English system, was the poorhouse or almshouse.[6] The poorhouse was introduced to America as a multipurpose institution that provided shelter for the aged and the infirm and required work of the able-bodied. It was used as an instrument of control, threatening the loss of freedom to any who failed to attain and maintain self-sufficiency. The advent of the poorhouse proved to initiate a shameful chapter in American welfare history. According to an 1857 municipal report:

> The Yard was uncleansed—the surface drain filled with offensive matter—the Privies in a most filthy state—the floors most unwashed, many of the windows obscured by apparently many months accumulation of dust and cobwebs—nearly all the beds and bedding in a disgustingly neglected state, and in some localities, swarming with vermin.[7]

The poorhouses were overcrowded and filled with sickness, alcoholism, and mental illness. Efforts at work rehabilitation failed for lack of suitable work opportunities and discipline; liquor was easily available; and, according to Michael Katz's review of nineteenth-century reports, poorhouse administrators failed to monitor admission and discharge policies so that the poorhouse "became a temporary refuge for the degenerate poor, 'a winter resort for tramps . . . a place where the drunkard and the prostitute' recuperated 'between debauches.'"[8] Despite the wretched conditions and widespread suspicion about abuse of them, the poorhouses proved to be peculiarly resilient institutions. By the late nineteenth century, reformers successfully campaigned to close them, only to have similar deplorable conditions reappear with the introduction of the successors to the poorhouse: the municipal lodging houses of the early twentieth century and the shelters for the homeless in the 1980s.

Finally, the basic English philosophy about the poor, the distinction between poverty and pauperism, was unconditionally incorporated into the ideology of American welfare as the deserving and the undeserving poor, a distinction that remains today. Katz, quoting an analysis written in 1834, stated that:

> Poverty resulted not from "our faults" but from "our misfortunes," and the poor should "claim our tenderest commiseration, our most liberal relief." But pauperism was a different story. "Pauperism is the consequence of wilful error, of shameful indolence, of vicious habits. It is a misery of human creation, the pernicious work of man, the lamentable consequence of bad principles and morals." Relief to the poor was charity; relief to paupers increased "the evil in a tenfold degree."[9]

Those who were considered poverty-stricken were the aged, widows and orphans, men responsible for families who lost their jobs, and those with incurable diseases and physical disabilities. Others, particularly the able-bodied who would not work, were the paupers. Early welfare practices treated the poor and the pauper very differently. The poor were cared for in what-ever ways the community could manage; the paupers were "warned out," that is, they "were often driven out of the colony to freeze or starve, or were left to the mercy of the wilderness."[10] This approach—intended to staunch the spread of indolence as well as to remove the specter of destitution from public view—would take many different forms over the next hundred and fifty years and would be incorporated into antivagrancy laws, including the Tramp Acts in the late nineteenth century and what are being referred to as "antihomelessness laws" in the late twentieth century.[11]

The Frontier

> *If the settled communities turned against a misfit, he . . . had the option of escaping to the boundless frontier. . . . In the beginning everybody was a frontiersman or a pioneer; later, this way of life became an option—for the ambitious, for the adventurer, and also for the failure and the misfit.*[12]

The pioneers were the subject not only of real history but also of romantic mythology. They were the mountain men who became hunters, trappers, fur traders, Indian scouts, explorers, and cowboys, who were always on the move, pushing the frontier westward. Despite and in part because of their rejection of settled society, they became the embodiment of the heroic ideals of rugged individualism and personal dignity. Alone in the wilderness, they were free from social constraints; confronting the beauty of nature and the hardship of the elements, they treasured independence, autonomy, and anonymity. The stuff of legends and fantasy, these loners were, nevertheless, first and foremost social isolates—unmarried men, detached from family and friends, members of no communities except the temporary societies they formed with their wandering comrades. Today, some continue to romanticize the rugged individualism of homeless men and women who "valiantly" survive the hardships of the streets, the grates, and the alleys of America's cities.

The first explorers of the West were followed by wagon trains of settlers seeking land and, often, a new beginning. Then, in 1848, gold was discovered in California and thousands of young men set out to make their fortune in the California gold rush. Others joined crews to build America's railroads. According to Henry Miller, professor of social work:

> Their hallmark was a mobility that verged on nomadism; they had no permanent residence, and were unattached to kin or community. They embodied, to an extreme perhaps, the country's ethos: pick up and move. They suffered from illness; they were lonely; they had many of the marks that had been ascribed to their counterparts of earlier generations: the tendency to abuse chemical substances, a bit of roguery, and a touch of mental illness.[13]

Life during this era was rugged; alcohol and narcotics, mostly opium, were plentiful. By the 1870s large numbers of drug addicts and alcoholics ended up in the alleys of San Francisco's Chinatown and the Barbary Coast, where panhandling became a way of life[14]—a life that we see again more than one hundred years later among many of today's homeless.

Economic, Social, and Political Change

As America expanded westward, other major economic, social, and political forces swept across nineteenth-century America. Industrialization—the decline of home industry, the movement of manufacturing into shops and factories, and the advent of mechanization in farming and manufacturing—brought displaced workers to the growing cities, dramatically increasing unemployment and poverty through the 1850s.[15] At the same time, between 1820 and 1860, a massive wave of immigration brought more than 5 million people to America. This wave included many refugees from the Irish potato famines who joined displaced workers looking for new work and swelling relief rolls. Many immigrants arrived almost penniless, having spent most of their money to make the trip to America; many were sick when they arrived and others could not find work. According to Katz, contemporaries reported that many "had been accustomed to receiving relief in their old homes, and so were not abashed to ask for it when they came to the new world."[16] American cities became the hub for these growing concentrations of the unemployed and the homeless, but not always happily. As one New York State official claimed, "Cities are the great resorts for the struggling and vagrant poor, who although having no permanent settlement amongst us, still at times call loudly for relief and assistance."[17]

The rise in dependency and the increased cost of relief in the 1850s placed the issue of poverty at the center of political debate, and there were various efforts, not unlike those of today, to understand the causes of poverty and pauperism. Analysts of the nineteenth century concluded that these conditions resulted not only from the growth of the cities and immigration, but also from a combination of "intemperance . . . and the indiscriminate generosity of private charity" that "undermined the relation between work and survival."[18] According to some, "of all the causes of pauperism, intemperance, in the use of spiritous liquors, is the most powerful and universal."[19] Nineteenth-century analysts were unapologetic about the relationship between alcohol and pauperism. Analysts and public officials continued to recognize the connection between alcohol and economic dependence, originally articulated in this country in colonial days, until attitudes changed in the 1960s. Only since then has it become unacceptable to connect poverty (and homelessness) with personal behavior for fear of "blaming the victim."

The concurrent processes of immigration, urbanization, and industrialization that would continue to change the face of America well into the twentieth century were abruptly interrupted by the War between the States. As wars have historically done, the Civil War provided an opportunity for work, adventure, and bravery; both the Union and the Confederate armies attracted, among others, many unemployed, rootless, poor, and homeless men.[20] Once it was over, the Civil War and its aftermath produced a gargantuan wave of destitution, displacement, and dispossession. Wounded war veterans, freed slaves, and widows and orphans now joined the ranks of America's homeless—the immigrants, the urban poor and unemployed, and the victims of nascent industrialization. The need for assistance was beyond the capacity of local governments and charity organizations, and for the first time, the federal government became an actor in helping the destitute and the homeless. In 1862 Congress enacted a system of pensions for Union soldiers and families that was extended to cover Confederate veterans and families in 1890. Moreover, in 1865, Congress established the Freedmen's Bureau to assist in the resettlement of newly freed slaves.

In addition, after the Civil War, many surviving soldiers, their homes destroyed and their way of life changed, joined the pioneers and fled West to the promise of cheap land, work on the railroads, and jobs as cowboys in the cattle industry, which in the late 1860s started to drive cattle to new railheads for mass distribution. According to Henry Miller, cowboy life differed greatly from the romantic and heroic legends that pervade American culture. Usually young, cowboys "moved from ranch to ranch—always with the belief that things would be better elsewhere. . . . [O]ut-of-work, [they] 'usually degenerated, drifted, disappeared.'"[21] By the turn of the century, most of the opportunities for unlimited adventure and easy-to-find work on the frontier were gone. The railroads were built, the gold rush had ended, the land was fenced, and in many places, the transient cowboy was replaced by the settled farmer. What remained was a large marginal work force, "a 'reserve,' a *residuum* of the untrained, unskilled, and unsettled, many of whom lived on the edge of convention and law" (emphasis in original).[22]

Hoboes and Tramps

Much of the residuum consisted of migrants, who often illegally rode and slept in train boxcars on the same rails that they had helped to lay. They sought work as ranch hands, miners, lumberjacks, ice harvesters, workers in the growing building and construction trades, or as farmers. Those making up this vast army of itinerant workers came to be known as "hoboes," a word derived from "hoe-boys," migrant farm workers who used hoes. The hoboes were different from their middle- and working-class contemporaries; while they believed in hard work, they were employed in jobs that paid daily or hourly wages, jobs that were of short duration, were seasonal, and were scattered across the country. But the hobo was ultimately attracted to the urban hubs of industrialized nineteenth-century America. As Charles Hoch and Robert A. Slayton explained:

> The hobo's existence was tied to the city; his work and travel were in distinctly urban patterns . . . traveling from the city to a job on a farm, then back to the city for rest and recreation, then out to another farm or to a forest or to a fishing or mining community. Sometimes they worked as skilled or unskilled labor in shops or factories. . . . [These men are in contrast] to today's migrant laborers, who never connect with city centers in the course of following the harvests.[23]

Another group of wanderers in the late nineteenth century were the tramps, who, unlike the hoboes, did not work but similarly wandered across the country hitching rides on the railroads, panhandling, begging, stealing, and drifting from town to town in search of food, places to sleep, and easy ways to find spare change. Because the hobo worked, he was not economically dependent nor a recipient of public assistance, even though his itinerant life-style often made him an object of fear and ridicule. The tramp, on the other hand, was a frequent claimant on public resources, and his failure to work engendered considerable animosity. Katz reported that the public believed "tramps were lazy, dishonest, agitators living off the sentimental generosity of soft hearted women and the public bounty of poorhouses, where they retreated to spend their winters in warmth and comfort. Able-bodied tramps had absolutely no redeeming qualities, and they should be ejected from poorhouses as surely as they should be cut from outdoor relief."[24]

Despite their social and economic differences, hoboes and tramps shared one important characteristic—a life of constant wandering and frequent use of the country's developing network of railroads. These men were not welcome riders: they traveled for free, they stole goods from the freight cars, they often left behind trash from their rummaging. Perhaps most important, they were often the victims of serious injury and many died. The railroad companies hired "Pinkerton men," private police, to monitor the cars and eject the hoboes and tramps; these "railroad bulls," exceeding their authority, often beat or clubbed these unwelcome riders.[25] Codifying intolerance into law, states eventually enacted Tramp Acts that prohibited tramping and required "imprisonment at hard labor in the nearest penitentiary."[26] By 1898, all but four states had such acts—laws still on the books in some places that are being used today to drive the homeless out of city centers.

It was not only the railroad companies that were hostile to these itinerants; local communities, particularly those close to railroad junctions and highways, made every effort to discourage the tramps and hoboes from taking up even temporary residence. Forced out of town, the tramps and hoboes formed their own communities, the "hobo jungles," or "hobohemias." The jungle offered amenities such as water, nearby stores, and companionship while at the same time permitting privacy and anonymity. Not surprisingly, descriptions of hobo jungles, like those of the poorhouse, suggest conditions that we see again today in public shelters.[27]

> Theft was widespread—hobo jungle codes of behavior notwithstanding. Violence sometimes occurred. The drinking of spirits often led to unpredictability of behavior. Children and teenagers were often the targets of older "buzzards." Sexual abuse of young boys was a hazard they all had to face; many did not escape the coercion of the "wolves" who stalked them. Hobo life was a life without women: in all such societies homosexuality is rampant.[28]

The Bums

> *The hobo works and wanders,*
> *the tramp dreams and wanders,*
> *the bum drinks and wanders.*[29]

Historians identify a third distinct group among the homeless at the turn of the century. Different from the hobo and the tramp, the "bums" were both workers and nonworkers who stayed in one place, living hand-to-mouth, often on the streets or in cardboard boxes. This "home guard" was joined by the hoboes and the tramps during the cold winter months or at any time of the year when the transients were no longer capable of living the life on the road because of old age, illness, or infirmity.

According to Hoch and Slayton, there was a hierarchy among the bums. First was the home guard, the stationary residents who had encountered problems in the job market and were unemployed casual laborers.

> The next social rank down, after the home guard, was that of beggar. . . . Even among beggars, there were categories. . . . There were those who sold their skill, like the "mush fakers," beggars who had learned, while in a penal institution, to repair umbrellas. Others sold particular items; peddlers such as "timbers" sold pencils, a "wangy" sold shoe laces, and "wires" sold articles made from stolen telegraph wires. More common, however, were the beggars who claimed any of a variety of afflictions. They beseeched the pity of all passersby, crying out for a little dose of mercy. Among the established types were the "flopper," who sprawled on the sidewalk in crowded business thoroughfares; the "stiffy," who simulated paralysis; and the "dummy," who pretended to be deaf and dumb. There were distinctions between a "straight crip" (someone who was actually crippled) and a "phoney crip" (someone who was faking a deformity, or whose problem was self-inflicted). . . . Below them were the drug addicts ("hop heads" or "junkies"), "mission stiffs" and "grafters." Mission stiffs faked conversions in return for bed and board; grafters exploited charitable organizations. . . . At the very bottom of the heap was the "tomato can vag" (for "vagrant"). . . . They lived in boxes, cellars, and doorways; they picked the refuse of restaurants, in alleys, and from tomato cans for food.[30]

As much as people would like to believe otherwise, many of these characters reappear among today's homeless.[31] In an effort to avoid pejorative labeling of the homeless, we have lost a rich and colorful vocabulary that was developed almost a hundred years ago to describe an important cultural phenomenon. Today, by homogenizing the homeless population, mainstream society can view it as a group with a single problem, and, as a consequence, American culture has not only lost the richness of the description but also the capacity to understand the heterogeneity of the homeless population—both its variety and its underlying problems.

Skid Row

In small towns, the home guard stayed in the hobo jungle; in larger urban areas, these jungles came to be known as skid row, named for the street in Seattle where logs were skidded down to the waterfront docks. The term came to be applied to those sections of urban centers, including such places as Chicago's Main Stem and New York's Bowery, that were home to destitute people. The vast majority of them were single unattached men—those who were between travels and those who did not travel, those who sometimes worked and those who did not. The economic recessions of the 1870s and the 1890s and the Tramp Acts, which made travel risky, drove many hoboes into the cities to look for work. There, they coexisted with other tramps, the home guard, and the bums. Skid rows became complex social and economic communities, and there were a variety of institutions that catered to the men who lived on the row: bars, package stores, inexpensive restaurants, secondhand stores, barber colleges, tattoo parlors, all-night movies, burlesque theaters, and employment agencies. Overall, the goods and services were cheap, priced suitably for low-income residents.[32]

As the populations of skid row grew, local communities had no choice but to respond. By the latter part of the nineteenth century, the poorhouses had disappeared. These closings were the result of successful campaigns by reformers concerned about both their conditions and their costs. In their place, police stations, including jail cells, became the primary source of public shelter throughout America. In 1890, for example, police stations in New York provided 150,000 lodgings a year, and in 1898, the comparable number in Chicago was 139,578.[33] Gradually, because of the miserable conditions of police station lodgings (cold, bare stone floors) and the prevalence of tuberculosis, venereal disease, and lice, the municipal lodging house was created as an alternative, thus repeating the history of the original poorhouse. Municipal lodging houses, the major source of shelter for unemployed and homeless residents of cities during the period preceding the Great Depression, inherited the three major purposes of the poorhouse: shelter, punishment, and deterrence. Because a distinction was made between the deserving and the undeserving poor, able-bodied men were frequently required to perform hard labor like chopping wood and collecting garbage, requirements imposed to limit the demand for shelter at public expense.[34]

There were other options for shelter for those who, for whatever reason, did not stay at the municipal lodging houses. These included, in descending order of quality and cost: boarding and rooming houses for working men and women, what Miller called the "elite lodging house";[35] the cubicle or cage hotels, where large rooms were subdivided into cubicles just big enough to hold a bed, chair, and occasionally a locker; dormitory lodging houses, where up to 200 men could rent cots or bunks; the flophouse, which provided literally nothing more than several square feet of bare space for a lodger to flop down; barrelhouses, where tavern patrons paid to sleep all night in a chair, on a table, or in a beer barrel; establishments that permitted people to sleep in the hallway; and for a penny, the most appalling kind of accommodations, where people hung on a series of ropes stretched across a room. For those who lacked even a penny, there were charitable hotels run by such not-for-profit organizations as the YMCA, the gospel missions, and the Salvation Army, which all sought religious conversion in return for respite from the elements.[36] Because of this array of housing alternatives, unattractive as they may seem today, few skid row residents actually slept on the streets. As recently as 1958, one study found only 100 men sleeping on the streets out of a total skid row population in Chicago of 12,000.[37]

For those who did not work, like so many of today's homeless, life on skid row was supported by begging, panhandling, and petty theft, and there was the constant challenge of finding something to eat and a place to sleep. Run-ins with the police were common, especially when skid row residents crossed the boundaries into middle-class neighborhoods. These run-ins are similar to the practices in many of today's cities, where police sweep the homeless out of downtown areas, and foreshadow today's "Not in My Back Yard" (NIMBY) phenomenon, where middle-class residents refuse to allow the development of homeless services in their neighborhoods. In addition, there was the "dominance of alcohol abuse in the lives of [skid row] citizens. . . . Booze . . . was a serious component of Skid Row life and a fulcrum about which much of that life revolved."[38] Despite the shift in focus in the 1980s to the "new homeless" and denial about alcoholism, the rate of alcoholism among today's homeless is about the same as it was during the skid row era.[39]

The abundant variety of people and human behavior made skid row an appealing subject for early sociological research, and many rich histories of skid row were produced between 1920 and the early 1960s. A virtually universal finding of this research was that skid row attracted primarily single white men, who became stereotyped as the "skid row bum" and formed the standard against which today's homeless population is judged to be significantly different. Several social historians, however, suggest that sociologists ignored comparable social enclaves, complete with the kind of diversity found among skid row's residents, in racially segregated areas. The racial bias of the research prevented the recognition of the totality of America's destitution and diminished understanding of both the common and distinctive features of white and black skid rows.[40] Today's homeless population may not in actuality be so racially different from that of the skid row era. What is more likely is the scattering of the entire destitute and homeless population throughout today's urban areas as a result not only of desegregation but also of slum clearance, urban renewal, and gentrification, processes that largely bulldozed skid row out of existence in the second half of the twentieth century.

The Emergence
of the American Welfare State

The second half of the nineteenth century saw major developments in American social welfare practices. For example, Dorothea Dix campaigned for improvements in the care of the indigent mentally ill, who had been labeled as "deviants" and housed in jails and poorhouses. She successfully opened St. Elizabeth's Hospital for the Mentally Ill in 1852 in Washington, D.C., as well as some thirty other asylums throughout the country. By 1890 New York State adopted the first State Care Act, under which the state assumed full responsibility for the care of all the "insane poor." As state institutions for the mentally ill were established throughout the country, they tended to be large and bureaucratic and were not wholly accepted as being sufficiently humane and responsive to the needs of their patients.[41] These complaints culminated in the 1940s and 1950s in widely publicized documentation of mental hospitals as "snake pits."[42] This publicity, along with advances in psychiatry, led to the deinstitutionalization movement of the 1960s.

"Scientific charity" was another major development of the period. At the heart of this concept was the belief that overly generous "indiscriminate charity" had previously created a core of individuals who felt that they had entitlements to relief and shelter. Scientific charity, a movement that preceded the formal development of social work, was an effort to make private philanthropy more rational and systematic and to introduce programs to rehabilitate individuals so they could become economically independent. The motives behind this notion were very similar to the ones that drive welfare reform, "workfare," and transitional programs for today's homeless. "Friendly visitors" from the not-for-profit charity societies called upon poor families to help them identify and address their problems. As Katz explained, however, scientific charity was an anachronism.

> Charity organization society agents and visitors . . . were to inspire confidence and radiate warmth as they intruded into the most intimate detail of their clients' lives. They were to be welcome guests in the homes of people who had no choice but to receive them, if they wanted to eat or keep warm. . . . Over and over again, charity organizations' sponsors claimed their overriding goal was to restore the very poor to independence. Dependence on private or public charity was their great enemy. Yet, their very method taught dependence, because only an outward show of deference merited relief. Any display of independence they translated into ingratitude, and gratitude was everything. Clients had to show their appreciation cheerfully; they had to accept the advice so freely offered; they could not resist attempts of agents or visitors to reorder their lives. In fact, increased dependence became the price of continued support.[43]

These "lady bountifuls" of the late nineteenth century, by encouraging dependence in return for continued support, ultimately, "taught the poor to be paupers"[44] and insured the need for a "helping" industry not unlike the "homelessness industry" seen now. As criticism of scientific charity mounted in the 1920s, emerging professional codes of social work placed increasing emphasis on professionalism and detachment, and the "friendly visitors" of scientific charity were replaced by trained social workers. But even a newly

professional cadre of social workers could not be prepared for the poverty
about to overwhelm the entire country.

The Great Depression

The stock market crash of 1929 ushered in an era of national poverty unlike
anything this country had previously experienced. Breadlines, soup kitchens,
and massive unemployment spread across the nation. Shantytowns sprang
up to house the dispossessed. Farmers escaping the dust storms and fore-
closures joined millions of other dislocated workers as migrants looking for
new homes and new work. Homelessness and the need for temporary
housing expanded exponentially: In Chicago, the number of lodgings
provided by various agencies grew from 1 million in 1930–1931 to 4.3 million in 1933–1934; in New York, the city's municipal lodgings increased
from 159,000 in 1929 to almost 2.3 million in 1933, an increase on a daily
average basis from 434 to 6,110.[45] According to one congressional investi-
gation, some 5 million people were migrating from state to state looking for
work and housing as late as 1937.[46]

The severity and universality of the Great Depression required remedies
that were very different from existing policies and practices for assisting the
impoverished, the unemployed, and the homeless. Before 1930, America
had relied extensively on private, not-for-profit charity organizations and on
local governments that ran poorhouses, municipal lodging houses, and
provided "outdoor relief." At the state level, some governments had enacted
provisions for unemployment compensation and welfare relief for mothers.
Illinois and Missouri, for example, had passed the first mothers' pension
legislation in 1911, and a number of other states had quickly followed suit,
establishing the precedent for the federal Aid for Dependent Children
(ADC), established in 1935, and its successor, AFDC, Aid to Families with
Dependent Children.[47] Before the depression, the federal government's role
was still limited to providing relief for Civil War survivors and emancipated
slaves. The depression changed all this, as it became apparent to many that
the poverty and destitution were national problems and their redress, therefore, a federal responsibility. The New Deal, comprising the variety of
programs enacted over the period prior to World War II, was the vehicle that
redefined the role of the federal government and dramatically extended its
reach in addressing the problems of the homeless and the destitute.

For the first three years of the depression, charity organizations, cities,
and states continued to bear the burden of feeding and sheltering the homeless. Shelter facilities created in response to the burgeoning demand, like the
poorhouses and the municipal lodging houses that preceded them, were
filthy and squalid places filled with disease, alcohol, drugs, and mental
illness, and they had grossly unsanitary toilet facilities; in New York City, one

shelter had "1,724 beds in one enormous room, a situation described as 'like nothing else under the sun, [except] perhaps a scene from Dante.'"[48] As we have seen, this scene unfortunately would be repeated again at public shelters for the homeless in the 1980s.

In 1933, Congress created the first of the New Deal emergency and public assistance programs with the Federal Emergency Relief Act. This act created the Federal Transient Bureau to provide assistance to the huge and mobile population of the depression. By 1935, the Federal Transient Bureau had become very unpopular, "plagued by the familiar and very stubborn conviction held by the community at large that transients were dangerous degenerates."[49] It was replaced by the Works Progress Administration (WPA), and the focus for relief shifted from helping transients to creating new jobs for the unemployed. By establishing stringent residency requirements similar to those based on the English Settlement Laws introduced 300 years earlier, the New Deal incorporated the now familiar elements of American social welfare policy—residency, work, relief, and with the creation of the original ADC program, assistance to women and children.

The revolutionary part of the New Deal reform was the introduction of federal unemployment insurance and Social Security, both intended to help the broad spectrum of the American working population facing the hard times of the depression. Unlike the relief and welfare programs that preceded them, these programs were predicated on workers paying into the system as a kind of insurance against which they could draw in times of need or retirement. By creating a clear and conscious distinction in federal policy between work-earned benefits on the one hand and relief or public assistance on the other, policymakers played a role in the ongoing process of defining the deserving and the undeserving poor.

> The American welfare state emerged in the 1930s divided between public assistance and social insurance. Social insurance benefits were entitlements; they reflected the assumption that workers and employers paid into funds on which they drew in times of unemployment or when they retired. . . . Public assistance is means tested. That is, it serves only people who meet strict income and asset requirements. . . . Public assistance has become synonymous with welfare; it carries the old stigma of relief. Its recipients are the modern paupers.[50]

Much of the political debate since, including today's debate about homelessness, has focused on two issues: to what benefits the poor, including the homeless, are entitled; and how to construct a system that overcomes the stigma attached to being in need of public benefits. The depression produced substantial agreement about the centrality of federal involvement in addressing the problems of poverty and economic crisis; what remained was the continuing process of sorting out those who deserved to be helped from those who did not and deciding under what conditions help would be offered.

The Fraying Safety Net
for the Homeless

Although the national economy was beginning to rebound by the time America entered World War II, it was the war itself that stimulated tremendous recovery. World War II, called the "greatest public works project ever conceived,"[51] enlisted some 15 million men and provided wartime factory jobs to millions of others, including women. On December 7, 1941, unemployment was 17 percent; as the war economy heated up, unemployment virtually disappeared.[52] The confluence of military service and wartime work essentially eliminated the economic blight of the depression and fueled economic expansion after the war. To insure participation in the new economic boom, the new GI Bill provided substantial benefits for returning World War II veterans—housing, education, lifelong health benefits, and pensions. As with the pension programs for Civil War veterans, the GI Bill conferred upon World War II veterans the status of being deserving of government support. Three decades later, negative attitudes about the Vietnam War prevailed, and veterans of this unpopular war, lacking needed support, are now among today's homeless population and often viewed as the undeserving poor.

The economic recovery and expansion brought about by World War II continued for approximately twenty-five years and generated, among other things, the high birthrates that produced the baby boom. It was a period of unprecedented prosperity and optimism during which, as Nathan Glazer explained, "we believed . . . that our rich country had both the material resources and the intelligence to eliminate poverty, eradicate slums, overcome the differences between the educational achievement and health of the rich and of the poor. Social scientists—economists, sociologists, political scientists, anthropologists—were pulled into the design and administration of new government programs aiming at these results."[53] During the 1960s, there was a sense that no problem was too difficult or intractable to solve.

The growing prosperity, however, stood in stark contrast to the lingering and persistent poverty in America, and this contrast forced Americans to examine the disparity between the rich and poor. This was one of those periods when "the myth [of the middle class], somewhat like a great fog, lifts, and the reality of poverty is discovered once again . . . [as it is] every twenty years or so."[54] The publication of such books as Oscar Lewis's *The Children of Sanchez*, which introduced the concept of the "culture of poverty," and Michael Harrington's *The Other America* gave rise to a renewed national effort to understand the causes and the nature of poverty. As policymakers and reformers digested these new insights, a new generation of government programs to deal with social ills proliferated under the auspices of the Great Society.

As they set about designing new programs to address poverty, the social scientists, civil rights activists, poverty warriors, and modern reformers of the 1960s were far less comfortable with sorting the poor into categories than their predecessors had been, particularly when such sorting was based on moralistic judgments such as "indolence," "intemperance," "laziness," and "wilful error." Instead, most considered the problems of the poor and the destitute to be the result of racist and discriminatory economic, political, and social systems that failed to provide opportunity for all to participate fully in the life of this country. Reinforced by William Ryan's influential book *Don't Blame the Victim,* activists and policymakers believed strongly that the problems were in the system and not inherent in the people who were destitute and disadvantaged. The injunction was clear: To acknowledge personal conditions or behaviors as playing a role in poverty, destitution, and later, homelessness or to ascribe personal responsibility to individuals in trouble was to "blame the victim."

Unfortunately, America's most active social reformers, fearful of blaming the victim, ignored what had been a commonplace connection between alcohol, mental illness, abject impoverishment, and the homelessness that existed on white and black skid rows. Therefore, they failed to take advantage of advances in both the science of alcoholism and psychiatry that could have been marshaled to help those who were destitute and suffered from these conditions. At the same time, reform-minded advocates within the professional spheres of alcohol treatment and psychiatry, riding on the tide of sweeping legislative changes, were successful in promoting two major initiatives that ultimately had the unintended consequence of increasing homelessness. The first, the Community Mental Health Center Act signed into law in October 1963, signaled the beginning of deinstitutionalization of the mentally ill—or what E. Fuller Torrey called the "signpost to a grate society."[55] The second was the Uniform Alcoholism and Intoxication Treatment Act of 1971 (also referred to as the Hughes Act), which decriminalized public drunkenness. This act had the effect of shifting the focus of responsibility for the public inebriate from the criminal justice system to the health care system, transforming the "revolving door" from the jails to the streets into the "spinning door" from detox centers to the streets.[56]

Most of the Great Society efforts focused on creating new programs and institutional arrangements for those for whom no such programs or institutional arrangements had previously existed—the poor, the disenfranchised, and the disadvantaged. The Voting Rights Act and the Civil Rights Acts provided voting opportunities as well as access to the political and economic systems in ways previously unavailable for poor and minority citizens. Moreover, the War on Poverty programs were intended to educate and train people for participation in these systems and to empower poor and minority citizens through "maximum feasible participation" and community action.

Great Society reforms went hand in hand, however, with deinstitutional-ization and decriminalization, which aimed to eliminate existing institutions, social settings, and programs. Although these were to be replaced by more humane and less restrictive programs, implementation fell far short of deliv-ering the hoped-for alternatives in community-based treatment and detoxifi-cation services. Furthermore, the expansion of slum clearance efforts, urban renewal, and gentrification, propelled by Great Society initiatives to redevelop America's decaying inner cities, essentially razed skid rows, effectively dis-placing their residents but offering no alternatives. The result during the 1960s and early 1970s was the irreparable fraying of the well-established safety net that had been in place for the homeless for generations. State mental institutions for the "insane poor" and the entire panoply of public and private lodgings, missions, soup kitchens, stores, and other community amenities in place in skid row since the era of the hobo jungles fell victim to the Great Society. This series of developments set the stage for the increased visibility of homelessness in the 1980s.

The Deserving
and the Undeserving Poor

Despite the common perception that it was a new phenomenon in the early 1980s, homelessness has always been part of the American social experience. The homeless were the rejects of the colonies, the rugged explorers of the frontier, the tragic wreckage of the Civil War, the hoboes, tramps, and bums of the late nineteenth century, the denizens of the skid rows of both white and black America. They were the products of the depression who continued to live in the rows until slum clearance and urban redevelopment forced them to scatter throughout urban areas, and, finally, they are now the unfor-tunate members of the baby boom who "lost their inner maps" or who became the isolated poor of inner cities, plagued by poverty and drugs. For all these individuals, rejection by mainstream society has been the norm, as has a life filled with alcohol, drugs, and mental illness and the constant hassle of finding food and lodging.

Public officials and private citizens have been reasonably consistent over time in accepting homelessness as a fact of life and in differentiating the deserving from the undeserving poor. The deserving poor have been the aged, widows, orphans, war veterans, and those who are sick, infirm, and unemployed through no fault of their own. Throughout American history, most of the homeless have been considered members of the undeserving poor—by virtue of their transience, their economic dependence, and the centrality of alcohol and drugs in their lives. Society has ejected them from the community and excluded them from shelters and has refused them par-ticipation in welfare by using residency requirements or by making them work as a condition of assistance. People have worried that "indiscriminate charity" has been too generous and that charity, though offered in the name of promoting independence, has had the effect of undermining the work ethic and promoting dependency.

In the 1980s, political advocates attempted to change American attitudes about the homeless and portrayed them as the deserving poor by framing the issue as one of poverty and victimization. Society has responded to that challenge by believing that the homeless are deserving, but ironically, it has not changed its ways of treating them. The worst conditions of the poorhouse are recreated in today's public and private shelters. By instituting exclusionary rules that deny services to those who are drunk, high on drugs, or exhibiting the bizarre symptoms of mental illness, today's shelters repeat the practice of earlier times when misfits were driven out to starve or left to the mercy of the elements. Although there has been an outpouring of public support, many programs for the homeless, especially transitional programs, have "creamed" today's homeless population, setting strict standards as conditions of continued support. In addition, there is growing concern that "indiscriminate charity" has increased dependence and that the expectation of shelter, food, and clothing as an entitlement has undermined motivation for becoming independent and self-sufficient.

In the 1990s, efforts to manipulate public opinion are in large measure failing. Across America, citizens are experiencing "compassion fatigue"[57] and public attitudes toward the homeless are shifting; once again, the American public is coming to believe that the homeless are undeserving and is becoming less generous and more careful about its support. City officials are using a variety of laws to prevent their cities from becoming "havens" for homeless people.[58] They are sweeping the homeless from downtown areas and enacting antihomelessness laws intended to prevent the homeless from begging and sleeping in public and to insure that the homeless remain hidden from sight. Some of today's antivagrancy laws are actually revivals of the Tramp Acts enacted in the nineteenth century; San Francisco's law prohibiting sleeping in public, for example, enacted in 1870, is currently being "liberally enforced" to control what is regarded today as a major public problem.[59] In short, despite the vast expenditure of financial and human resources during the 1980s, the public continues to see the homeless on the streets and in public places and is beginning to blame the victims after all for the "moral failings" of substance abuse and mental illness.

As frustration at the seeming inability to solve the problem mounts, the public is becoming afraid and angry. A 1990 California study of public attitudes about homelessness reports that "a principal factor in community concerns . . . is fear";[60] but the angry battle cry of the 1990s could well become, "Brother, Don't Spare a Dime," the title of a 1991 *Newsweek* article whose author worked with an alcoholic homeless man. This author wrote:

In a society that has mastered dodging responsibility, these homeless prefer a life of no responsibility at all. . . . Was "society" to blame for this man? Hardly. It had provided free medical care, counseling and honest effort. Was it the fault of the economy? No. This man never gave the economy a chance to solve his problems. The only person who can be blamed for his failure to get off the streets is the man himself. To argue otherwise is a waste of time and compassion. . . . Unless the homeless are willing to help themselves, there is nothing anyone else can do. Not you. Not me. Not the government. Not anyone.[61]

Much like Steinbeck's "comfortable people," today's Americans first felt pity; this pity is changing to distaste, fear, and finally to anger. To understand why public opinion has come to this point, we turn now to the politics of homelessness.

7

The Politics
of Homelessness

Contemporary American homelessness is an outrage, a national scandal. Its
character requires a careful, sophisticated, and dispassionate analysis ... but its
tragedy demands something more direct and human, less qualified and detached.
We have tried to present the facts and figures of homelessness, but we were unable to
capture the extent of our anger and dismay. ... [H]omelessness in the United States
is an inexcusable disgrace and must be eliminated.[1]

The statement above, prepared by ten members of the Institute of Medicine's Committee on Health Care for Homeless People, reflects the passion and intensity felt by those engaged in the debate about homelessness. To understand this intensity, it is necessary to understand the context in which the debate emerged, define the major participants, and explore the issues that have formed the substance of the debate. The politics of homelessness have been complicated and controversial. Underlying much of the debate is the unfortunate fact that many of those who brought homelessness to national public attention framed the public discourse around the wrong issues, namely poverty and the absence of "affordable housing"; as a result, little progress has been made in addressing the real problems and homelessness has continued unabated.

The 1970s

When homelessness first became a public policy issue at the beginning of the 1980s, Americans were still coping with the effects of a decade of economic and social disruptions. In 1973, the Organization of Petroleum Exporting Countries (OPEC) placed an embargo on oil that lasted for six months and sent oil and gasoline prices skyrocketing. The embargo marked the beginning of an inflationary cycle that would affect the entire U.S. economy, from every household's "market basket" to the cost of housing to the cost of industrial production. "Stagflation" was the newly coined euphemism for extraordinary inflation, high unemployment, and slow growth. Because its attention was so focused on the Watergate scandal, the nation was slow to

110

recognize the immediate impact of OPEC's action; however, as Nicholas Lemann suggested, the imposition of the oil embargo "now appears to have been the pivotal moment at which the mass upward economic mobility of American society ended, perhaps forever. . . . As it slowly began to sink in that everybody wasn't going to be moving forward together anymore, the country became more fragmented, more internally rivalrous, and less sure of its mythology." The mythology Lemann was referring to was the idea that children would always do better than their parents and that upward mobility was the defining characteristic of the national culture.[2]

When President Jimmy Carter spoke to the nation about "malaise," he was reflecting upon the public's loss of optimism about the future as well as its loss of control over the present—gasoline lines that first appeared in 1973 reappeared in 1979, and no one seemed capable of rescuing the hostages held by Iran. Just fifteen years earlier, social and economic optimism had permitted the government to wage the War on Poverty and to increase federal spending for health, education, jobs, welfare, and the environment—in short, Americans had believed that "all of the nation's ill and shortcomings, from poverty to the heartbreak of psoriasis, could be vanquished by bureaucratic phalanxes of social and health programs backed by billions in appropriations."[3] Now, pessimism was spreading through America, and the national political climate was changing in response. One indication of this change was that people no longer believed that problems could be solved by increasing the government's financial commitment; instead, reluctance to "throw more money" at all the nation's problems prevailed.

By 1978, citizens in California launched a tax revolt with Proposition 13 that quickly spread to Massachusetts and then to other states, opening up "a new schism in American politics, pitting taxpayers against tax recipients."[4] In 1980, Ronald Reagan was elected president, in part because he promised to cut taxes, to increase defense spending, to reduce the size, cost, and regulatory power of the federal government, and most important for our analysis, to diminish the government's role in caring for America's poor. Just as important as the presidential election in 1980 was the surprising congressional election, which turned control of the Senate over to the Republican party and, with a strong cadre of "Reagan Democrats" in the House of Representatives, created a conservative governing majority in Congress for the first time in fifty years.[5]

As Thomas and Mary Edsall recount in their political history *Chain Reaction*, the election of 1980 created a political realignment in the United States. The Democratic party's historically broad-based coalition, which had engineered much of the progressive agenda of the post–World War II period, was splintering. Traditionally Democratic working- and middle-class voters, concerned with what they perceived to be a disproportionate tax burden to support services and benefits less and less responsive to their own needs, elected Democrats to Congress who would support the conservative initiatives of the Reagan administration and the Republican agenda.[6] The results of the political realignment were nowhere more evident than in 1981 when, with overwhelming support, Congress enacted the Omnibus Budget Reconciliation Act. This act abolished many categorical programs, created block grants that devolved much of the responsibility for running programs to the states, and reduced spending for social programs that had formed the social safety net for poor Americans. With this major piece of legislation in place, the Reagan administration was ready to implement its conservative agenda of tax relief, draconian cuts in domestic spending, a reduction in federal regulatory authority, and increases in defense spending. The debilitating result was a huge federal deficit that will continue to curb federal social and domestic initiatives for decades to come.

An Issue for the New Left

Such was the economic and political situation that faced political activists on the Left as the 1980s began. In addition, issues that ten years earlier had served as central mobilizing forces for these activists—the Vietnam War and Watergate—were now history. At the same time, conservative attacks on Great Society programs that a decade earlier would have been politically unthinkable were now greeted by tax-weary voters as welcome reform. With no single issue around which to mobilize, some activists on the Left turned their attention to global issues: the nuclear freeze movement and arms reduction and the civil wars in Latin America. Others focused their attention on domestic issues, continuing the struggle to gain passage of the Equal Rights Amendment, full employment, pay equity, reproductive rights, and gay rights or working to alleviate the suffering of the inner-city underclass, particularly children. One other issue, the increasingly visible phenomenon in the late 1970s and the early 1980s of street people, gave still others a new cause to pursue, one that had the potential for wide popular and political appeal.

As we have seen, the Great Society and reform movements of the 1960s and 1970s, although beneficial to many segments of America's poor and minority citizens, had the unintended consequence of fraying the generations-old safety net for the homeless. Gone were the state mental hospitals; gone for the most part were the skid rows and flophouses of the major cities; gone, too, was a consensus about how to treat public drunkenness. No alternative systems of care adequate to the tasks ever materialized to take their place. Efforts to organize and empower the poor and disenfranchised to take their rightful place in the social and economic systems were irrelevant to individuals who suffered from severe psychiatric illness or whose lives and families were destroyed by the ravages of alcoholism, drug addiction, and domestic violence. Without the old safety net, many became homeless. At the same time, the huge cohort of baby boomers was entering their thirties and was beginning to put pressure on existing social service and helping systems; some joined the ranks of the homeless. As their numbers and their visibility increased, the new homeless provided a fresh opportunity for liberal activists to mobilize around a phenomenon that looked like incomparable poverty and deprivation.

In 1980, activists Mitch Snyder and Mary Ellen Hombs testified before Congress and launched the political campaign to address homelessness.[7] By bringing with him a box containing the ashes of a dead homeless person, Snyder introduced a flamboyance that was both reminiscent of the social activism of the late 1960s and characteristic of much of what was to follow. In a book they coauthored, Snyder and Hombs described their appearance before Congress:

> On September 30, 1980, Community for Creative Non-Violence [CCNV] members Mary Ellen Hombs and Mitch Snyder appeared before the House [of Representatives] District Committee, accompanied by the cremated remains of "John Doe," the first homeless person to freeze to death during the previous winter. Snyder was specially released, for a few hours, from a 60-day jail term that he was serving for an unlawful entry conviction, resulting from accompanying homeless friends to St. Matthew's Cathedral for shelter during a snow storm on February 9, 1980. Hombs and Snyder made the following comments: . . .
>
> "Envision, if you will, an infinitely long line of people, stretching—five, ten, twenty abreast—as far as the eye can see. There are literally millions of them— men, women, and children. . . . Since these are times of modest expectations, our goal is simple: the creation of adequate, accessible space, offered in an atmosphere of reasonable dignity, for every man, woman, and child who needs and wants to get off the street."[8]

Thus began the effort to define homelessness as an issue of shelter and housing. The specific content of the political debate about homelessness, this new breed of visible poverty, passed through several iterations during the 1980s and included legal rights issues—the right to shelter, the right to housing, involuntary commitment to institutions, and residency requirements—as well as service issues—emergency shelters, emergency financial assistance, welfare benefits, disability entitlements, and universal access to health care. The basic parameters of the debate have remained unchanged. On one side, those determined not to focus on personal attributes of the homeless—that is, not to "blame the victim"—consider homelessness a problem related to poverty, housing, economics, disenfranchisement, powerlessness, government failure, and social inequality in America—in short, the consequence of systemic failure. On the other side, those who feel that the homeless choose their lot argue that homelessness is a moral failing and a personal choice that absolves the community of any responsibility; under this assumption, no public response is needed.[9] In the middle, many who examine the immediate problems confronting the homeless to develop appropriate programs to address their needs are vilified by the advocates of systemic change for "medicalizing the problem" or warned that their data about alcohol and drug abuse and mental illness will be misused and misinterpreted by the proponents of doing nothing.

Mitch Snyder and the Homelessness Movement

More than even the homeless themselves, Mitch Snyder made homelessness a major political issue of the 1980s and set the tone for the political debate. Robert Hayes, counsel to the National Coalition for the Homeless and the first to use the courts to secure a legal right to shelter for the homeless in New York City, on hearing of Snyder's suicide in July 1990, credited Snyder with creating "almost single-handedly a movement" for the homeless.[10]

Snyder was born just three years too early to be called a baby boomer, but in 1969 at the age of 26, during the heyday of the New Left and the counterculture, he left behind his middle-class life and took to the road, searching for answers to the questions of the time: the Vietnam War, competitive individualism, civil rights, community, and equality. He spent time in jail with the Berrigan brothers, Roman Catholic priests and charismatic leaders of the antiwar movement; there, "Snyder's personal rebelliousness was increasingly channeled into political protest."[11] In 1973, Snyder received an invitation to join the nascent antiwar group known as the Community for Creative Non-Violence in Washington, D.C., just at the time the group was searching for a new agenda. The CCNV, built on the Ghandian traditions of nonviolence and community, soon began to turn its attention to the privation in the inner-city neighborhood where the organization's communal house was located. Offering shelter to an evicted tenant one night, Snyder found his issue:

> We live in a disposable society, a throwaway culture. The homeless are our human refuse, remnants of a culture that assigns a pathologically high value to independence and productivity. . . . The homeless are simply surplus souls in a system firmly rooted in competition and self-interest, in which only the "strongest" (i.e., those who fit most snugly within the confines of a purely arbitrary norm) will survive.[12]

CCNV proved to be the perfect setting for Snyder to develop his newfound ideology and learn the tactics of aggressive activism and confrontation. Ed Guinan, creator of CCNV, served as both Snyder's mentor and trainer. Guinan's political tactics had a profound influence on Snyder; one example of a tactic that Snyder incorporated into his own style is Guinan's 1972 twenty-one-day fast to dramatize the right of the poor to eat. At the end of his fast, he took food from a Safeway shelf, sat down in the aisle, ate it, and said, "This bread has been stolen by Safeway from the children, from the elderly, from the hungry, from the farmers and farm workers. It is here in this store so that this monopoly may now steal from the consumers. *People have a right to eat*" (emphasis in original).[13] During the 1980s, hunger strikes on behalf of the homeless were to become both Snyder's trademark and his most powerful political weapon. Like Guinan, he claimed rights for the homeless: "They demand dignity and not the demeaning that comes from sleeping on the streets. . . . They demand that, here and now, in the wealthiest nation on the face of the earth, basic shelter be recognized politically, philosophically, and programmatically as an absolute and inalienable human right."[14]

Victoria Rader described CCNV's creative ability to capture public attention. Reminiscent of the political antics of the Yippies, CCNV conducted "illegal occupations of buildings, pray-ins, eat-ins, cage-ins, jump-ins and even laugh-ins. And most of all, Mitch Snyder's fasts."[15]

> Snyder is the first one to admit that he is doing theater. "Yes, we time the fast to fit the presidential election and the cold weather, when people are more sympathetic to the homeless." But Snyder is transparently rather than deceivingly "the actor." He dresses and lives like a street person. He begs and yells, he carries around the cremated ashes of a homeless friend, he pours blood on cathedral altars and prays in the middle of the street and gets arrested. If the audience still does not respond, he starts starving himself to death, always, always, in front of the cameras.[16]

Snyder and other CCNV staff fought for the rights of the homeless, collected enough signatures to put Washington's right-to-shelter ordinance on the ballot, and campaigned for its successful adoption by the voters. They ran soup kitchens and drop-in centers, staffed shelters, collected information about the homeless, and testified before the first congressional hearings on homelessness since the Great Depression.

By waging a protracted battle with the Reagan administration that included a long, closely watched fast, Snyder won possession of a huge building where he vowed to create America's largest shelter for the homeless. Opening their own model shelter permitted CCNV to create an environment organized around their principles of love and community, claiming that the only real rule at the shelter was the Golden Rule. Shelter organizers eliminated bureaucratic rules that they believed were dehumanizing and put the tolerant attitudes of the counterculture into practice. The shelter accepted "those among us who are different"[17] and required nothing for admission. "People shouldn't have to do anything to get shelter. A shower doesn't get rid of lice anyway. *This is their home*" (emphasis in original).[18] Rehabilitation was not CCNV's goal; according to one staff member, "For many of these people, getting back into the mainstream is never a possibility. . . . Besides, for those of us who have come out of the mainstream, we are not comfortable putting people back into the culture that creates the problem in the first place."[19] The result was that CCNV's shelter, according to some, was the ultimate "crash pad"—drugs and alcohol were openly tolerated; according to others, it had "an atmosphere reminiscent of a psychiatric ward before the advent of major tranquilizers."[20]

Snyder and CCNV, along with Robert Hayes and the National Coalition for the Homeless, also inspired a nationwide network of advocacy groups claiming the right to shelter for the homeless.[21] But, most important, Snyder worked hard to convince the national media that homelessness was important. CCNV "framed the issue in terms of justice rather than charity . . . until, finally, the media adopted much of the Community's initial perspective as their own. . . . Homelessness became a legitimate problem only when the media certified it as reality."[22]

The Media as Messenger

Preferring the word "homeless" to pejorative labels seen as blaming the victim, Snyder convinced the press to present the homeless in sympathetic ways, as victims of Reaganomics and severe cutbacks in social welfare programs. With help from CCNV and other advocacy groups, the media helped transform the homeless into the deserving poor—people with dignity, people without homes who needed shelter. In his sharp critique of TV journalism, Walter Goodman, commenting on the 1992 report of the New York City Commission on the Homeless, noted the degree to which such a portrayal differed from reality.

> The report this week that more than two-thirds of the single men and almost a third of the adults in families housed in New York City's shelters are on drugs or alcohol may startle people who are addicted to television news. More often than not, a news story or documentary on the homeless will feature a hardworking, straight-living young couple or an attractive teenager and her child who have run into a spell of bad luck. . . . If you want to arouse sympathy for the homeless, you do not put forward off-putting specimens. Television news producers can count on advocacy groups to supply them with model victims for viewing purposes. . . . Reports on the homeless often tend to imitate depression-movie scripts: hard-working folks in heart-wrenching situations. If only jobs and housing were provided, they would be like you and me.[23]

Advocates found willing messengers among the print media as well. A study that analyzed major magazine and TV reporting of the homeless between November 1986 and February 1989 revealed that the media identified only 7 percent of the homeless as substance abusers, rarely mentioned mental illness, indicated that over 50 percent of the homeless were employed, and consistently exaggerated the proportion of women and children.[24] The authors of this report concluded that the portrait conveyed is of the "deserving poor who differ from other Americans mainly in their lack of housing, not in any social, psychological, or behavioral deficiency," and they quoted CBS's Martha Tischener as saying, "People who once gave to the needy now are the needy."[25] The homeless, according to advocates and their media allies, are people just like us, victims of unemployment, inflation, and recession, and most important, victims of Reaganomics.

There is no doubt that Snyder and the advocates he inspired succeeded in putting the suffering of homeless people into the national spotlight. Although the advocates did not always articulate the issues in the following way, most of the rhetoric and political posturing focused on five central themes:

What do we mean by homelessness?
How many homeless are there?
Who are the homeless?
What are the causes of homelessness?
What should we do to solve the problem?

In the following pages we will explore the first three of these questions and set the stage for addressing the final two; these we will examine in Chapters 8 and 9.

What Do We Mean by Homelessness?

Everyone who has read newspapers or magazines or watched television during the past fifteen years assumes he or she knows what homelessness means. There are, however, major differences in the definitions used by various reporters, analysts, and advocates. In fact, when the U.S. Census Bureau decided to include the homeless in the 1990 census, census officials made a decision not to "try to impose a definition on what is a hotly debated concept."[26] In explaining this decision, a Census Bureau document offers the following:

To most people, the homeless population includes at least those who sleep in the streets at night or who live in emergency shelters or subsidized housing because they do not have regular access to conventional housing. They are obviously and literally homeless. Even here, however, there is not universal agreement about who to include. Some persons stay at a shelter for only a night or two because of domestic disputes or violence. Others have small monthly incomes and stay in cheap rooms part of the month and in shelters the remaining days when money is low. Some data users include in their definition of "homeless," families doubled up with others in conventional housing. Others include those "at risk" of losing their homes because they have unsteady incomes or spend a large portion on the cost of housing. Some data users would include all persons in single-room-occupancy (SRO) units even though the people living there may not consider themselves to be homeless.[27]

The Census Bureau resolved the problem of definition by including in their special count only those persons found in emergency shelters or visible in street locations at the time of the census, thus limiting their count and provoking heated objections from those who would use broader and more inclusive definitions.

One of the first attempts at defining homelessness was made by Ellen Baxter and Kim Hopper in a 1981 study in New York City. In *Private Lives/Public Spaces,* they stated, "We define the homeless as those whose primary nighttime residence is either in the publicly or privately operated shelters or in the streets, in doorways, train stations and bus terminals, public plazas and parks, subways, abandoned buildings, loading docks and other well-hidden sites known only to their users."[28] Three years later, the U.S. Department of Housing and Urban Development added to this definition such places as armories, schools, church basements, former firehouses, government buildings, and places not designed for shelter, such as airports, cars, or trucks; HUD also included people who were given vouchers to stay in hotels, apartments, or boarding homes.[29] The National Institute of Mental Health used as a working definition "anyone who lacks adequate shelter, resources, and community ties";[30] Peter Rossi, in his careful study of Chicago's homeless, used the definition of "not having customary and regular access to a conventional dwelling."[31]

Others have developed even broader definitions that include the pre-homeless or those "at risk" of becoming homeless at some point in the future. Perhaps the most inclusive definition was that summarized by Gregg Barak as including "the hidden or invisible homeless, the prehomeless people, the renters and even the home owners at risk, or people who are without a fixed domicile,"[32] to which Barak also added Hopper and Hamberg's definition, which includes being "without an address which assures them at least 30 days' sleeping quarters which meet minimal health and safety standards,"[33] and Hopper's "undomiciled person who is unable to secure permanent and stable housing without special assistance."[34]

All of these definitions define homelessness in terms of where people stay or sleep at night, but others incorporate the concept of occurrence into the definition. Most researchers study the homeless at one particular point in time, that is, on the night or nights of their study; a few have examined the occurrence of homeless over the course of a period of time, usually a calendar year. Toro and McDonell argued that it is appropriate to examine a lifetime estimate for risk of homelessness—the potential for homelessness at any point during a person's lifetime.[35] Most people know individuals or have themselves experienced situations that could be considered homelessness under one of the many definitions above, if only for a night or two when for one reason or another they spent the night waiting for a plane or a bus, staying with friends or relatives before securing a job or finding an apartment in a new city, or even "sleeping it off" in a car on the highway or in a public place. A definition that includes being at risk of becoming homeless at any point in one's life is so broad that it begins to lose all meaning; certainly, such a definition bears little relevance for serious development of policy.

There is more here than legitimate disagreement. Some use a broad definition in order to inflate the size of the homeless population and stimulate greater political attention; others use a more limited definition to minimize the sense of urgency; and still others limit the definition either to focus their analyses or to design ameliorative responses to specific categories of homelessness. Clearly, different people with different purposes can, "by the touch of the definitional wand,"[36] radically change both the nature and the size of the homeless population.

As we will discuss at length in Chapter 10, we believe the word "homeless" is inappropriate because it focuses on a single consequence for many people who are not receiving treatment for addictions to alcohol and drugs or for serious mental illness; we recommend, in fact, that we stop using the term. For the purpose of this discussion, however, we define the homeless as those persons whose ability to function in ordinary social and economic interactions has been so impaired by their disabling conditions that they are socially alienated from their various support networks and society's institutions and are unable to maintain independent housing.

How Many Homeless Are There?

This absence of shared definitions naturally reinforces the tendency toward counting. It may not always be clear exactly what researchers are counting, but at least numbers give the appearance of a convincing portrait. If this activity seems almost ritualistic, it is nonetheless easy to understand: The problem is complex, the size of the population is daunting, and researchers know that funding constraints are likely to obstruct the implementation of any recommendation they might make. So, hemmed in on all sides, they count the homeless.[37]

The size of the homeless population is probably the most highly charged issue in the debate surrounding homelessness because it ultimately focuses on political claims for public resources and attention. The estimates range from 250,000 to 350,000, the range reported in the federal effort to count the homeless population in 1984, to more than 3 million, or about 1 percent of the American population, the number introduced by CCNV's Hombs and Snyder in 1982.[38]

At the low end of the range, HUD's first estimates were castigated by advocates as being woefully misrepresentative of the magnitude of the problem and indicative of the Reagan administration's desire to ignore the issue. At the high end, Hombs and Snyder's original testimony before Congress was almost whimsical. "How many [homeless people] nationally? Millions. Of that much we are certain. Precisely how many? Who knows?"[39] Four years later, Snyder "confessed that 'these numbers are in fact meaningless.' When asked why he uses 'meaningless' numbers, [he] told a congressional panel that he was trying 'to satisfy your gnawing curiosity for a number.'"[40] Nevertheless, Snyder's speculative 3 million became a magic number for the media, many politicians, and homeless advocates and is still widely used.

Those who consistently use the figure of 3 million have not, by and large, conducted research; however, many others have—in local, regional, and national studies. According to a 1988 General Accounting Office analysis of eighty-three of these studies, the number of the homeless estimated in the better-designed studies averages out to about 325,000.[41] A national study conducted by the Urban Institute suggested that the total number of homeless people in the United States is between 500,000 and 600,000. Based on this volume of good research, Rossi asserted that "There are no grounds for regarding the [CCNV] estimates as valid. . . . [I]t is surely strange that guesstimates of the sort issued by local advocate groups and CCNV should be cited in the press as serious and valid calculations."[42]

The political ramifications of definitions and estimates are most apparent in studies that include all potential people "at risk." Several analysts, in examining the nation's housing stock, have concluded that shortages of affordable housing place anywhere from 4 million to 19 million people "at risk" of becoming homeless. Some claim that many American families are "now living on the knife edge of homelessness; they are doubled and tripled up in the (mostly overcrowded and deteriorating) apartments of friends and families; they are one paycheck, one domestic argument from the streets. In a mild recession, homelessness in America is likely to double and triple overnight."[43] Written in 1989 before the 1991–1992 recession, the worst since the early 1970s, this prediction has fortunately proven to be vastly overstated, but it stands as a good example of the hyperbole that characterizes the numbers game of homelessness.

Perhaps the most extraordinary estimate is the one presented by Toro and McDonell in their 1991 study. Although they did not specifically define homelessness, they estimated, based on telephone interviews with a sample of people in the Buffalo, New York, area, that 12.2 million people, or 6.7 percent of the U.S. adult population, are at risk for homelessness sometime during their lives. They explained that

> this 6.7 percent figure is likely to be an underestimate for a number of reasons: Persons without phones as a group are probably at a higher risk for homelessness, some persons may have been reluctant to reveal on the phone that they had been homeless, the rate of homelessness may be higher in areas other than the site of this study, and the rate of homelessness may be increasing . . . and continue to do so over the adult life-span of the current U.S. adult population.[44]

Toro and McDonell went on to report that, if individuals are included who are "living temporarily with friends or relatives," the percentage of people at risk of homelessness over their lifetime may reach 12 percent of the American adult population, about 22 million people.[45] Some ten years after Hombs and Snyder's 1980 congressional testimony, Toro and McDonell finally quantified Snyder's vision of the homeless as "an infinitely long line of people, stretching—five, ten, twenty abreast—as far as the eye can see. There are literally millions of them—men, women, and children."[46]

To account for the extreme variations in numbers, a considerable amount of time, energy, and research money has been dedicated to defending or disproving one or another estimate, and the literature is filled with debates about research strategies, statistical methodologies, sampling differences, and definitions. But as Anna Kondratas, assistant secretary for Community Planning and Development, U.S. Department of Housing and Urban Development, stated, "There is no equivalency, for example, between the validity of those estimates that put the number of homeless in the hundreds of thousands and those that claim millions. Methodological discrepancies cannot account for estimating errors of 500 percent."[47]

Only politics can.

Three Questions in the Numbers Game

A further complication in the numbers game is that the question of how many homeless there are is actually three separate questions: What is the total size of this needy population on any given night, how many people have been homeless during a given year, and is the size of the homeless population growing? It is often very hard to know which of these questions is being answered when numerical claims are made about homelessness. For example, the Urban Institute estimate of between 500,000 and 600,000 is based on a calculation of how many individuals were homeless for one night in 1987. The authors of this study, Martha R. Burt and Barbara E. Cohen, made clear that "since data suggest that the number of people homeless during the course of a year is approximately double the number homeless at any given time, these figures imply that more than 1 million persons in the U.S. were homeless at some time in 1987."[48] Most of the time, authors are far less specific about the time period for which they are reporting numbers and readers are left to discern for themselves what the numbers mean.

Answers to the question regarding the growth of the homeless population are even harder to decipher than answers to the first two questions. Every year since 1982, the U.S. Conference of Mayors has conducted a survey on hunger and homelessness in major U.S. cities. Every year they ask, "Has the total number of people requesting emergency shelter in your city increased, decreased, or stayed the same during the last year? By what percentage?" These and other questions are addressed not to researchers but to staff in each city's mayor's office and to service providers—hardly a disinterested group since the mayors' reports are used to support claims for increased funding. The results are in no way subjected to statistical or scientific analysis of any kind; nevertheless, every year's national press release of their findings reports a substantial growth in the homeless population. This annual survey is what Rossi calls a key person survey; "the main problem with key person surveys," Rossi wrote, "is that they are of unknown validity—probably better than no information at all, but how much better no one knows."[49] A more sardonic reaction to the annual reports of increases in the size of the homeless population was offered by Kondratas: "Every year since [Mitch Snyder's 3 million estimate], the advocates and the mayors have been telling us that the numbers have been rapidly increasing, as much as 38 percent a year, but we still have 3 million homeless."[50]

Some thoughtful people, like Burt and Cohen from the Urban Institute, have suggested the possibility that there has been little growth in the homeless population during the past fifteen years: "One likely possibility is that larger and larger proportions of the homeless use shelter services as more and more shelters are developed." When shelter operators are asked questions about increases in homelessness, they might be accurate in saying that the number of sheltered homeless has increased dramatically, but "it might also be true that the total number of homeless persons has changed little."[51] Referring to the only two studies from the mid-1980s that allowed direct comparisons, Burt and Cohen found little statistical evidence of growth;[52] however, more recently, Burt, comparing earlier estimates with those that she and Cohen developed, speculated that there was a 22 percent increase in the size of the homeless population between 1984 and 1987.[53]

Although it is hard to know exactly how much the homeless population has increased since 1980, there can be little doubt that there has been an increase. As we discuss at length in Chapter 2, there was a virtually automatic and predictable increase in the homeless population as a demographic consequence of the baby boom. The first of the huge cohort of boomers turned thirty-four in 1980, the year when homelessness became a national phenomenon. Throughout the decade, baby boomers continued to reach the age for leaving their parental homes, exhibiting serious mental illness, and increasing their involvement with alcohol, drugs, and crime, and they have continuously swelled the ranks of the homeless.

The Census Counts the Homeless

The Bureau of the Census and homeless advocates energetically played the numbers game as each prepared for the 1990 census. The game opened with a barrage of numbers. In a June 1989 *Washington Post* report on preparations for the census count of the homeless, Maria Foscarinis, director of the National Law Center on Homelessness and Poverty, disputed the recently published Urban Institute estimate of 600,000, calling that figure too low and stating that "our estimate is 3 million." At the same time, Mitch Snyder was quoted as saying that "just about everybody in America who is involved thinks the figure is 2 million to 3 million."[54]

Despite efforts by the Census Bureau to identify and secure the cooperation of shelter providers and other people who work regularly with the homeless, the National Coalition for the Homeless heatedly debated whether they should participate with the census. Some feared cooperation would be tantamount to co-optation—the census would produce low estimates and "reduce public concern and lead policy-makers to cut services."[55] Others, including Kim Hopper, a National Coalition for the Homeless board member, hoped that "by cooperating, [advocates] will be taken more seriously as critics."[56] On the actual S-Night, March 20, 1990, Mitch Snyder refused to permit census takers to enter the CCNV shelter. Having burned his census form in protest of the predicted low count, Snyder railed, "By misusing the census data, politicians can take from the homeless what little they have left: their very existence."[57]

The final result of the S-Night count of the homeless nationwide was an especially low count: 178,828 in shelters and 49,793 in visible street locations for a total count of 228,621.[58] Having threatened to sue if the Census Bureau did not publish a disclaimer that the numbers did not represent a total count, the advocates' immediate response to the announcement was predictable. Foscarinis, claiming that the bureau's list of shelters was incomplete and that counting in the shelters was chaotic and haphazard, stated that "The shelter count is not as bad as the street count, but even the shelter count is extremely inaccurate."[59] In a similarly predictable and somewhat defensive statement made after the results were announced, the Bureau of the Census reported that the S-Night count was "not intended to, and did not, produce a count of the 'homeless' population of the country. S-Night," they explained, "was designed to augment traditional census procedures to insure the fullest possible count of America's population."[60] Despite the cost of $2.7 million for the special S-Night count and the use of more than 22,600 census workers specially recruited and trained to count the homeless under the watchful eye of paid independent observers from homeless advocacy groups, it is now not clear exactly what the census found.

Counting the homeless, although it can be done, is a difficult proposition at best. The homeless are mobile and often hidden, and the disabilities from which most suffer often make them difficult to approach and interview; they are often frightened or confused and sometimes stay hidden for fear of being arrested, committed, or attacked. According to Rossi:

> Under even the most inclusive definitions of homelessness, it is still a very rare condition that affects at most . . . 1.5 percent of the adult population (and most likely) affects less than 1/10 of 1 percent of the adult population. The study of rare populations is not impossible, but it is expensive. For example, if we undertook a random sample of any urban area, in order to obtain a sample of homeless persons, we would have to approach anywhere from 70 to 500 adult persons in order to encounter one homeless person.[61]

Although some researchers have made respectable efforts in this direction, the politics of numbers continue to plague anyone trying to make sense of the dimension of the problem of homelessness in America. Despite the growing acceptance of the estimates from the Urban Institute, the public continues to be confronted by outlandish claims and posturing by those who are interested in creating as large or as small a number as they need to support whatever political claims they choose to make.

Who Are the Homeless?
Just "Ordinary People"

Politics and political perspectives also surround the descriptions of who makes up the homeless population. Most common are the efforts by advocates to portray the homeless as people just like everyone else who happen to be suffering from the effects of stagflation, recession, and unemployment. Such descriptions discount the disabling conditions found among the majority of the homeless. A congressional report stated:

> Typically, we think of the homeless as drunks, drug addicts, or mentally disturbed people and, at one time, a majority of the homeless may have fit these categories. But, as the witnesses today will make clear, many homeless people are perfectly normal. They are like us, except that we have the good fortune to have a place in which to live.[62]

In this short statement, Congressman Charles E. Schumer, a Democrat from New York, confirmed the effectiveness of the political crusade to portray today's homeless as people just like anyone else; those who do have homes, according to this portrayal, are just a paycheck or a streak of bad luck away from homelessness. The homeless are ordinary members of our community: "The older woman next to you on the bus may be going nowhere in particular, riding only to keep warm or dry or seated. . . . [T]he well-dressed man nursing a cup of coffee at the lunch counter is not necessarily an executive mulling over a tough business decision, nor is the family at the local campground necessarily on vacation."[63]

The homeless "are just like the rest of us. . . . [They] want the same things you do—sometimes they want to talk, sometimes they'd rather be private."[64] Susan Baker, chairman of the National Alliance to End Homelessness, said that the homeless "miss the comfort of conversation, books, music, and peaceful reflection that we take for granted. It's the simple things in life—having conversations with friends, being complimented when you've done something well, hearing music or seeing beautiful things—that can give you the reinforcement you need. We shouldn't neglect this side of life when we think about what we can do to help homeless people."[65] The message is that the homeless or the prehomeless or the potential homeless are just like members of the general public and, therefore, helping them is like helping our neighbors.

Another approach is to portray the homeless family as the two-parent, rust belt family sleeping in cars, temporarily out of work, suddenly unable to afford housing in a market of skyrocketing housing prices and declining government subsidies to help the poor. This is despite almost universal findings that the vast majority of homeless families consist of single adult women accompanied by children.[66] A fine example of this error appears in Jonathan Kozol's book about homeless families in New York City, *Rachel and Her Children*. To be sure that readers understand that homeless families are just like other families, Kozol's first chapter is entitled "Ordinary People." The family that Kozol described is a two-parent family: "He was a carpenter. She was a woman many people nowadays would call old-fashioned. She kept house and cared for their five children while he did construction work. . . . When they were told about the fire, they grabbed the children and ran home. Everything they owned had been destroyed."[67] Purveyors of the two-parent family message go to great lengths to promote this image of homelessness; in 1988, Tom Brokaw left New York City, where there is as high a proportion of homeless families as anywhere in the nation, and traveled to rural Iowa to find white, two-parent homeless families for an NBC special on homelessness; he informed viewers that the homeless are "people you know."[68]

If the potential homeless includes ordinary people, then even more engaging are the children. From one service provider, we hear: "But nowhere does my heart ache more than in the family shelters, where I see the children and where I have known parents who stay awake at night to protect their children from rats. What we are sowing in our children, we will reap as a nation."[69] Such portrayals evoke strong emotions: These are our children and our future. Again, the implication is that everyone must help because everyone is at risk.

Children have always been and will continue to be the most appealing and deserving of the poor. By focusing on children, the advocates for the homeless may be trying to guarantee that America will view the homeless as deserving, but by failing to acknowledge the extent of drug use by homeless mothers and the horrifying consequences for their children, they have instead failed to help us understand what in fact they are deserving of—drug treatment for crack-addicted homeless mothers and pregnant women.

The case of Jacqueline Williams demonstrates the fallacy of thinking that the homeless are ordinary people. Mrs. Williams, the mother of fourteen children and a resident of a large welfare motel in the District of Columbia, confronted the mayor of Washington on "The Donahue Show" about the city's responsibility to provide her and her family with housing. Under public pressure generated by the TV show, the city placed the family in a newly renovated house, despite the concern of professionals familiar with the family's case history. The city subsidized the monthly rent and seemed to have fulfilled the obligation articulated by advocates who claimed that all Mrs. Williams needed was a decent place to live and raise her children. One year later, city inspectors declared the house unfit for human habitation.[70] Many of the indoor plumbing fixtures had been ripped out, the kitchen cabinets were gone, little furniture was left, the house was filled with trash, debris, and human waste, and windows, doors, and walls had been destroyed. The city welfare agency determined that the children in the family were suffering from continuing patterns of abuse and neglect and removed those under the age of eighteen to foster care. The house was boarded up and taken out of the stock of available low-income housing, only to become an object again of the claim by some that the city was not doing enough to provide housing for the homeless.

Mrs. Williams's family was not ordinary, and helping her and her children required more than publicity and housing. As Goodman concluded, "Any plan to address the pathologies that rage through America's cities requires a sustained commitment, and that requires public understanding and acceptance of what is sure to be a heavy long-term burden. Pretending just won't do."[71]

The Deserving Poor

The strategy for assuring the worthiness of the homeless has been to deny the commonplace characteristics that have defined some of the poor as undeserving throughout history. Congressman Schumer said that today's home-less are not drunks, drug addicts, or mentally disturbed people like those of years past. In classic "I think thou doth protest too much" fashion, the advo-cates tell us that "the traditional and persistent picture of street people as 'dirty, lazy, drunken bums' bears scant resemblance to today's chronically homeless person"[72] and that "the homeless include no small number of rather respectably attired people who do not fit the tattered 'derelict' and 'bag lady' stereotypes. . . . [N]or by any means are they all chronic 'psychos' or 'winos.'"[73] More recent examples from the research literature include statements that "the homeless are [not] lazy misfits who brought their plight upon themselves";[74] that the new homeless are not "roaming idlers and shirkers";[75] and that only 5 percent of the homeless are "lazy, shiftless bums."[76] Perhaps the most eloquent example of this form of denial is Rossi's attempt to fashion a politically acceptable statement given his knowledge of research findings.

> It is important to stress that (according to the best estimates) two-thirds of the homeless are not mentally ill, three-fifths are not alcoholics, three-fifths do not suffer disabling physical disorders, and 90 percent do not abuse drugs. Hence the discussion centers in all cases on minorities—large and significant minor-ities, to be sure, but minorities nevertheless.[77]

Plainly said, one-third of the homeless *are* mentally ill, 40 percent *are* alcoholics, 40 percent *do* suffer from disabling physical disorders, and ten percent *do* use drugs—all data supported by the voluminous research that we summarized in Chapter 1 and that Rossi knows only too well. Rossi's attempt to distance homelessness from the disabilities of the homeless is patently transparent given the numbers he himself uses in this statement—up to 83 percent of the homeless are seriously impaired by mental illness, alcoholism, or drug addiction, not including the two-fifths who have "disabling physical disorders."

Responses to the Homelessness Movement

The federal response to homelessness is a confusing but not surprising attempt to respond to the image of the homeless that the movement created. Faced with Snyder's frenetic political activities, often conducted on the grounds of the Capitol building, Congress enacted the Stewart B. McKinney Homeless Assistance Act in 1987. The federal government had already formed a task force based in the Department of Health and Human Services (HHS) that addressed homelessness primarily as a problem for people with health and health-related social services needs. But, given the agenda of the homelessness movement, the advocates had successfully redefined the issue primarily as a shelter and housing issue, and although the act reauthorized many existing programs for the homeless, it shifted the responsibility for coordination and leadership to the Department of Housing and Urban Development. This serious institutional mismatch still plagues implementation of federal homelessness programs.

At the local and state levels, services for the homeless are the province of agencies that are accustomed to dealing with HHS, its vocabulary, its funding mechanisms, its regulatory provisions, and its grants-making calendar. Under the McKinney Act, these same state and local agencies must work with HUD, whose requirements are tailored to the terminology and work cycle of the building industry and the financial mechanisms used to support construction, mortgages, and building subsidies. Consequently, for the first several years under the McKinney Act, many local service providers ignored McKinney Act funding. According to Burt and Cohen's extensive review of McKinney programs in six states, state and local officials found the application process "excruciating."[78] These officials were intimidated by HUD requirements for information and long-range community plans (Comprehensive Homelessness Assistance Plans, or CHAPS), which are very different from the kinds of records and materials they were used to preparing and maintaining. Moreover, there was unrealistic turnaround time for preparing proposals, and HUD requirements regarding control (ownership) of buildings prior to application approval discouraged small service providers from applying for McKinney funds.[79]

Because it is a "bricks and mortar" bill, the McKinney Act still provides few funds for services; where services are called for, funds are limited to a small percentage of total grants or are expected to be provided by state and local governments as matching grants. Significantly, in the fields of mental health and alcohol and drug treatment, federal grants under the McKinney Act are limited to research and demonstration funding. Because local advocates focus their campaigns on shelter, however, local public officials are only too happy to have funds from any source to provide emergency shelter—as two prominent researchers wrote, the emergency funds allow them to do "something almost biblical in its simplicity, and not particularly costly"[80]— and shelters are still the primary institutional setting for caring for people with a myriad of problems. As one writer explained, over the past 225 years we have come full circle and "we [now] have the most poorly organized system of care since we started with the almshouses in 1750."[81]

The Research Community Responds

The research community, in responding to the need for information on which to base policy, incorporated the agenda of the homelessness movement into much of its research. Research about homelessness—its dimensions, its characteristics, and its causes—grew exponentially during the

1980s. In 1980, the literature indexes in *Psychological Abstracts* contained only four articles about homelessness; by 1990, there were 265 listings. Similarly, 285 of the 488 entries in a current bibliographic listing of books and articles about homelessness have been published since 1985.[82] Despite all this information, little real light has been shed on the problem.

The homelessness movement placed the same political pressure on the research community to present the homeless in a sympathetic light as it placed on the press and electronic media. Ellen Bassuk, who has contributed valuable information and insight into the plight of homeless families and children and who created a foundation to provide grants for services for this very needy population, reported in a December 1991 *Scientific American* article that "researchers, such as myself, studying these problems were accused of stigmatizing an already disenfranchised population—of blaming the victim. In an effort to protect the homeless, some advocates and providers refuse to acknowledge mental illness or substance abuse. They simply concluded that permanent housing would eliminate homelessness."[83] In describing the hostile reaction from the advocates to his presentation of his findings concerning the number of homeless people in Chicago, Rossi said, "Those two hours were the longest stretch of personal abuse I have suffered since basic training in the Army during World War II. . . . It was particularly galling to have to defend our carefully and responsibly derived estimates against a set of estimates whose empirical footings are located in a filmy cloud of sheer speculation and guesses."[84] Rossi was accused of having "sold out to the conservative forces of the Reagan administration and of having seriously damaged the cause . . . by providing state and local officials with an excuse to dismiss the problem as trivial."[85]

Under such pressure from the advocates, some analysts have struggled to present their findings about substance abuse and mental illness in the most acceptable ways possible, minimizing the importance of these disabilities and focusing instead on broader policy issues less subject to criticism from the movement.

Denial

The politics of homelessness is the politics of denial. The most invidious result of the homelessness movement's crusade to define homelessness as the absence of housing has been to reinforce the nation's natural tendency to deny substance abuse and mental illness as major health problems that confront middle- and upper-class families as well as the homeless. People are so overwhelmed by their inability to address the devastation of alcohol, drugs, and mental illness in society that they are more than willing to ignore the fact that the homeless are those most devastated by these problems.

Defined in its technical sense, denial is "the inability to recognize a problem in the face of compelling evidence."[86] The compelling evidence is plentiful. An estimated 17.7 million Americans have serious, debilitating problems with alcohol that cost the nation an estimated $85.8 billion a year in reduced or lost productivity.[87] In 1987, an average of 300 people died each day from alcohol-related causes; in 1988, more than 23,000 people died in alcohol-related automobile accidents and nearly 1.8 million arrests were made for drinking and driving.[88] One in four American families is affected by alcohol-related problems.[89] Up to 74 percent of alcoholic and drug-dependent women report sexual abuse, including rape and incest.[90]

According to a 1990 report, an estimated 141,000 deaths were caused by alcohol abuse (95,000), drugs (6,000), and mental illness (40,000); each victim lost an average of 28.1 years of life.[91] Calculated in terms of the direct cost of diagnosis and treatment and the indirect cost of loss of earnings due to reduced productivity or death, drug abuse cost the nation some $58 billion and mental illness cost the nation more than $129 billion.[92] The most devastating result of drug use is that an estimated 100,000 babies are born exposed to cocaine every year; by the year 2000, there may be anywhere from 0.5 million to 4 million children in America who have been exposed to drugs.[93] Drug arrests and drug-related crimes are filling jails and over-whelming the U.S. court system; drug-related murders are filling the morgues, and AIDS is epidemic among drug users, who are infecting their sexual partners.

In the face of such numbing information, it is no wonder that people feel helpless and overpowered. Despite all efforts, the numbers continue to stagger the imagination. And so society pretends the problems do not exist. People deny the facts; they want to ignore these problems "in the face of compelling evidence." And, because the homeless are so obviously affected by the ravages of these problems, people distance themselves from the visible suffering and call them people without homes.

There is no doubt that Snyder and the advocates he inspired succeeded in putting the suffering of homeless people on the national political agenda. The philosophy underlying the homelessness movement, however, was misguided. By using the word "homeless," by defining the problem as one of shelter and housing, and by denying the extent of substance abuse and mental illness, the crusade not only inhibited the development of real help to the very people who were the supposed beneficiaries but also warped the nation's understanding of the problem. This result constitutes the great irony and paradox surrounding the politics of homelessness. The movement manipulated the facts about homelessness and was successful in capturing public attention and public dollars, but the movement ultimately failed because it did little to raise the public will to address the serious problems that perpetuate homelessness. As we will see in the next chapter, neither the movement nor much of the voluminous research and analysis has helped to explain the real causes of homelessness in the 1980s, and as a consequence, both have failed to inform the development of solutions that have any genuine chance of ameliorating the problem.

8

Causes and Solutions:
Confusion and Denial

The literature on homelessness, both empirical and popular, is a morass of speculative, value-laden and overblown generalizations about both the causes of the condition and who should be responsible for meeting the needs of homeless people.[1]

The political debate about homelessness raises a number of serious public policy issues. To improve opportunities for the poor and the working poor in America in the 1990s, policymakers should address: the availability of affordable housing (both privately developed and publicly funded); welfare and the reform of the welfare system; job training and the development of entry-level and low-skilled jobs; the adequacy of the minimum wage; and finally, access to health insurance and adequate health care, including treatment for substance abuse and mental illness. Although advocates often attempt to relate all of these issues to the plight of the homeless, we must distinguish between the homeless and the domiciled poor if we are going to make any real sense of the direction in which U.S. policies must go to address the problems of each population.

Failure to distinguish between the poor and the homeless has not achieved the advocates' intended purpose. Although they have typically hoped to convince the public that the homeless are like ordinary people and therefore members of the deserving poor, the effect has been quite the contrary. By refusing to acknowledge alcoholism, drug addiction, and mental illness as major characteristics of the homeless population, the homelessness movement has failed to grasp the opportunity to educate the public about these disorders and about the nation's failure to help those impaired by them. Instead, the politics of denial have let stand the age-old perception that people with these problems are the undeserving poor, and society has treated them accordingly—provided them with unclean and squalid barracks, excluded them from some shelters, screened them out of transitional programs, and in many cases, left them to sleep or die on the streets. Due to the blurring of distinctions between the homeless and the poor during the past decade, the majority of the homeless continue to suffer without relief and most of the struggling poor persistently receive inadequate support.

In order to clarify the distinction between the homeless and the poor, we need first to better understand what causes homelessness. Said another way, those who hope to help the homeless need to know why some poor people become homeless while most do not. Despite this seemingly obvious need for information, good research about causality is conspicuous by its absence in the literature on homelessness; virtually no one has engaged in inquiry that specifically examines the factors that cause people to become literally homeless. Instead, a few researchers have tried to approximate causes by examining whether homelessness precedes or follows the onset of the many personal disabilities and problems that their data reveal are overwhelmingly present among the homeless, and a few ask the homeless themselves, in simplistic ways, about why they are homeless. Most, however, derive causality from their own politically oriented perspectives. None of these approaches provides anything close to a satisfactory answer to the question of why people become homeless.

As recently as 1992, after the publication of hundreds of studies, reports, books, and articles on the subject and seven years after the 1985 statement from the Ohio researchers that opened this chapter, the New York City Commission on the Homeless, confronted by the paucity of good information about the causes of homelessness, concluded that the "dearth of current, reliable information about the causes of homelessness is at least partially responsible for the superficiality of the public debate on the issue, and has allowed discussion to be driven primarily by ideology and politics rather than by facts. . . . The position that one takes on the matter has become a litmus test of political ideology."[2]

Housing, Housing, and Housing

Passing the litmus test with curious, if not flying colors, Victoria Rader, biographer of CCNV and Mitch Snyder, suggested that "the most important event for the homeless in 1980 was Ronald Reagan's election as president."[3] She recounted, as if they were victories, Reagan's immediate moves to impose major cuts in social programs and his intense efforts to dismantle the safety net of social services that some claim precipitated the increases in homelessness in the early 1980s. What Rader was saying, of course, was that the Reagan administration presented social activists with an exquisite opportunity to mobilize public opinion in opposition to the domestic policy initiatives and long-term policy agenda of the newly elected conservative government.

The movement took immediate advantage of the opportunity, and advocacy pieces began to appear early in the decade suggesting that a wide variety of macroeconomic and social forces were responsible for creating the increasingly visible problem of homelessness. First and foremost of these was the issue of affordable housing. If the definition of homelessness is being without a home, then the three main causes of homelessness, according to Robert Hayes, were "housing, housing, and housing."[4] Because the movement focused so much attention on the lack of housing as the cause and the availability of housing as the solution, the most consistent theme in the policy debate surrounding homelessness has centered on housing, its availability, its cost, and the extent of crowding and doubling up. To evaluate the advocates' claims about the housing "crisis" of the 1980s and its direct linkage to homelessness, we need to look at these issues in some detail.

Housing and the Baby Boom

There can be no doubt that the 1980s was a period of major changes in America's housing market. First, in 1976 the leading edge of the baby boom began to turn thirty. Most of the boomers began to settle down, marry, take jobs, and start families, and they needed housing.[5] The absolute numbers of the baby boom generation put enormous demands on the American housing supply between 1970 and 1990; in 1970, there were only 63 million households in the United States, but by 1990, there were 93 million, making for an increase of almost 50 percent over the twenty-year period. The increased demand for housing units was compounded by a number of life-style patterns characteristic of the baby boom: fewer young married couples were living with their parents than in past decades; divorce increasingly turned one household into two; single-parent families became more common; and more single adults left their parental homes to set up their own households.[6]

Interestingly, the major increase in demand was not in the rental market. In 1970, 64.3 million people lived in 23.6 million rental units; by 1980, 65.1 million people occupied 28.6 million units.[7] This increase in renters of slightly less than one million suggests that most people were buying instead of renting during this period. In their study "The Baby Boom—Entering Midlife," Leon F. Bouvier and Carol J. De Vita calculated that, during the 1970s, 32 million Americans turned thirty, the typical age for buying a first home, and another 42 million turned thirty during the 1980s. Bouvier and De Vita maintained that "the number of new *homebuyers* was a prime factor in pushing up the cost of housing in the late 1970s and early 1980s" (emphasis added).[8]

The changing standards of what constituted acceptable living conditions also drove up prices. To remind readers of living conditions that only a generation earlier had been common for many Americans, Irving Welfeld, in his 1988 book *Where We Live: A Social History of American Housing,* described his childhood living conditions:

Once upon a time in America my family tree grew in Brooklyn. The family, consisting of two parents, a girl, and two boys, lived in a three-and-a-half-room apartment above the store. When it was time for bed, my sister would roll her roll-away into the living room. The boys would retire to their large sixty-square-foot closet. If nature should call, they would have to traipse through their parents' bedroom and trip over the bed in the living room to reach the bathroom.[9]

What was common earlier is now defined as inadequate. Grace Milgram, housing specialist for the Congressional Research Service, reported that in 1940 a dwelling unit was considered "crowded" if there were more than 1.5 persons per room; by 1960, a unit with more than one person per room was considered "crowded" and one with 1.5 persons per room was considered "seriously overcrowded." Based on the criterion of 1.5 persons per room, crowded households accounted for 9 percent of America's housing stock in 1940; by 1989, only 0.6 percent were considered "crowded." Based on the higher standard of one person per room, the incidence of crowding still dropped, from 20.3 percent in 1940 to 2.9 percent in 1989.[10] Moreover, the 1990 U.S. Census found that the average number of persons living in each U.S. household also declined—2.63 persons per household in 1990, down from 3.11 persons per household in 1970.[11] Looking specifically at the rental market, Martha Burt also found less crowding, from 2.73 persons per unit in 1970 to 2.28 in 1980.[12] Thus, as the standard for decent housing became one person or less per room, the number of "crowded" or "seriously overcrowded" housing units nevertheless *decreased* between 1940 and the late 1980s. These decreases raise serious questions about the claims that homelessness or being at risk for homelessness increased during the 1980s because of overcrowding or doubling-up.

Meanwhile, housing costs skyrocketed. The increases were fueled by several factors, including the size of the aging baby boom cohort, life-style choices, the new definition of what constituted acceptable space, and increased construction costs, which resulted from the OPEC-driven infla-tionary cycle of the 1970s. The resulting increases gave pause to the entire population, especially first-time homebuyers, newcomers to the rental market, and not incidentally, their middle-class parents, who found their baby boom children returning home after an initial foray into the housing market. The rhetoric of the homelessness movement, therefore, found fertile ground in the middle class and played on this very real concern about housing. By portraying the homeless as ordinary people, the advocates successfully tapped into the national anxiety about the rising cost of housing in the 1980s.

Despite the claims of the homelessness movement, analysts have never established a definitive causal linkage between the increased demand for housing, along with the rise in costs, and the rise in homelessness during the

1980s. Instead, they have cited information about the high cost of housing, the numbers of poor and middle-class people paying larger and larger proportions of their incomes for housing, and the declining government subsidies for housing and implied that all these factors account for the increase in homelessness.

The Lack of Affordable Housing

If the strategy of the homelessness movement was to play upon the fears of the many Americans confronted by rising housing costs, its success derived not from the public's gullibility but from the sheer complexity of the issue of affordable housing. Because government subsidies—tax deductions for mortgages, construction subsidies to builders, and direct housing grants for rent subsidies in both government-owned and private-sector housing— are an integral part of most affordable housing programs, the debate has focused in large measure on making changes in these various governmental subsidies. There is considerable disagreement, however, over the question of whether government assistance has declined during the past fifteen years, and if so, how much it has declined and what effect this has had on housing for the poor. For example, how much has the rehabilitation of existing housing, as opposed to the development of new housing, affected the supply of housing for the poor? Did budget appropriations for the major federal housing programs show the same degree of decrease as authorizations for those programs? Did outlays for subsidizing low-income housing in future years change housing opportunities available under current expenditures? Has there been an actual increase in the number of people being subsidized, and if so, has the rate of increase in the number of new people being subsi- dized declined during the 1980s? Should housing subsidies be in the form of Section 8 certificates, which guarantee that the renter pay only 30 percent of income, or should they take the form of vouchers, which permit renters to search on the open market and make decisions about what percentage of their income they are willing to pay?

In summarizing all of the often contradictory data about affordable housing, Burt concluded that, even though federal outlays for future subsi- dized housing decreased by more than 80 percent during the Reagan years, these decreases would not affect low-cost housing until the 1990s and that the impact of these funding decreases on homelessness in the 1980s was "not as straightforward as it might seem."[13] Michael Carliner agreed:

> There has been no . . . extraordinary deterioration in the national housing supply or affordability in recent years. By many measures, the housing situation actually appears to have improved. Construction has accelerated, vacancy rates have increased, overcrowding has diminished, and, despite sharp cutbacks in

new budget authority for housing programs since 1979, the number of households benefitting from federal assistance has continued to increase.[14]

For most people the issue of affordable housing is an enormously confusing
puzzle, and the arguments made on each side of the debate are almost as
arcane as those used in the controversies surrounding the research methodologies employed to count the number of homeless people. Despite the
difficulty in untangling these arguments, there is no doubt that changes in
government subsidies for housing affect the poor and the very poor, but as
Milgram pointed out, "It is not clear . . . that homelessness results from a
physical lack of housing units rather than from other social ills."[15]

Those who argue that the lack of affordable housing is the primary cause
of homelessness imply that the main problem confronting the homeless is
their lack of resources to participate in the American housing market, either
because they cannot earn enough money or because the cost of housing is
beyond their reach. For those who take this position, the solution is simple—
provide housing that does not overtax their financial resources. One way of
testing the effectiveness of such a solution is to examine what would happen
if housing units for all the homeless were provided. On one level, of course,
the problem would be solved and homelessness would be eliminated; all the
homeless would now be living in their own houses. The real question is how
long the problem would stay solved.

The story of Jacqueline Williams, the woman with fourteen children who
obtained housing from Washington, D.C., authorities after appearing on
"The Donahue Show,"[16] provides some indication of the answer. Mrs.
Williams' family needed much more than housing. They were not able to
maintain the housing that was provided, child welfare officials eventually
removed her children under the age of eighteen to foster care, and after one
year's occupancy, the house was condemned as being unfit for human habitation. Further evidence is provided by statements from others who have
studied or worked with homeless people. The New York City Commission
on the Homeless reported in their 1992 study that fully half of all homeless
families placed in permanent housing returned to the shelter system.[17] The
social worker at the Capitol City Motor Inn in Washington, D.C., reported
similar recidivism rates for families placed in housing.

In short, simply providing housing is *not* the primary solution to the
problem of homelessness because the lack of affordable housing is *not*
the primary cause. Without help for their many disabling conditions, most of
the homeless will continue to be unable to maintain themselves in permanent
housing. The futility of simply providing housing is underscored by the data
about the long-term chronicity of homelessness among the single homeless
population and its episodic nature. Those disabled by addictions and mental
illness or both, who drift in and out of homelessness, staying intermittently

in shelters, hospitals, jails, detox units, transitional programs, and back on the streets in a continuous cycle, are particularly at risk of not being able to maintain independent housing.

The absence of affordable housing as a primary cause of homelessness is advanced by advocates for mainly political reasons—to promote consideration of systemic macroeconomic problems that they believe need to be addressed. For example, Kim Hopper and Jill Hamberg asserted that, because the shortage in affordable housing results from profit-driven housing policies that produce a declining proportion of low and moderate rent units, "anything short of a massive public subsidized housing effort" will not address the problem; "only if housing is recognized as a social good and its provision seen as a necessary public service [will] appropriate action be taken."[18] By first mobilizing for the right to shelter for the homeless, advocates were actually pushing for a national entitlement to housing, an entitlement that extends well beyond helping the homeless. Hopper and Hamberg admitted: "A right to shelter is not the same thing as a right to housing—much less a right to appropriate housing—although it may be an opening wedge."[19]

We are not suggesting that the issue of housing is irrelevant to the homeless. Instead, we would argue that policymakers and the public must address the disabilities that make maintaining stable housing impossible before making the issue of affordable housing the central issue for today's homeless. Appropriate, affordable, and often specialized housing for homeless people with different types of problems will eventually be required; before then, space in various types of treatment programs, followed by structured living arrangements that support continued recovery, where appropriate, are necessary. It is only when individuals have made substantial progress in overcoming their disabilities that independent living in affordable housing will become relevant.

Focusing solely on affordable housing without first addressing the disabling conditions of the vast majority of the homeless is analogous to simply providing a walking cane to someone who has suffered a broken foot without first resetting the bones in the foot and encasing the foot in a cast. In the case of a broken foot, the use of a cane is only appropriate after the broken bones have been treated; providing a cane without first treating the broken bones will only make future recovery more difficult. In the case of homelessness, permanent, affordable housing is appropriate only after the immediate disabling conditions that prevent independent living have been treated. Failure to treat the disabling conditions will only make recovery from them and emergence from homelessness more difficult. In the meantime, the indiscriminate call for affordable housing, especially when it is used by advocates as an "opening wedge" to solve all of America's housing problems, is not helpful.

The Decline in SRO Housing

Another familiar theme in the literature on homelessness is that the widespread destruction of single-room occupancy (SRO) hotels caused the homelessness of the 1980s. Ironically, the same 1949 federal housing act that promised decent housing for all Americans—a promise often cited by the advocates as the foundation for their position—also set in motion the elimination of housing in the name of slum clearance and urban renewal. The prototypic slums were skid rows, blighted geographic areas filled with undesirable places—flophouses and SRO hotels, burlesque theaters, bars, taverns, mission halls, and cheap stores—all of which were targeted for elimination by the urban renewers. Neighborhoods were razed, and buildings that used to house occupants of skid row were either demolished or rehabilitated and converted to higher income residences. With few exceptions, the skid rows of U.S. cities became parts of revitalized downtown commercial and residential centers. Between 1970 and 1982, more than one million SRO units, nearly half the nation's total supply, disappeared;[20] in New York City alone, where one study found that half of the homeless women had lived in SROs before becoming homeless, there was a loss of 110,000 SRO units during the same period, a full 87 percent of the city's stock.[21]

On one level, those who make this argument are correct; there can be little doubt that the massive elimination of SROs and other cheap housing units has meant that former residents of these units no longer have a place to stay, and many are among the homeless today. As the loss of SROs and other cheap housing became accepted as a cause of homelessness, the obvious solution was to replace facilities of this kind, which has been achieved by opening shelters and in some cities actually building new SROs. But, as we have seen, this solution neither eliminated homelessness nor prevented its increase.

On a deeper, more important level, skid rows were more than just its buildings. According to Blumberg and colleagues, the "natural area perspective" provides only a limited view of the social phenomenon of skid row. They argued in the early 1970s that skid row was a special kind of slum "occupied by the unfit, the unfamilied, the poor, the personally inadequate, the aged and the chronically ill, especially those afflicted with alcoholism or tuberculosis," people whose ties with the larger community had disappeared. Skid row, for them, was "not merely or even primarily a specific neighborhood. Rather, 'Skid Row–like' people are found wherever there is poverty, in the slum neighborhoods, the low-income ethnic enclaves, even in the suburbs."[22] The purpose of this analysis was not to "blame the victim" but to lay the foundation for the development of the Diagnostic and Rehabilitation Center (DRC) in Philadelphia. This center, still in existence, was designed to address the full range of addiction, health, and social needs of "Skid Row–like people," wherever such people happen to dwell. To describe their work, Blumberg and his coauthors coined the phrase "Operation Bumblebee"

> after the aerodynamic engineers who concluded that bumblebees cannot fly according to any scientific principles but, being too dumb to know it, fly anyway. The case work team was flying in the face of the overwhelming opinion that Skid Row alcoholics could not be rehabilitated.[23]

The DRC has been successfully rehabilitating homeless alcoholics and drug addicts for more than twenty-five years. By mid-1990, the DRC was providing sufficient treatment to homeless, crack-addicted pregnant women for their babies to be born drug-free.[24]

The insightful perspective that skid row was more than just buildings helps explain why the life-style that characterized earlier skid rows has not disappeared even though much of the physical landscape of skid row throughout America has. The homeless of today are little different from the residents of skid row. Mental illness and drug addiction are now far more common aspects of this life-style than they were in the past, but as we have shown, alcoholism, serious health problems, tuberculosis, and chronic incapacity, early death, joblessness, and disaffiliation are still the norm among the skid row–like people of the 1980s and 1990s.

The elimination of SRO housing may have caused the displacement of former skid row residents and made them more visible, but it did not cause the many conditions that produce a skid row–like existence; recreating marginal facilities that duplicate the skid row buildings may provide shelter but would do nothing to resolve the other multiple problems of today's homeless; and so homelessness continues.

Structural and Economic Causes of Homelessness

Moving beyond housing, some researchers and analysts advance a full compendium of economic forces as causes of homelessness: poverty and extreme economic deprivation, inflation and the resulting reduction in the earning power of wages and social welfare benefits, economic recessions, the U.S. job market and the shift from an industrial to a service economy, unemployment, and Reaganomics and the reduction in social safety net programs. Although each of these factors has played an important role in the overall economic hardships facing many in the United States, there is no conclusive evidence that any of them had been the direct cause of homelessness or its increase in the 1980s.

Robert Hayes of the National Coalition for the Homeless, who in pursuit of a right to shelter on demand addressed the issue of "housing, housing, and housing," also called the homeless the "poorest of the poor."[25] Similarly,

James Wright, lead researcher for the Health Care for the Homeless Project (HCH), claimed that "homelessness is basically a poverty problem; it is created by a large group of extremely poor and socially marginal people who cannot compete successfully in an ever-dwindling low-income housing market. . . . [T]he solution to homelessness is ultimately easy: Do away with poverty and you will simultaneously do away with homelessness as well."[26]

A California study of 400 families commissioned by the state legislature to look at the causes of homelessness, however, compared stably housed poor families with homeless families and found that the homeless are often not as poor as their domiciled counterparts and that "their more severe legacy of personal distress . . . [and] distinctive histories of personal and family trauma"[27] were major factors in their homelessness. Wright and Weber, in their HCH report, stated that "the immense majority of the extremely poor manage to secure housing, despite the tightness of the low income housing market."[28] Comparisons to earlier decades raise additional questions about the validity of the argument that poverty causes homelessness. According to Hopper and Hamberg, "There was little or no homelessness as we know it today . . . during the early postwar period, at a time when poverty and hunger were more prevalent and benefit levels lower."[29] Indeed, if poverty is the cause of homelessness, why are there so many very poor people in this country who are not homeless? What these analyses still have not done is to explain the difference between poor people who do not become homeless and the homeless. As we have discussed at length in earlier chapters and will look at again in Chapter 9, the problem is far more than simply being poor and without a home.

Many have argued that it was the reduction in safety net benefit programs in the early 1980s that pushed the poor into homelessness. The most salient and immediate of the Reagan era policies was the drastic reduction in Supplemental Security Income (SSI) benefits paid to elderly and disabled single individuals. By changing the eligibility requirements in 1981, some 150,000 people, including many who were mentally ill, lost their benefits; but after several years, the more restrictive requirements were relaxed, and under congressional pressure, benefits were reinstated to most who had lost them and new homeless individuals were added to the rolls.[30] Homelessness did not decline, however, as benefits were restored. Another safety net program, Aid to Families with Dependent Children, had been declining in purchasing power since the late 1960s, and the decline continued during the Reagan years. This decline in benefits is tragic for its many recipients, but only 10 percent of all homeless households are families and, in Peter H. Rossi's Chicago study, only 6 percent of homeless adults, including those in family groups, received AFDC.[31] Since very few homeless are thus directly affected, the declining value of AFDC cannot be cited as a primary cause of homelessness.[32] Furthermore, in her careful, quantitative analysis of factors associated with homelessness in the 1980s, Burt revealed what she called an "unexpected finding" that contradicts the argument that decreased benefits play a significant role in increasing homelessness; she found that increases in benefit payment levels are associated with increases in homelessness, not with decreases in homelessness.[33]

National recessions and rises in unemployment are assumed to affect those in poverty and propel them into homelessness. According to this argument, homelessness will increase during recessionary periods when unemployment rates are high and will presumably decline during periods of recovery. The sharp increase in visible homelessness in the early 1980s appeared to be directly connected to the recession of 1981–1982. According to a 1985 GAO report, the 1979 unemployment rate of 5.8 percent rose to 10.8 percent by December 1982. However, contrary to expectations, as the recession ended and unemployment declined to 7.4 percent by January 1985, only slightly above the prerecession level,[34] homelessness continued to increase. Writing in 1986, Peter H. Rossi, Gene Fisher, and Georgianna Willis noted that they found little or no evidence in their Chicago survey that individuals with middle incomes, much less those with high-paying incomes, who had been laid off during the 1981–1982 recession had become homeless.[35]

It is not true that we are all just a paycheck away from homelessness; the magnitude of the homeless population does not ebb and flow to correspond with changes in the overall economic well-being of the country. Despite projections, the deep and prolonged recession of 1991–1992 that generated major plant closings and massive industrial sector layoffs has not produced a marked increase in homelessness. In fact, according to some, the 1991–1992 recession has had the opposite effect. The recession and the general economic downturn depressed the housing market with two results beneficial to low-income renters. First, landlords were slower to evict tenants for nonpayment of rent than they would be during a more competitive real estate market when they could expect to find replacement tenants easily. Second, because of the overall economic downturn, vacancy rates increased, and the opportunity for poor renters seeking housing also increased.[36]

Global Causes

On a somewhat broader note, some advocates have claimed that homelessness results from political and economic oppression of America's poor—disenfranchisement and dispossession. For example, Hombs and Snyder suggested that homelessness has been caused by the "virtually total disenfranchisement of the poor," those who are "victims of the long-term effects of alienation and oppression."[37] Joel Blau suggested that the cause of homelessness can be traced to the business response to macroindustrial policies of the postwar period during which deindustrialization, a shift to a service economy, and international competition required a transformation in the nature of the U.S. economy. As business sought to

> regain its competitiveness . . . it did so by lowering everyone else's standard of living. From deregulation to tax policy and the assault on labor unions, this response left the bottom four-fifths of the U.S. population with less money. Hence whatever form the lack of money takes, this business response is the true economic cause of contemporary homelessness.[38]

For Blau, homeless people are part of the bottom four-fifths of the U.S. population who lack enough money to pay for housing. Because the U.S. economy is "organized for the pursuit of profit," and because such basic human needs as food, housing, and medical care are commodities that are rationed for those from whom no profit can be gained, Blau suggested assembling a progressive political coalition of poor and middle-income people to organize around these needs.[39] Blau himself suggested that "this may seem all very dewey-eyed," and he indicated why he thinks it may not happen—social policies designed to eliminate homelessness violate the underlying principles of the U.S. economy: private profit, self-sufficiency through work, and the commodification of basic human needs. Thus, he concluded that such policies "cannot be granted serious consideration."[40]

Others go even further in their analysis and would reform the entire global economy and polity. Gregg Barak, for example, whose examination of homelessness is "grounded in an appreciation of the forces of globalism and the internationalization of capital,"[41] called for a new social order, without which "by the end of the 1990s, if we stay the present course, the homeless population is estimated to grow as high as 20 million."[42] He concluded that what is needed is a change in "the fundamental class nature of U.S. society" and in "the underlying contradictions of the capitalist state and political economy."[43] Barak's solution included

> the establishment of a maximum wage (or absolute limits on income) and a minimum guaranteed income for all; requirements that contingent or part-time workers receive full benefits and equal hourly wage with full time workers; comprehensive child care and national health care; urban renewal of buildings and infrastructures and ecological cleanup; and the creation of non-capitalist spheres of economic social activity or the decommodification of certain goods and services for the needy such as housing and education.[44]

By 1991, American society had apparently moved beyond the "times of modest expectations" that Mitch Snyder identified in his congressional testimony in 1980. Then Snyder's goal was "simple: the creation of adequate, accessible space . . . for every man, woman, and child who needs and wants to get off the street."[45] Eleven years later, empowered by the homelessness movement, Barak articulated a more ambitious goal: a radical overhaul of American and international economic, political, and social systems. The relevance of such a transformation to the realities of homelessness in America today seems tenuous; Barak's proposals serve to illustrate what others have observed—that "as the distance from city streets increases, understanding of the problem of homelessness decreases."[46]

Alcohol, Drugs, and Mental Illness

What is missing from all of these analyses is a serious discussion of the extent to which alcoholism, drug addiction, and mental illness may be primary and direct causes of homelessness for many and the extent to which these problems are very real in the day-to-day lives of America's homeless. There now exists a vast research literature that indisputably confirms the existence of these problems among today's homeless population, so it is not the absence of information that prevents analysts from addressing these issues. Rather, it is the ideological inclination to refrain from "blaming the victim" and the refusal to look at what many analysts apparently regard as negative personal characteristics. By acknowledging the role of alcoholism, drug addiction, and mental illness, analysts would be forced to confront problems that they understand in only a limited fashion because they lack experience in treating them and which, under the best of circumstances, are difficult to treat. Ignoring these conditions, however, precludes constructive understanding of the dynamics and causes of homelessness and inevitably prevents serious consideration of proposals to address these real problems. As the American Psychiatric Association's Task Force on the Homeless Mentally Ill stated, "A psychiatric diagnosis is not in any sense an indictment; it is merely an attempt to classify and help us know how best to respond to service needs among homeless individuals."[47] Given the volume of information about alcoholism, drug addiction, and mental illness among the homeless, people must go to extraordinary lengths to deny the compelling evidence that the research presents.

Many of the homelessness movement's most vocal advocates have chosen to simply ignore the evidence, and a substantial quantity of the homelessness literature never even mentions these conditions. Academic researchers and analysts do discuss alcohol, drugs, and mental illness but take considerable pains to minimize their importance. A prime example is Rossi's statement quoted in Chapter 7 about the percentages of the homeless who are *not* mentally ill, alcoholic, addicted to drugs, or physically disabled.[48] The statistics Rossi presented suggest that up to 83 percent of the homeless population *do* suffer from mental illness, alcoholism, and drug addiction.

Others not only deny the importance of these conditions but also deny the causal relationship between them and homelessness. For example,

Charles Hoch and Robert Slayton, in their otherwise excellent history of skid row, asserted that:

> The difference between those facing daily shelter uncertainty and those with housing security is not, we believe, based on vulnerabilities such as alcohol addiction or mental illness, but on the social and economic advantages our class standing allows us. . . . What we share across class lines is increasing shelter uncertainty, not increasing physical vulnerability.[49]

Findings from the Health Care for the Homeless Project

Perhaps the best example of the effort to minimize the centrality of alcohol, drugs, and mental illness is the book *Address Unknown: The Homeless in America* written by James D. Wright. In 1987, he and Eleanor Weber co-authored a report about the findings of the Health Care for the Homeless project. In this study, they amassed an extensive and well-regarded collection of information about the health problems among the homeless based on clinical data collected from the HCH's nineteen demonstration health clinic projects across the country. To summarize, Wright and Weber found that only a third of all adult clients did not suffer from alcohol, drug abuse, and/or mental illness;[50] that the leading health problem of the homeless was alcohol abuse, followed by mental disorders of various kinds;[51] that a wide variety of physical health problems was substantially more common among alcohol abusers and drug abusers than among nonabusers;[52] that the overall death rate among the homeless was 3.1 times the "expected" rate, the average death was twenty years earlier than expected, and alcohol was the direct cause of death in at least 16 percent of the cases and a contributory factor in about 50 percent;[53] and finally, that among health care providers, alcohol, drug abuse, and mental illness were rated as the most significant reasons for people becoming homeless.[54] Wright and Weber concluded that "these results make it plain, *as if further evidence were needed,* that no account of homelessness in America could possibly be complete without some systematic attention to these three elements"—alcohol and drug problems, mental illness, and chronic physical disorders (emphasis added).[55]

Despite these findings, Wright's statements in *Address Unknown* stand as a testament to the achievement of the homelessness movement in confusing even those whose own empirical evidence commands acknowledgment of the tragedy of substance abuse and mental illness among the homeless—from a humanitarian point of view, if not a scientific one. Wright tried to minimize the role that alcohol plays in the lives of homeless people by suggesting that "the difference in the rate of alcohol abuse between homeless people [40 percent] and people in general [10 percent] is a *matter of degree*. . . . It certainly is not as though all homeless people were alcoholics; in fact, the most plausible conclusion one could reach given the available research studied is that more than half—the clear majority—are not" (emphasis added).[56]

Like many of his colleagues who have speculated that people drink because they are homeless, Wright rationalized the use of alcohol by the homeless: "Like many alcoholic and even 'social drinkers' in the population at large, homeless people often drink to alleviate, however temporarily, the miseries of life—to cope, as Shakespeare wrote, with 'the slings and arrows of outrageous fortune.' The main difference between homeless alcoholics and the rest of us is perhaps only that their fortunes are more outrageous."[57] In another passage of consummate rationalization, Wright suggested that "it is well-known that alcohol and many other drugs induce euphoria, and among the homeless, euphoria is in singularly short supply. . . . What hope remains for people like this? What solace can they hope to find? Is there, in short, a better alternative than getting and staying drunk?"[58]

These are unfortunate statements, given Wright's own findings about the health and mortality consequences of alcoholism among the homeless. As we will show in Chapter 10, there are better alternatives, and the refusal to acknowledge them consigns chronically homeless alcoholics and drug addicts to lives of continuing misery.

Wright did not end his rationalizations with alcoholism and drug addiction, however. Like many colleagues who surmise that mental illness among the homeless is a function of interpretation, he explained that:

> Many of the apparently crazy, bizarre, or abnormal behavioral patterns observed among the homeless are adaptations to the rigors and dangers of street or shelter existence and should not be interpreted as signs of psychiatric impairment. In a very deep sense, homelessness *itself* is an insane condition. . . . [W]e should therefore take pains to avoid mistaking the conditions of homelessness itself, and adaptations to those conditions, for signs of mental disorder among the homeless population (emphasis in original).[59]

Wright later contradicted himself by stressing that "no serious researcher doubts that much mental illness is organic, biochemical, and/or neurophysiological in character"; and that "no serious researcher believes that people with problems of this sort will show dramatic improvement in their mental health simply because others *no longer treat* them as though they are mentally ill" (emphasis added).[60]

The confusion continues in Wright's discussion of the causes of homelessness. On one hand, Wright acknowledged that "only chronic psychiatric difficulties rival alcohol abuse as the precipitating condition for a homeless existence."[61] Moreover, he reported on a study of homeless alcoholics in Los Angeles that found that three-quarters had serious alcohol problems before their first episode of homelessness,[62] and he cited the 1988 statement by the Institute of Medicine's Committee on Health Care for Homeless People that "major mental illnesses, principally schizophrenia and the affective disorders (bipolar and major depressive disorders), are unlikely to result from the trauma of homelessness."[63] On the other hand, Wright ultimately concluded that

> in some sense, of course, these factors [alcohol abuse, drug abuse, mental illness] are appropriately cited as the "cause" of a person's homelessness, just as consistent bad luck can be cited as the "cause" of losing at cards. Given a game that some are destined to lose, in other words, it is appropriate to do research on who the losers turn out to be. But do not mistake an analysis of the losers for an analysis of the game itself.[64]

The game itself, he said, consistent with the themes promoted by the homelessness movement, is housing for the very poor.[65]

Wright was honest about his pessimism concerning the ability of homeless alcoholics to benefit from treatment:[66] "They are for all practical purposes beyond help. . . . Indeed, one is tempted to conclude that . . . [chronically homeless alcoholics] are destined to die in much the same circumstances as they now live—homeless, besotted, broke, useless to any collective social purpose, dependent for survival on the largesse of society."[67] Unable to discern a programmatic approach to so disabled a population, Wright suggested a triage approach: "The existence of such elements within the homeless population is no excuse for diminished, mean-spirited or cold-hearted efforts on behalf of the remainder. The solution is not indifference, but careful marshalling of available resources to help those who can be helped and those most in need."[68]

The most serious and dangerous consequence of this kind of denial, characteristic of so much of the research on homelessness and of the homelessness movement, is to promote solutions that ignore the problems of the vast majority of the homeless. For example, Charles Kiesler, in his article that ends the American Psychological Association's (APA) special volume on homelessness, wrote:

> Alcohol and drug abuse and mental health (ADM) services should not be among the top three priorities in public policy responses to the problem of homelessness. That is not to say that ADM services and considerations are unimportant or cannot have an effect on the problem. It is to say, however, that ADM actions tend to be ameliorative in nature: They will soften the effects of the national homelessness problem, but they will not solve it. They are directed neither at the real causes of homelessness nor at the root solutions.[69]

There are other examples of specific policy recommendations that ignore the realities of alcohol, drugs, and mental illness for the homeless. Peter

Rossi, though acknowledging the extent of these disorders, made the case that homelessness results when poor families use up all their material resources dealing with "destitute, unattached adult" family members; his policy solution is to create a new income supplement for these families, "Aid To Families With Dependent Adults."[70] Wright called for additional sums to be added to already existing income support programs for the poor and suggested some new ones, including rent insurance (similar to "national flood insurance"), expanding the range of people covered by unemployment insurance, and finally, "federally sponsored flophouses," or boarding houses and expanded access to public housing.[71]

Others have argued for solutions that are in fact addressed to the problems of the poor, not to the problems of the homeless. Some advocates call for voter registration drives to empower the homeless, because "when homeless people cannot participate in the electoral process, policy makers are left uninformed, unequipped, and often become unresponsive to the legitimate concerns of the very poor."[72] Others support community organizing as a method of empowering the homeless or the working poor.[73] Burt, while admitting the extent of substance abuse and mental illness among the homeless, nevertheless proposed the most typical collection of remedies: providing subsidies for renters, creating more affordable housing, improving benefit levels, and creating better jobs, educational opportunities, and training programs. She concluded that "by reshaping the work environment and improving education and training . . . we will solve not only the problem of homelessness, but also the problem of declining living standards for a much broader spectrum of American workers."[74]

Burt's concluding remarks indicate the extent to which analyses of homelessness, like programs for the homeless, have moved further and further away from addressing matters of relevance to homelessness. By proposing to solve problems for a "much broader spectrum of American workers," Burt implied that the homeless are part of the American work force, despite significant evidence that some of the homeless have never worked, that many work only sporadically, and that most have not worked for far longer than they have been homeless.[75] Analyses such as this are similar to the homeless prevention programs in public housing projects where "homelessness" programs address the needs of people who are not and have never been homeless.

The full compendium of wholesale social reform to benefit America's poor is both laudable and, in the context of Lemann's observation that the 1973 OPEC oil embargo marked the end of uniform upward mobility for all Americans, an appropriate political challenge. But such reforms have nothing to do with those who suffer from substance abuse problems and mental illness and who, without appropriate treatment and long-term care where needed, will continue to live skid row–like life-styles in the shelters and on the streets.

In the midst of the denial and the resulting panoply of inappropriate solutions, there are some who are neither afraid to confront the problems at hand nor fear being co-opted by the homelessness movement. Fischer and Breakey, writing in the same APA volume as Kiesler, argued that

> research evidence consistently supports the high prevalence of alcohol, drug, and mental disorders in the contemporary homeless population. . . . Publicizing such findings also arouses protest from advocates on the grounds that such findings can be used negatively by persons who are unsympathetic to the homeless population. It is certainly a perversion of science when research data such as those reviewed here are used to blame homeless persons for their own predicament, to stir up prejudicial sentiments, or to suggest that they are somehow less worthy of public sympathy because of their many problems. On the other hand, denial of the extent of their problems will make it all the more difficult to ensure that the services they so badly need are made available. Knowledge of the high prevalence of major health problems should increase the sense of public outrage that the most disadvantaged suffer most.[76]

Although their work is far less publicized than those who deny the importance of substance abuse and mental illness, there are many who, along with Fischer and Breakey, are not only willing to tell the truth about homelessness and its causes but are also engaged in developing ways to help those who are the most disadvantaged and who suffer most. They are neither perverting science by stirring up prejudicial statements nor perverting science by ignoring and misrepresenting their findings. The work of these researchers lays the foundation for developing a more reasoned approach to the subject of homelessness.

PART THREE

A More Reasoned Approach

9

The Truth
About Homelessness

If the lack of affordable housing, poverty, declining social benefits, and the nature of America's political and economic systems are not the primary causes of homelessness today, then what are the causes? Specifically, what caused its growth in the 1980s, and what causes it to continue into the 1990s? Moreover, if recreating facilities similar to the SROs has done little to help the homeless, then what other solutions are viable?

Disaffiliation

> *Homelessness suggests an extreme condition of disaffiliation, a continuing marginalization and finally a complete loss of community, a loss of sense of self.*[1]

Homelessness is a condition of disengagement from ordinary society—from family, friends, neighborhood, church, and community; perhaps most important, it is a loss of self. In Chapter 4 Franklin says, "The first time, I felt like this is not me. I felt like less than a man." Homelessness means being disconnected from all of the support systems that usually provide help in times of crisis; it means being without structure; it means being alone.

Disaffiliation does not cause homelessness, but rather is the most universal characteristic of the homeless. Poor people who have family ties, teenaged mothers who have support systems, mentally ill individuals who are able to maintain social and family relationships, alcoholics who are still connected to their friends and jobs, even drug addicts who manage to remain part of their community do not become homeless. Homelessness occurs when people no longer have relationships; they have drifted into isolation, often running away from the support networks they could count on in the past.

Leon was married and had two daughters whose college graduation pictures he still carried with him. He had served with distinction in the Korean War; when he left the service he returned to his job. His life-style was both middle class and family oriented, until he started drinking again at a family gathering. Leon knew he was an alcoholic. He had been able to stay sober for almost five years by never taking a

153

drink, but that one drink started him off again. He began to miss work; his wife couldn't take another round of drinking and the abuse she had suffered before; his daughters were ashamed of him; his mother had to ask him not to stop by because she was afraid her neighbors wouldn't understand.

Leon knew what was happening, but he couldn't stop it. He began to avoid his family and friends—he too was ashamed. He stopped working when he was sure he would be fired anyway. With no income, he couldn't pay rent, clean his clothes, or buy food. Now, his only friends seemed to be the guys on the corner, the bottle gang with whom he shared the money he could panhandle, whom he joined at the soup kitchen for meals, and with whom he shared his drinking. But they couldn't help him when he was too drunk to reapply for his disability benefits, so he just let the benefits drop. They couldn't help him when the hospital refused to operate on his knee because he always had too much alcohol in his system, so he just let it go. Leon had lost everything—his wife, his children, his job, his benefits, and his health. Sometimes, someone in the neighborhood would let him sleep on the couch or the floor, but most of the time, he slept in the alley only three blocks from his mother's house.

William Breakey has suggested why "affiliative bonds" disintegrate and how this disintegration precipitates the downward spiral that so often ends on the streets, in jails, in shelters, in soup kitchens, and on park benches: (1) There may never have been strong personal attachments because of life-long patterns of shyness or isolation; (2) individuals may feel they have to withdraw; or (3) they may be forced to withdraw by others.[2]

> Substance abusers or the mentally ill are especially at risk in all three categories. In many cases they were shy solitary individuals before becoming ill. Then, the effects of the illness itself may have acted to distance them from others; socially inappropriate behavior in an alcoholic, for example, or persecutory delusions in a person with schizophrenia. Finally, stigma, fear, or resentment on the parts of others may cause the person to be excluded from family or community interactions, to lose a job, or to feel unwelcome in social gatherings. The addiction or [mental] illness thus creates or fosters a pattern of disaffiliation, the very condition that is the hallmark of homelessness.[3]

Stigma

American society still stigmatizes alcoholics, drug addicts, and the mentally ill. People avert their eyes, laugh, or feel afraid when they see obviously addicted or mentally ill people on the street. People who exhibit these problems make others very uncomfortable. As people withdraw from them, those who suffer from these problems withdraw as well—to protect themselves from the sense of failure that comes from comparison with their peers; to achieve autonomy to continue what to others appears to be destructive behavior; or to insulate themselves from the stigma of being different. "Insulated by his alienation, protected by identity beliefs of his own, [the stigmatized person] feels that he is a full-fledged normal human being, and that we are the ones who are not quite human."[4]

James Wright explained that many health-care workers and other social service workers perceive the homeless as undesirable, but "the alcohol impaired, the drug abusive, and the mentally ill are 'more undesirable' than others, and those who are both alcoholic or drug abusive and mentally ill are the most undesirable of all. To be drunk, crazy, and homeless is about as low as one can fall."[5] Given such intensity, is it any wonder that Wright and his colleagues attempted to distance their policy recommendations from their research findings? Many who claim that they do not want to blame the victim by focusing on the personal problems of the homeless may, in fact, be distancing themselves from these behaviors because they find them distasteful. By ignoring the obvious, however, they merely reinforce the stigma attached to these characteristics and further isolate those who feel stigmatized by them.

Ashamed, abandoned, rejected, fearful, and sick, the homeless give up, not "because they choose to live this way" nor because they are "lazy, shiftless bums" but because alcoholism, drug addiction, and mental illness are conditions that, if left untreated, propel people into a downward spiral. Impaired by the effects of alcohol, drugs, or psychosis, they cannot work or continue relationships with others, so they drift away from settled society, which at the same time rejects them; thus, they become homeless. For substance abusers, as their very existence is consumed with alcohol-seeking or drug-seeking behavior, it becomes impossible for them to work; they use whatever money they have to replenish their supply of alcohol or drugs. Their behavior often hurts family members and friends who finally lose patience and stop giving them money, shelter, food, and care; they are evicted; they are frequently rejected by helping institutions; and they eventually end up on the streets or in jails, homeless, friendless, and alone. For the mentally ill, delusions, fears, and hallucinations (exacerbated if they use alcohol or drugs to relieve the symptoms of their mental illness) make it difficult if not impossible to work. Relationships with family and friends disintegrate; money is hard to manage, as are other aspects of daily living; and, often lacking appropriate care, they drift into a life of isolation on the streets or in jail.

By failing to acknowledge alcoholism, drug addiction, and mental illness, our society also fails "to encourage individuals to deal with intrapersonal issues or to seek the treatment for a psychiatric or addiction problem that may be crucial to their escaping from homelessness."[6] Some pessimists think it is useless to encourage the homeless to seek help because they see little hope for them. Harold Moss of the Community for Creative Nonviolence stated, "Since the jig is up—there is hardly any further to fall. . . . For many of these people, getting back into the mainstream is never a possibility."[7]

Such pessimism, if accepted as truth, consigns the majority of the homeless to isolated, lonely lives, illness, and early death.

But we need not accept this point of view. Those who work with homeless alcoholics and drug addicts and with the chronically mentally ill are realistic about the difficulties they face but nevertheless urge treatment. According to four treatment professionals, whose work with the Manhattan Bowery Project in New York City gives them a basis for optimism,

> [homeless] alcoholics have a rate of recovery from alcoholism that is far lower than that of the general population, yet they, like their middle-class counter-parts, suffer from a disease that can be arrested with treatment. Proper treatment for the public inebriate involves a variety of therapeutic interventions used over an extended period of time. Success is possible and should be sought.[8]

Similarly, drug addicts respond to long-term intensive treatment. The crack cocaine epidemic is daunting, and crack is considered the most addictive drug known to medical science. Even so, a 1990 report suggests that "there is no reason for the public and policymakers to despair about the prospects of successful treatment" for crack addicts, even for very poor inner-city users.[9] As for the mentally ill, Breakey suggested, "it is wise to keep in mind that the prognosis is often extremely poor"; nevertheless, "this should not be a cause for despair in the service provider but rather a stimulus to develop more creative or effective approaches."[10]

In short, many homeless people can be helped to return to lives of promise. The biggest obstacle they face is society's unwillingness to admit that their "personal characteristics" or "attributes" are contributing or causal factors in their homelessness. These are not signs of moral weakness nor of personal failure but are all conditions that, given the advances in medical science and treatment knowledge, can be treated and from which people can recover.

The Increase in Homelessness

Homelessness has been part of the American social experience since colonial days, as have isolation, rejection by the community, alcoholism, drug addiction, and mental illness. If these are not new problems, what happened in the early 1980s to suddenly produce street scenes never thought possible in America—large numbers of people huddled in blankets, begging, and without a place to stay at night?

First and foremost, as homelessness burst into public view in the early 1980s, there were simply many more people affected by the problems of substance abuse and mental illness because of the baby boom. Similarly, members of the underclass left behind in America's cities faced a future with little hope, and many have become trapped in a cycle of poverty, drugs, and despair. Just as the population bulge of 76 million people born between 1946 and 1964 overwhelmed community systems such as schools in their early years, by the late 1970s many more people were at risk of becoming alcoholic, drug addicted, and mentally ill and were straining the resources of community and welfare agencies as well as straining their relationships with family, friends, and other support systems.

Many analysts fail to examine these demographic factors in accounting for the increases in homelessness. For example, Martha Burt argued that a large proportion of the homeless exhibit mental illness, alcoholism, and drug addiction but added that "many people have had these vulnerabilities in past decades." She said, "Only the changes in structural factors [poverty, unemployment, benefit levels, lack of affordable housing] can explain why the vulnerabilities led to a much larger homeless population during the 1980s than in earlier times."[11] Burt simply ignored the enormous increase in the actual number of people with these vulnerabilities, let alone the social and political characteristics of the baby boom generation that encouraged drug use and cultural deviance, that viewed mental illness as heightened awareness, that romanticized autonomy and freedom to be unattached and unsettled, and that, for some, meant being part of the emerging inner-city underclass, confronted by the combination of poverty, desperation, and drug addiction.

The impact of the baby boom cannot be overstated. In 1970, there were only 73 million people between the ages of eighteen and forty-four, the age group most at risk for the onset of mental illness and most likely to be seriously involved with alcohol, drugs, and the criminal justice system. By 1980 there were 94 million Americans in this age bracket, a 29 percent increase, and by 1990 there were 108 million, 48 percent more than in 1970.[12] Remember that the average age of the homeless population is about thirty-four and that the leading edge of the baby boom reached this age in 1980. Clearly, the aging of the baby boom goes a long way toward explaining the sudden increase in homelessness in the early 1980s, especially given the failure of various helping systems to keep pace with the increasing demands that would be placed on them.

Decriminalization of Alcohol

Much has been written about the impact of the deinstitutionalization of mentally ill patients in relationship to homelessness; however, less has been said about the effects of decriminalization of alcoholism and public drunkenness.

In the early 1940s, a loose coalition of groups (Alcoholics Anonymous, founded in 1935, the National Council on Alcoholism, and the Yale Center of Alcohol Studies[13]) joined together to redefine the problems of alcohol for the American public. The members of this coalition based their work on four principals that they hoped would revolutionize the way people would think about alcoholism: (1) The problem drinker is a sick person, exceptionally reactive to alcohol; (2) he or she can be helped; (3) he or she is worth helping; and (4) the problem is therefore a responsibility of the healing professions, as well as of the established health authorities and of the public generally.[14] With the adoption of the disease concept by the World Health Organization in 1955 and the American Medical Association in 1956, there was growing acknowledgment that alcoholism was a physiological disease characterized by dependence on alcohol, physiological withdrawal symptoms, and loss of control over drinking. In 1970, Congress enacted the Comprehensive Alcohol Abuse and Alcoholism Prevention, Treatment, and Rehabilitation Act, also called the Hughes Act, and in 1971, the Uniform Alcoholism and Intoxication Treatment Act. These two pieces of legislation mandated the development of publicly funded detoxification centers to treat public inebriates and provided the impetus to shift the responsibility for dealing with alcoholism away from the criminal justice system.

Although the number of public detoxification centers increased substantially, the increase was insufficient to handle the great influx of public inebriates who had been "clients" of the criminal justice system. Moreover, the detoxification centers that were established under the new laws proved inadequate to the task of providing the wide range of services needed by the seriously impaired skid row and homeless alcoholics—treatment plus social, vocational, and medical support as well as aftercare and attention to housing that supports recovery.[15] Furthermore, admission to the new centers was voluntary, and many who previously would have been held in drunk tanks refused to voluntarily enter detox centers or were unable to seek admission on their own. Meanwhile, public drunk tanks, home to thousands of public inebriates, were closed, leaving those who had relied on them for shelter to fend for themselves on the streets where, despite the intent of the law, some continued to be put in jails and others became homeless.

The inadequate number of new detox facilities and their inability to offer appropriate services were exacerbated by the increasing number of alcoholics produced by the baby boom. In 1940, estimates indicated that there were 750,000 alcoholics in the United States, but by 1980, the National Institute on Alcohol Abuse and Alcoholism (NIAAA) estimated that there were 6 million alcoholics.[16] (It should be noted that some of this growth must be attributed to increasing self-identification owing to growing public awareness and acceptance of alcoholism as a disease for which treatment is possible.) In 1990, the secretary of Health and Human Services reported that there were approximately 10.5 million alcoholic or alcohol-dependent adults in the United States and that by 1995, this number was expected to rise to 11.2 million.[17]

Simultaneous to the growth in the number of alcoholics, skid row neighborhoods were disappearing as slum clearance and urban renewal efforts expanded. In 1940, there were 150 well-established skid row neighborhoods throughout the United States; by 1980 there were only 35 and their total population had dropped from 750,000 to 135;000.[18] Dilapidated buildings and SRO hotels in slum neighborhoods were converted and gentrified into middle-class housing, restaurants, and shops in boutique neighborhoods, in large part to accommodate the housing and recreational needs of the aging middle-class baby boomers (the Yuppies). The only options for former skid row and SRO residents and growing numbers of others who would have joined their ranks before gentrification were jails, the streets, and shelters, that is, homelessness.

The Gentrification of Addictions Treatment

Skid row neighborhoods, however, were not the sole arena for gentrification; services were also gentrified. As the nation became disenchanted with the drug and alcohol culture of the 1960s and 1970s, people became more aware and more fearful of the many dangers of failing to treat these addictive disorders—domestic violence, drunk driving, industrial accidents, fires, suicides, deaths from overdose, crime, and gang violence. Mothers Against Drunk Driving (MADD), the "Just Say No Campaign," the War on Drugs, lobbying efforts to put warning labels on alcohol products, and a host of other campaigns warned against the dangers of alcohol, drugs, and most recently, AIDS. The result was an explosion in books, information pamphlets, public service announcements on radio and TV, educational materials for schools, and an exponential growth in twelve-step self-help groups. Alcoholics Anonymous (AA) grew from its beginning in 1935 to 22 groups in 1940 and to an estimated 73,000 groups throughout the world by 1987,[19] and it spawned Narcotics Anonymous (NA), Al-Anon, Adult Children of Alcoholics, Alateen, and hundreds of clones like Overeaters Anonymous and Gamblers Anonymous.

Whereas American society once condemned "intemperance" and designed methods to exercise punitive control over public drunkenness, interest in middle-class substance abuse has become very respectable. Many corporations, businesses, and governmental agencies have introduced employee assistance programs (EAPS) that offer counseling and treatment to alcoholic and addicted employees in lieu of job termination, and health insurance plans have begun to pay for both inpatient and outpatient addictions treatment. To meet the growing demand for treatment and recovery programs, stimulated in part by these incentives, both not-for-profit and private for-profit health care organizations have developed a variety of programs, most of which are modeled on a twenty-eight-day inpatient program that has proven to be very effective, particularly for middle-class alcoholics and addicts. Almost all introduce their patients to AA or NA, and participation in AA or NA is a required feature of most aftercare programs. There are estimated to be more than 1.6 million patients in substance abuse treatment programs at a cost of $1.6 billion, with a total medical cost of $15 billion.[20]

This is certainly very good news for most of the 76 million people in America who have been exposed to alcoholism in their families.[21] There is a serious downside, however, to this explosion in middle-class interest and attention that helps explain the increase in homelessness in the 1980s. Between 1978 and 1984, there was a 62 percent overall increase in hospital treatment beds for alcohol and drugs and a phenomenal 392 percent increase in private, for-profit treatment beds; during the same six-year period, however, there was a 17 percent *decrease* in treatment beds for alcohol and drug abuse controlled by state and local jurisdictions.[22] For-profit beds increased from 5 percent to 15 percent of the total, while federal, state and locally controlled beds decreased from 64 percent of the total to only 40 percent.[23] According to Ken Schonlau, a participant in a 1989 NIAAA conference,

> Slowly but surely they're shifting services from the people who are really destitute to people in the middle and upper classes. There's been an awakening about drug and alcohol recovery in the middle and upper classes in our country, and they're really going for services. . . . I'm convinced that back in the 60s before we had any public funding, or researchers interested in the subject, we had more residential recovery opportunities for the real down and out alcoholic than we have today.[24]

Shortages in public treatment beds create acute problems for homeless substance abusers who are ready to enter treatment. "Same-day admission" is essential for maintaining motivation for treatment, but according to a recent study by the National Coalition for the Homeless, homeless people were denied immediate admission at some 80 percent of treatment programs in a national sample.[25] Because of the shortage of beds, eligibility requirements are frequently imposed to prevent the use of expensive detox and in-patient beds from being used to provide the "three hots and a cot." Some facilities also require that an individual be drunk in order to be admitted to detox and permit only one admission per month.[26] These rules can lead to bizarre consequences.

> *We had been working with George for almost two years when he declared himself ready to enter the D.C. General Hospital's alcohol and drug treatment program. Because it was Friday and the admissions office was closed, it was necessary for George to enroll in the detox program to ensure that he would still be willing to enter the treatment program after the weekend. The receptionist who answered our*

phone call to the detox center kept asking, "Has he had a drink today?" We assured her several times that he was an alcoholic and heroin addict and we wanted to get him into the detox program in order for him to be able to transfer to the treatment program on Monday. Again, "Has he had a drink today?" Finally, we got the message, but George happened to be stone cold sober—a rare event. Much to his amazement, we piled George into our car, took him to a liquor store and bought him a pint of gin and a ginger ale chaser. Before we were out of the parking lot, George had downed the pint, ignoring the chaser. By the time we arrived at the hospital, he was very drunk, and therefore eligible, under the rules, for admission to detox.

Although there is not as much recent information about separate drug treatment in the United States as there is about alcohol treatment, it is a truism that drug treatment, particularly publicly funded treatment, is woefully inadequate, and the recent crack epidemic has made the shortage even worse. Nationwide, congressional figures suggest that only 12.5 percent of the nation's 6.5 million drug users have access to publicly funded treatment.[27] In Washington, D.C., for example, city officials estimate that almost 128,000 people (including 80,000 alcoholics) need drug treatment, but there are only 105 publicly funded drug and alcohol detoxification slots, 339 residential treatment beds, and 2,500 outpatient treatment slots. This totally inadequate supply of treatment facilities means that addicts in need of treatment have to wait for up to two months for detoxification and up to nine months for an inpatient treatment bed. According to a March 1992 report, D.C. General Hospital had 1,200 names on a waiting list for *twenty* beds. The situation has become so bad that addicts sleep in the hospital's emergency room, calling the treatment program every few hours until a bed opens; others threaten to commit a crime or to kill themselves to persuade staff to let them in.[28] Being placed on long waiting lists or being denied treatment for lack of space is not what addicts need; they need a quick response to requests for treatment. According to Ron Clark, executive director of Rap, Inc., a highly successful drug treatment program, "When you try to find them [addicts who were awaiting treatment], they have been arrested, moved, disappeared and in some cases, they have died."[29]

Homeless mothers are more likely to be addicted to drugs than mothers who are not homeless.[30] Nevertheless, in New York City, a shocking 54 percent of the drug treatment programs surveyed in 1990 refused treatment to pregnant, addicted women; 67 percent of the programs denied treatment to pregnant addicts on Medicaid; and 87 percent denied treatment to pregnant women on Medicaid who were specifically addicted to crack.[31] The national picture is no better: In 1989, only 10 percent of all women and 12 percent of pregnant women needing drug treatment received it.[32]

As disturbing as this information may be, it still only tells part of the story. A report issued by the National Institute on Drug Abuse indicates that in

1989 almost 40 percent of all treatment units across the country were out-patient and that more than half of the clients in treatment were treated in outpatient facilities,[33] despite almost universal professional agreement that in order to succeed, homeless alcoholics and drug addicts need long-term, highly structured inpatient programs followed by aftercare that includes alcohol-free, drug-free housing that supports continued sobriety. Out-patient treatment not only fails to provide sufficient structure but also fails to address the most salient factor in relapse, that is, continuing to live in an environment that strongly encourages alcohol and drug use and abuse, an environment certainly found on the streets and in shelters for the homeless.

Perhaps the worst failing of the treatment system available to the homeless is the lack of attention paid to what happens to the individual after each step in the treatment process. Without appropriate regard for aftercare and arrangements for housing, perhaps structured or supervised housing, all too often homeless individuals leave treatment facilities only to return immediately to the streets where they are confronted by the same conditions that reinforced their pre-treatment behavior. According to the National Coalition for the Homeless report, the single most significant impediment to recovery among homeless substance abusers was the absence of "recovery housing."[34] The result is the "revolving padded door"—revolving because individuals must enroll in detox or treatment over and over again; padded because detox facilities, emergency rooms, mental hospitals, and substance abuse treatment facilities, although not necessarily of lasting benefit without follow-up, are gentler than jails or prisons.

In summary, it would appear that the ability to obtain substance abuse treatment has become a function of class, that is, wealth and income. Just when the nation is accepting the dangers of alcohol and drug abuse, and middle- and upper-class alcoholics and drug addicts are entering treatment in ever-increasing numbers, publicly supported treatment for those who cannot afford it is declining—there are fewer facilities, waiting lists are growing, and inpatient care with follow-up and support is in increasingly short supply. The baby boom created a large group of people at risk for developing alcohol and drug problems; the gentrification of skid rows displaced thousands who formerly were housed; and decriminalization was not accompanied by the development of alternative facilities. Now the dearth of affordable and appropriate alcohol and drug treatment programs essentially guarantees that the most severely impaired are likely to remain homeless.

Deinstitutionalization

It has become virtually axiomatic that a major cause of homelessness in the 1980s was the deinstitutionalization of the mentally ill. This term refers to the removal of mental patients from state mental hospitals, a phenomenon that began in the mid-1950s and was codified into law with the passage of the Community Mental Health Center Act in 1963. The release of the mentally ill from treatment facilities was premised on new scientific developments in understanding the organic nature of mental illness and the development of psychotropic medicines to treat these disorders. By stabilizing patients with medication, medical professionals said, patients could enjoy relief from their psychotic symptoms and, with community-based care and monitoring of their medication, could function outside of institutions.

The basic facts of deinstitutionalization are well known. Between 1955 and 1985, there was an 80 percent decline in the number of patients in the nation's state mental hospitals, from 552,000 in 1955 to 110,000 in 1985. E. Fuller Torrey has explained that most of the reduction came between 1960 and 1980, during which time slightly more than 400,000 patients were released.[35] Actually, the situation is somewhat more complicated. In the early years, 1955 to 1970, the patients who were released were the best candidates for community living or were elderly patients who were transferred to nursing homes.[36] In the following decade, however, it was the less able patients who were released, often with no adequate provision for aftercare or follow-up, either to the totally inadequate system of board and care homes or to the streets. In addition, during the first fifteen years of deinstitutionalization, the number of long-term patients in residence in state hospitals declined sharply, but the number of total admissions actually doubled. Then between 1970 and 1980, admissions also dropped significantly. In California, for example, admissions declined from 42,000 to 19,000, and in Massachusetts they went from 13,000 to 6,000.[37] Perhaps the most glaring mistake of deinstitutionalization was the 59 percent reduction in psychiatric beds in the nation's Veterans Administration hospitals between 1963 and 1980, the period during which veterans were returning from service in Vietnam with trauma disorders and significant needs for psychiatric treatment.[38] Many of them became homeless.[39]

The Community Mental Health Center Act of 1963 provided significant fiscal incentives to states to reduce the number of state hospital patients. By releasing patients to the federally funded community mental health centers (CMHCs) authorized by the act, state officials shifted fiscal responsibility for the mentally ill from the state to the federal level. In addition, liberalization of the federal Aid to the Disabled Program (now Supplemental Security Income, SSI) permitted mentally ill persons to receive federal benefits. By releasing the mentally ill from their care, states reduced their share of the cost for the mentally ill from 96 percent in 1963 to 53 percent in 1985.[40]

The primary intent of the Community Mental Health Center Act, however, was not to shift fiscal responsibility but to provide less restrictive community-based care in a national network of some 2,000 CMHCs. But this national network never quite materialized—fewer than 800 were actually created.[41] Furthermore, while the congressional mandate was for the CMHCs to "provide community treatment facilities for the individuals who had been released from, or would go to state mental hospitals,"[42] the CMHCs rarely performed this function, and very little provision was made for follow-up, aftercare, and monitoring of patients released from hospitals to the CMHC system. Between 1968 and 1978, an average of only some 5 percent of CMHC admissions were patients released from mental hospitals; in the 1970s, 50 percent of the CMHCs had no inpatient beds; and in 1977, 32 percent of the CMHCs had no emergency services at all.[43]

The failure of the CMHC system can be traced to the transformation of its primary mission. Originally designed to care for the mentally ill, the CMHCs later became the organizing base for community empowerment groups in the 1960s and then began providing therapeutic counseling to those whom Torrey called "the worried well." This gentrification was accompanied by a shift within the psychiatric profession itself—from mental illness professionals who treat severely disabled psychotic patients to mental health professionals who treat those with less serious problems.[44]

This gentrified mental health system is ill suited to providing treatment services for the chronically mentally ill, many of whom become homeless. According to Levine and Kennedy, "The homeless don't fit our usual program models . . . because so many homeless are change-resistant, let alone unmotivated, so unattractive, so seemingly helpless, that [serving them] is not appealing."[45] Analysts who have looked at changes in professional norms suggest that many helping professionals are trained to help people recover relatively quickly and are reluctant to treat the chronically mentally ill, who may require repeated treatments over long periods of time and who may stay dependent or need domiciliary care. Among the homeless this group might include late-stage chronic alcoholics as well as the seriously mentally ill who have long-term chronic problems.[46] A 1987 study reported that professionals who treat chronic patients experience "feelings of hopelessness, helplessness, dislike or disgust, and discomfort"; they lack "adequate training in the skills required to overcome" such feelings; and they do not receive "peer support and validation" for working with this population.[47] Therefore, professionals prefer to treat more desirable clients, "those with fewer, less complicated problems and better prognosis who are also more likely to have medical insurance."[48] When patients also are substance abusers, professional resistance is even greater.

As we have already seen, the dually diagnosed are viewed as the least appealing of all patients. Writing in a helpful handbook for psychiatrists, Richard J. Frances and John E. Franklin warned that dual diagnosis patients can be antisocial, paranoid, histrionic, and "may become belligerent, distrustful, unappreciative, uncooperative, or violent—possibly reflecting the patient's fear and low self-esteem—making management and history taking difficult."[49] The authors alerted their readers to the negative reactions evoked by these patients and suggested that therapists take a simple "time-out" to collect their feelings and clarify diagnoses.[50] Given the negative attitudes of treatment professionals toward such patients, it is not surprising that the dually diagnosed are the most likely to fall between the treatment cracks, rejected by addictions treatment services because of their mental illness and excluded from mental health services because of their substance abuse. With literally nowhere to go and with no help from family, other support systems, or professionals, they more often than not become home-less. Furthermore, the difficulty in treating them that results from the complexity of their multiple problems, combined with their often hostile attitudes toward helping professionals, leads many to believe that the dually diagnosed do not want help; this notion in turn reinforces the denial about their problems and permits family, other support systems, and even profes-sionals to regard them as misfits unworthy of help.

Disinstitutionalization

The dismantling of the nation's system for treating the most severely disturbed members of society, those with the psychotic disorders of schizo-phrenia and manic depressive psychosis, was taking place at the same time the number of people with serious mental illness was exploding. As we reviewed in Chapter 2, as the baby boomers reached the age of onset for mental illness, eighteen to forty-four, the number of people at risk for becoming mentally ill increased exponentially—by more than 30 million between 1960 and 1980 and another 14 million between 1980 and 1990.[51] Using the 1990 prevalence estimates for mental illness—which claim that some 22 percent of the population will suffer from some form of mental illness, excluding alcohol and drug abuse, during their lifetime and that 1.5 percent of the population will suffer from schizophrenia[52]—we estimate that the number of people likely to suffer from mental illness increased by 6.8 million between 1960 and 1980 and by an additional 3.2 million between 1980 and 1990. The number of people likely to suffer from schizophrenia increased by almost 460,000 between 1960 and 1980 and an additional 210,000 between 1980 and 1990. The enormity of the problem is underscored by the total number of people at risk for mental illness (21.1 million in 1980 and 24.3 million in 1990) and the total number at risk for schizophrenia (1.4 million in 1980 and 1.6 million in 1990).[53] Remember that in 1985 there were only 110,000 state mental hospital beds, and that few CMHCs have inpatient beds or emergency care capacity.

Given the enormous disparity between the number of people at risk and the decreasing number of publicly supported patient beds, we prefer to use the concept of *disinstitutionalization* rather than deinstitutionalization; by this term we mean that the seriously mentally ill were being deprived of the institutional care they needed. It is not the fact that people were being released from mental hospitals that caused homelessness to increase in the 1980s, but rather the total absence of institutional facilities to care for those who became psychotic after most of the state hospital beds were eliminated and too few alternative care facilities were made available. Compounding the problem of this gargantuan shortfall in treatment facilities, we must remember that the counterculture life-style phenomena of drug use, tolerance for deviance, and rejection of the very concept of mental illness also acted as disincentives for people to seek even the treatment that was available.

One result is that many of the mentally ill who formerly would have been in state mental hospitals now end up in jail. In 1986, there were 26,000 mentally ill persons in jails and prisons in the United States;[54] and according to Torrey, "It is likely that there are now more seriously mentally ill persons in jails and prisons than at any time since the early years of the nineteenth century."[55] Many others found their way first to skid row neighborhoods,[56] then to shelters for the homeless, the streets, park benches, and heating grates in cities across America.

The Law Firm
of Franz Kafka and Lewis Carroll

Apparently drafted by the law firm of Franz Kafka and Lewis Carroll, the laws on the mentally ill that have emanated from the deinstitutionalization era are both absurd and tragic.[57]

The erosion of medical services to treat mental illness coincided with the emergence of the mental health rights movement, part of the "rights" revolution of the 1960s. This movement voiced the growing concern about the indiscriminate use of powerful medications and treatments (like electroshock therapy), particularly when these were used on involuntarily committed patients. Some of the more extreme advocates advanced what has come to be known as the antipsychiatry movement. They hoped to prove that the concept of mental illness was a mechanism of social control used by the established society to discourage deviance and promote conformity. Popular books and movies, like *One Flew over the Cuckoo's Nest* and *The King of Hearts,* widely disseminated the basic philosophy of the movement's chief proponent, Thomas Szasz: "If there is no psychiatry, there can be no schizophrenics. . . . [T]he identity of an individual as schizophrenic depends on the existence of the social system of (institutional) psychiatry. Hence, if psychiatry is abolished, schizophrenics disappear."[58]

Others turned their attention to the issues of involuntarily restraining mentally ill patients and medicating them against their will. Rulings in the many lawsuits, quite properly brought on behalf of the mentally ill and intended to secure various rights and freedoms, paradoxically resulted in a tangle of legal doctrine not always in the best interests of the chronically mentally ill, many of whom became homeless.

Although the principles of freedom and self-determination are fundamental to the preservation of America's system of democratic rights, Torrey maintained that well-meaning lawyers "have grossly misunderstood what is wrong with most of these people. . . . To maintain the freedom to be insane is, itself, insane to me, yet that is what is happening."[59] Put another way, as the American Psychiatric Association's Task Force on the Homeless Mentally Ill said in its 1992 report,

> Should chronically mentally ill individuals have a right to "choose" a life on the streets without consideration for their physical health or the extent of their competence to make such a "decision"? We think not. We believe such practices cloak neglect in the banner of freedom and that they are a cruel interpretation of the basic civil rights that are so important to all citizens of the United States.[60]

At the very worst, legal advocates exploit the chronically mentally ill to advance legal doctrine relating to privacy and self-determination—in much the same way the homelessness movement exploits the homeless to pursue social and economic agendas. At the very least, some courts have handed down decisions that make very little sense and deprive the chronically mentally ill, particularly the homeless, of much-needed care. Roger Peele and his colleagues made the point that "[a]t the heart of the court system is a procedural style and a system of values that can be at cross-purposes with the needs of the homeless mentally ill." The legal process is an adversary one, in contrast to the cooperative and collaborative style necessary for providing services to the mentally ill who need care and continuous attention. Lawyers stress freedom and autonomy at all costs, while the best interests of the homeless mentally ill may require something quite different.[61]

As the rights of the mentally ill have wended their way through U.S. courts, three important doctrines have emerged: the right to treatment, the right to treatment in the least restrictive environment, and the right to refuse treatment altogether. As the issue of the right to treatment has developed in the judicial system, the focus has been on the adequacy and appropriateness of treatment for those already in the health and mental health systems, not for those outside the system. In an Alabama case, *Wyatt v. Stickney,* the court found that a patient had a constitutional right to treatment and then defined the treatment in terms of strict staffing and facility standards. Instead of increasing staff and improving facilities, the state responded by reducing the number of hospitalized patients to meet the staffing ratios required by the court.[62] The effect was to actually reduce the number of patients who could claim the right to treatment. The cost of meeting court-mandated patient-to-staff ratios creates a disincentive for states to provide hospitalization, especially since releasing patients or never admitting them in the first place insures that the fiscal responsibility remains at the federal level.

The second legal doctrine, the right to treatment in the least restrictive environment, was intended primarily to overturn various state civil commitment laws. In *Lake v. Cameron,* the court ruled that "a patient could not be involuntarily hospitalized if an alternative that infringed less on his right to liberty could be found."[63] Many psychiatrists argue that mental hospitals can provide more freedom than "available" community alternatives and that the goal should be the most optimal setting for the patient; nevertheless, the concept of least restricted environment has encouraged legislation, judicial decisions, and regulations that are based on the persisting view that hospitalization is the most restrictive environment.[64] Another case, *Lessard v. Schmidt,* also challenged civil commitment laws and produced the widely accepted standard of "dangerous to oneself or to others"—if the patient does not meet this criterion, he cannot be hospitalized against his will. Both of these judicial standards create narrow criteria for hospitalization that "ignore the treatability of mental illness" as well as "the effects of mental illness on free will and meaningful autonomy."[65]

Strangely, although the right to refuse treatment appears diametrically opposed to the right to treatment, it also emerged from lawsuits brought by the mental health rights movement. Patients who are "mentally competent" have the right to refuse hospitalization and medication; patients who are not competent are subject to a "tortuous" decision rule called "substituted judgment" developed by the courts to decide the best interests of the patient. Rael Jean Isaac and Virginia C. Armat quoted from the Massachusetts Supreme Judicial Court decision as follows: "In short, the decision in cases [where the patient cannot make a decision] should be that which would be made by the incompetent person, if that person were competent, but taking into account the present and future incompetency of the individual as one of the factors which would necessarily enter into the decision making process of the competent person."[66] Isaac and Armat offered their own explanation of substituted judgment as well:

> In other words, how would an incompetent person decide if he were competent taking into account the fact that he is incompetent? Note the court is not asking what an incompetent person would do if he were competent. . . . The court was saying a judgment had to be made on the basis of what a competent person would do if he were incompetent, a contradiction in terms.[67]

By 1983, twenty-five states had developed legal doctrine to permit individuals to refuse treatment,[68] and since then, other states have added comparable statutes. What this means in real life is that, for parents and loved ones of the mentally ill, "the biggest shock of all is to discover that the law supports the inalienable right of their family members to be crazy."[69] One mother who tried repeatedly to obtain treatment for her daughter asked the question:

> Can you imagine an ambulance driver or a policeman responding to a heart attack emergency looking down at the victim, shaking his head, and saying, "Well, there is nothing we can do. It's no crime to have a heart attack, you know. This person has smoked too much, is overweight, has not exercised, and there is nothing I can do. If he wants treatment, he will have to voluntarily agree to go to the hospital. Because he is unconscious, we cannot provide any assistance."[70]

The complexities and confusion do not end here. As in other areas of the helping systems, professional malpractice and civil liability have become issues in treating the mentally ill. These issues, as in other medical fields, have had the effect of reducing the availability of treatment. In a Florida case, a psychiatrist was held civilly liable for maintaining the involuntary hospitalization of a mentally ill patient even though the court had ruled on thirty different occasions that the patient needed hospitalization.[71] Alternatively, in two different but related California court cases, clinicians were held liable for failing to warn victims and possible victims of the potentially dangerous behavior of mentally ill patients whom they had released; but under the existing laws, they were not permitted to commit these patients involuntarily.[72] The result of these legal precedents, in combination with the difficulty in treating the seriously mentally ill, means that treatment professionals are understandably very wary of becoming involved with difficult patients, many of whom are among the homeless mentally ill.

H. Richard Lamb, former chairperson of the American Psychiatric Association's Task Force on the Homeless Mentally Ill, provided a good summary of the overall effects of the mental health rights movement:

> We still have not found a way to help some mental health lawyers and patients' rights advocates see that they have contributed heavily to the problem of homelessness—that patients' rights to freedom are not synonymous with releasing them to the streets where they cannot take care of themselves, are too disorganized or fearful to avail themselves of what help is available, and are easy prey for every predator.[73]

Charity

There is yet another issue that must be confronted in a frank discussion of homelessness. The role of charity, well intentioned though it may be, may inadvertently serve to maintain homelessness. Because some 90 percent of the shelters and soup kitchens operated for the homeless across the country are run by nonprofit organizations, the vast majority of which are religiously based, understanding the role of charity is important. Different from the "homelessness industry," where service providers have become defenders of the status quo in order to maintain their own roles and positions, charity is a fundamental principal of American society and is usually accepted as unquestionably beneficial. Charity, however, can be misused and misguided.

If charity is a way of maintaining hierarchical social relationships, with the more advantaged giver giving to the less advantaged recipient, charity becomes a mechanism of social control. It insures the existence of a less advantaged group and dictates how this group should respond to the generosity of the giver, namely with humility, docility, and gratitude.[74] Michael Katz recounted that "friendly visitors" of the late nineteenth century, by expecting gratitude for their charity, translated "any display of independence" into ingratitude and thus promoted dependence, not independence.[75] Are today's volunteers for charity offering help to the homeless so that they can feel their gratitude, while at the same time controlling them and making them dependent on the charity? Are charitable groups using the homeless to assuage their guilt by creating a group of "receivers," so that *they* can feel good as they give the homeless what they want to give them, not what they really need? We are not suggesting that society or individual communities should not act upon compassionate feelings for those in desperate need. Instead, we are suggesting that people be very careful about their motives. To perpetuate dependency and hardship by providing inadequate and inappropriate shelter and emergency services is not constructive; urging appropriate treatment for alcoholism, drug addiction, and mental illness is.

Telling the Truth

In marked contrast to many current analysts of homelessness, we do not consider major social, economic, and political forces to be at the root of today's homelessness. Inadequate housing, poverty, unemployment, declining social benefits, and governmental cutbacks have disastrous consequences for the poor and disadvantaged of America, but the homeless suffer from more immediate problems that prevent them from maintaining themselves in stable housing, from working, and from utilizing social benefits. If left untreated, these problems lead to isolation and alienation, misery, serious physical health problems, and early death. The effects of alcoholism, drug addiction, and/or mental illness are the precipitating cause of the downward spiral that ends with the disconnection from a society that stigmatizes the people who suffer from these diseases. Furthermore, significant changes in the U.S. population (the baby boom and the inner-city underclass), in combination with the impact of political and social movements over the past two decades—the decriminalization of alcoholism, the gentrification of substance abuse treatment, deinstitutionalization and disinstitutionalization of the newly mentally ill, and the perversities of the mental patients' rights movement—have increased the numbers of people suffering from these disabilities and have intensified their effects by denying treatment to the most disabled. This denial of treatment causes them not only to suffer but also to feel even more stigmatized and isolated. Homelessness is the result.

By denying the importance of alcohol, drugs, mental illness, and the loss of family and community for the thousands of people called the homeless, society shields itself, but not them, from the truth. Researchers and advocates have perseverated on the debate about numbers and have focused on the structural macroeconomic and political forces as the causes of homelessness; in so doing, they avoid the central question of how to help the growing population of very sick and disabled people who, because society has refused to tell the truth about them and their needs, became homeless during the 1980s and remain homeless today.

10

Tragedy on the Streets: A Call to Action

Why Should We Help the Homeless?

Having examined the causes and characteristics of homelessness, we are left with basic questions: Why should society help the homeless, and what types of programs would be appropriate for such an endeavor? Some have argued that the homeless constitute America's throwaways—that the homeless are beyond help, either because they are too "far gone," and therefore helping them is too difficult and too expensive, or because, since they have made their own bad decisions leading into alcoholism, drug addiction, or even mental illness, responsibility for the consequences belongs to the homeless individuals themselves, not society.[1] These formulations are what we call the "bad seed" hypothesis, namely that the homeless are unworthy of help because they are in some way inherently bad people and that society should therefore "give up," providing the truly homeless with only the most marginal shelter and food and otherwise leaving them to suffer their own fates.

Some who follow this line of reasoning believe that resources currently being expended on the homeless should be redirected elsewhere—to help those easier to help in transitional programs or low-income housing, to help those not yet homeless with homelessness prevention programs, or to address other problems that have nothing to do with homelessness. As in the past, when public resources are very scarce, as they are now, this justification for not expending dollars on behalf of the most troubled citizens becomes increasingly attractive. This option may be particularly popular because persistent denial about the true etiology of the decline into homelessness gives society license to ignore challenging problems that might require both changing ways of thinking and reordering priorities.

Since the very earliest days of our nation, however, Americans have always accepted at least some responsibility for providing for those who are unable to provide for themselves. If society is to preserve ideals inherent in the American democratic system—the promise of equality and justice and the declaration that citizens are intimately bound to each other to promote the common good—

society cannot eschew its responsibility to provide help for its least able members. This means helping those who can become truly independent and self-sufficient to do so and offering true sanctuary to those who cannot.

Furthermore, homelessness in the 1980s was caused in part by public policy decisions—well intended but ultimately with more complex consequences than had been imagined—that eroded many of the programs and care facilities that had evolved over the centuries to help the most disabled and destitute and replaced them with programs and care facilities for those able to pay for them. Although many current policy analyses focus on the presumed "failures" of social policies of the 1960s and 1970s that "threw money" at problems, few take the time to reflect carefully on policies that resulted in the actual elimination of various services and treatment for the poor. Before declaring the problems of the homeless to be of their own making or beyond the means of society to solve, people need to recognize that these failed policies, including the failure to prepare for the onslaught of millions of troubled baby boomers, played a major role in increasing the visibility of homelessness in the 1980s. Not only is there a civic responsibility, therefore, but also a moral responsibility to correct these policy mistakes in order to ameliorate the unintended but very real misery that they created.

Tell the Truth

It is not rude to help a sick person; it is not cruel to save someone's life.[2]

Society will continue to fail in all its efforts on behalf of the homeless unless people confront their denial about the realities of homelessness and start acknowledging the many problems that fill the lives of up to 85 percent of those whom we call homeless. A first step is to stop using the term "homeless," a word intentionally coined to avoid identifying personal problems and underlying disabilities and that has served for more than a decade to confuse the public and frustrate those trying to offer real help. Even worse, the use of the word "homeless" homogenizes a disparate population with an array of troubles in such a way that a single solution, the provision of shelter or housing, seems to suffice.

There is nothing wrong with "medicalizing" the problems if the purpose is to obtain medical treatment for those who need it. Identifying substance abuse problems with the purpose of encouraging substance abusers to seek treatment and communities to make such treatment available is not necessarily "blaming the victim." It is not wrong to identify mental illness if the intention is to engage the mentally ill in treatment and, if necessary, to offer them sanctuary and long-term asylum.

If those who live on the streets and in shelters should no longer be labeled as "the homeless," then what terms would be appropriate? Since people often call today's homeless "our friends," "our guests," "our brothers and sisters," or "people just like us," why not start referring to them by terms actually used for friends, brothers and sisters, or people just like us who are in trouble and who need help, namely, alcoholic men or women, people addicted to drugs, women battered and abused by their alcoholic or addicted partners, individuals diagnosed as seriously mentally ill, tuberculosis patients, people with AIDS, pregnant women with addictions problems, sexually abused children, crack-addicted newborn infants, or Vietnam veterans with trauma disorders? Shelter workers should not call them "guests" but should seek professional help for them, as they would for themselves or their children, and call them patients and clients.

Such a change in nomenclature requires a massive alteration in national attitudes. People must stop stigmatizing disease when continuing to do so merely prevents those who need treatment most from obtaining it and must stop the practice of sorting people according to artificial and blurred designations of who are the deserving and the undeserving poor. The past several decades have exposed most families in this country to all the maladies from which the people who stay in shelters or on the streets suffer; yet people continue to view strangers with these problems with disdain. It is time to put an end to such attitudes.

Scientific researchers recognize that alcoholism is a disease characterized by a clear symptomatology as a function of the way the liver metabolizes alcohol and the way the brain is affected by alcohol. Drug addiction is similarly accepted as a disease, and drugs that alter brain chemistry produce changes that affect behavior. Mental illness is understood as a neurophysiological brain disorder that manifests itself in impaired thinking, reasoning, and emotional processes. People who suffer from these disorders all have negative physiological, psychological, and behavioral side effects and are socially as well as medically impaired, but they *are* deserving, even if they are "homeless"—of treatment, care, and appropriate attention.

The Portland Model

It would be a cruel hoax to begin identifying what are regarded as stigmatizing conditions unless policymakers and program planners simultaneously developed appropriate programs to treat or ameliorate these conditions in the most professional ways. Fortunately, there are model programs that have already been successful.

In 1987, the city of Portland, Oregon, began an exercise in collaboration with Multnomah County, the Chamber of Commerce, the religious community, social service agencies, and local advocates for the "homeless" to clarify their values about helping substance abusers and mentally ill people who are troubled, fearful, and alienated. The planning document that guides the Portland Model makes clear that:

> Homeless people gathering on skid row, drinking and socializing, may make life look carefree. . . . In fact, being homeless, and finding enough food, clothing and shelter to stay alive, even *with* help from social service agencies, is a full time job. . . . Make no mistake about it: People are homeless because they do not have the ability to do anything else. It is clear that given the help they need, many homeless people can return to self-sufficiency. For some people, the road is difficult, but do-able. For others, breaking the cycle is so hard, so costly, that self-sufficiency is tactically impossible. Still, these individuals did not choose homelessness because it was a carefree way of life. These individuals can be accommodated so they do not jeopardize themselves or city vitality (emphasis in original).[3]

Modeled on the concepts underlying employee assistance programs,[4] Portland has created a "city assistance program," recognizing that

> effective intervention into the cycle of the disabling illness of alcoholism, this country's greatest drug problem, requires a change in public policy and attitude toward problem drinking. Tolerance and permissiveness with regard to the behavior of untreated public alcoholics and addicts must be replaced with sufficient understanding of the disease to know how to interrupt its enabling processes.[5]

The community declared that "while a person might have the right to drink [or drug] himself or herself to death, the city of Portland would no longer enable anyone to do so within its boundaries."[6] In their pioneering report, *Breaking the Cycle of Homelessness: The Portland Model,* the planners identified problems and articulated specific underlying values that helped to determine policies, program plans, and the assignment of responsibility for implementation.

Portions of the "12 Point Plan for the Homeless" illustrate this rational and realistic approach. Under the heading, "Initiative: Person Down," the statement of the problem is: "Individuals incapacitated by alcohol are vulnerable to exposure, victimization, or accidents. Some are suffering from illness or injuries which may be masked by alcohol." The value statement that follows this clear statement about the effects of alcoholic drinking is: "No one incapacitated by alcohol or drugs should be left untreated on the streets of Portland." The policy that emanates from these two statements is: "Anyone 'down' should be quickly assessed and taken to appropriate care." The planning document then lays out a series of program plans to offer outreach and transportation to detoxification facilities and assigns specific responsibility to specific city, county, or private agencies for implementing the program.[7]

Under the heading, "Initiative: Alcohol and Drug Treatment System," the stated problem is:

> The alcohol and drug treatment system lacks the capacity to assure appropriate treatment when it is needed. People are sobered, detoxified, and ready for longer-term care only to find they must wait for a vacancy in those programs. This often leads to having no place to go but back to the street, with the likelihood of returning to the dependency cycle.

The value statement that follows is: "Society and chemically dependent individuals can benefit from a sufficient quantity and variety of programs to provide appropriate treatment services to break the dependency cycle." The plan then provides a series of steps to develop sufficient treatment services.[8]

Under the heading, "Initiative: Chronic Mental Illness Treatment," the statement of the problem is:

> Many of the community's homeless population [are] categorized as chronically mentally ill. Policies of deinstitutionalization, predicated on delivery of services in the least restrictive environment, have proceeded without proper attention to providing adequate funding for community-based care. Additionally, inadequate attention has been paid to the recurrent need of some individuals, who often decline services, for periodic institutional commitment.

The value statement is: "Individuals suffering from chronic mental illness deserve adequate ongoing treatment of a type and in a location consistent with their present condition." The policy that derives from these is: "Provide adequate treatment services for chronically mentally ill individuals in an environment that is the least restrictive and most likely to protect the individual and others from harm," and the plan then lays out steps to provide services for the mentally ill.[9]

Other features of the Portland Model include attention to the need for changing involuntary commitment laws; providing employment for recovering substance abusers and mentally ill persons; providing appropriate housing opportunities, including substance-free housing for recovering alcoholics and drug addicts and supervised housing for the mentally ill; ensuring comprehensive and coordinated planning, implementation, and fund-raising from local, private, corporate, state, and federal sources; and developing strategies for involving the public in education about the nature of the problems and the needs in Portland. What is most remarkable about both the planning document and the overall tone of implementation is the readiness to acknowledge, accept, and plan for the treatment and recovery of substance abuse and mental illness.

We visited Portland in 1991 and saw how responsible a city's approach can be when denial is set aside, enabling behavior recognized and stopped, and proactive attention paid to people suffering from alcoholism, drug addiction, and mental illness. During our visit, we met with city and county officials and service providers, attended planning meetings, and visited emergency, treatment, and housing facilities. Despite financial constraints, the plan was being widely and faithfully implemented with exceptional enthusiasm and remarkable collaboration between the governmental, private, and business sectors. We talked with several men and women who were alcoholics or addicted to various drugs, a number of mentally ill individuals, and a few teenaged boys and girls—some still staying at the intake shelters, some living in specialized housing. All were engaged in or about to begin recovery programs, and all had real hope about their futures. We came away from our visit with a strong sense that Portland's approach, based on telling the truth about addictions and mental illness, should serve as an inspiration and resource for communities across the nation.

Develop Programs That Work

There are other examples of programs already in place that address the problems of even the most severely disturbed and disabled and that work to break the cycle of addiction, mental illness, abuse, victimization, violence, and social isolation and disconnectedness. Given the variety of good programs, it would be inappropriate to offer a single, comprehensive blueprint; local circumstances differ across the country, and there is significant evidence that various alternative strategies can be equally effective. What we will describe in the next few pages are not models but broad sketches of important program components needed to actually help the most isolated and ill-served members of society.

An important initial step must be active and aggressive outreach, offered in a nonthreatening way, usually over a long period of time—sometimes for months, sometimes for even longer. Many "homeless" people are fearful of others and distrust institutions with which they may have had previous negative encounters; others seem to prefer the isolation in which they exist or, as with the young chronically mentally ill, do not see themselves as needing help and often show contempt for traditional helping systems and traditional helpers. Outreach typically should include the dispatching of teams into areas where such people congregate to talk to them, build trust, and slowly, gently encourage them to accept the kind of help they need. The Manhattan Bowery Project in New York City includes former "homeless" people who are in recovery on outreach teams that make initial contact with people on the streets;[10] Project HELP in New York City sends teams of psychiatrists, nurses, and social workers in vans throughout Manhattan to transport homeless mentally ill people to psychiatric emergency rooms;[11] and the CHIERS wagon, an acronym for the Central City Concern Hooper Inebriate Emergency Response Service in Portland, Oregon, deploys deputized persons to respond to "person-down" calls and transports individuals to a sobering station.[12] Intentional outreach can be conducted in drop-in centers, day centers, shelters, soup kitchens, on the streets, or anywhere people in need of treatment spend time.

Outreach needs to be immediately followed up by or connected to treatment placement for detoxification or inpatient care or both or to treatment for psychiatric inpatient or community-based care. Immediate entry into treatment is an essential feature of the intervention strategies used by employee assistance programs and by professional intervention teams available to the middle class; the same focus on entry into treatment should hold true for the most debilitated substance abusers and the mentally ill. We emphasize the importance of not relying on referrals; substantial research shows that referrals to treatment are not effective and that seriously troubled people often fail to keep appointments made for them.[13] In addition, in some cases, even when clients attempt to follow up on referrals, they do not receive services; they are turned away for lack of space or for failing to meet exclusionary admissions criteria. Therefore, treatment needs to be offered in a treatment program where clients are assured of admission, and clients need to be accompanied or transported to the treatment site.

Comprehensive and effective programs provide short-term detoxification, longer inpatient care, half-way house settings, and finally, long-term alcohol-free and drug-free residential settings.[14] Addiction treatment programs that are modeled on the twenty-eight-day inpatient program developed for working and middle-class alcoholics assume a strong and supportive home environment after treatment. Experience has shown, however, that treatment for more seriously impaired street and shelter people who lack supportive networks must be offered for at least four to six months (some treatment programs, especially those that treat drug addiction, can take up to a year) and needs to be followed by aftercare in facilities that support sustained recovery, such as half-way houses and substance-free long-term living environments.

The Diagnostic and Rehabilitation Center (DRC) in Philadelphia, which has provided alcohol and drug treatment services to the homeless since 1963, incorporates residential treatment for an average of forty-one days and long-term outpatient treatment for both men and women who live in structured facilities connected with the program. The goal is for patients to remain in outpatient treatment for approximately six months and for patients to begin job training and job placement only toward the end of their treatment program, after their sobriety and renewed health are well established.[15] Phoenix House in New York and California and Daytop Village in New York are programs for drug-addicted "homeless" people who live in therapeutic communities that provide treatment in a residential setting where the patient lives for an extended period, sometimes as long as one to two years.[16]

It was a special day for Thomas. He was an alcoholic who had slept in alleys and in abandoned cars off and on for two years; he had been unable to stay in a job because of his drinking. When he first came to the employment office looking for a job, we had insisted that he start attending the AA meeting that met every week at the day center. Eventually, with encouragement from his sponsor, Thomas had entered a publicly funded twenty-eight-day inpatient program, participated in the six-week structured aftercare program at a half-way house, and completed a long stay in a residential employment training program for newly abstinent alcoholics and addicts. Now Thomas was sober, full of hope and no longer facing the life of despair on the streets from which he came. One day at a time, he hoped to stay that way. He was leaving for a job in Florida the next day and had come back to his AA group to say thanks. He promised to carry greetings to his new AA group in Florida.

Alcohol-free and drug-free residential settings are an essential step at the end of active treatment and need to be incorporated into a long-term recovery and aftercare process. Alcohol-free living centers or sober hotels, as they are often called, are intended to prevent the revolving door syndrome. Programs that ignore this step in the process have not worked because they "return the homeless back into his natural habitat, back into that permissive drinking culture where that homelessness/alcoholism cycle repeats itself over and over again. Clearly, therapeutic successes are doomed . . . unless somehow housing for the homeless alcohol and other drug abusers can be developed so that there's a place for sober, free and independent living."[17]

Substance-free living centers vary in size, in amount of on-site supervision, and in the kinds of ancillary programs provided either on-site or in connection with the center. For example, the Everett Hotel in Portland, Oregon, is linked to the substance abuse treatment program and provides housing for patients just completing treatment; the Cambridge-Somerville Program for Alcoholism Rehabilitation, the Railton Hotel in St. Louis, the Pine Street Inn in Boston, and the Alcohol Living Centers in Los Angeles all staff the facilities with house managers and maintenance personnel; the DRC provides on-site programs such as vocational counseling and life-skills training. Oxford Houses are self-governed and self-supported rental houses where groups of recovering alcoholics and drug addicts live in a "family-style residence."[18]

In developing such programs, providers have taken different approaches to acquiring funding for rehabilitating inner-city buildings, locating facilities (which should be away from areas where bottle gangs and addicts congregate but convenient to transportation), and avoiding restrictions created by local zoning ordinances and codes.[19] One universal feature of substance-free housing, however, is that residents work, pay rent, and maintain their sobriety by attending AA or NA meetings.[20] Failure to remain clean and sober is a cause for immediate discharge; however, the offer of renewed treatment and return to sober housing is pressed with the kind of assurance and enthusiasm that only recovering alcoholics and addicts can provide.

For the mentally ill who live in shelters or on the streets, there are also programs across the country that successfully engage people in treatment to ameliorate their psychotic symptoms and maintain a regimen of medication that permits them to function in sufficiently stable ways so they can live more satisfying lives. The report of the federal Task Force on Homelessness and Severe Mental Illness outlines a full range of services needed by the homeless mentally ill:

> In general, this population requires . . . needs assessment, diagnosis and treatment planning, medication management, counseling and supportive therapy, hospitalization and inpatient care, twenty-four hour crisis-response services (e.g., backup to landlords), and habilitation and social skills training. In addition, special efforts are needed to integrate substance abuse treatment for people who require both . . . and to improve hospital discharge planning policies to ensure that appropriate housing, mental health care, and support services are available in the community following hospitalization. . . . Complications or medication side effects should be anticipated, and problem-solving should occur ahead of time rather than during crises. Compliance with treatment plans must be monitored and supported, an important function of the care manager.[21]

The Task Force suggests that hospitals should be used only when treatment needs cannot be met elsewhere. Nonhospital programs often include "clubhouse" day programs as part of a structured living situation, where patients socialize, work, and at the same time are monitored to insure that they continue to take the medications that they need to function in normal ways. Fountain House in New York City integrates its clubhouse day program with both a jobs program and apartments for the members.[22]

Some of the more disabled among the mentally ill, as well as late-stage alcoholics or drug addicts who suffer from irreparable brain damage, may require long-term institutional care. Anyone with a parent or grandparent suffering from Alzheimer's disease understands this need. We are not advocating reinstitutionalization of all people who suffer from mental illness, but we are suggesting that institutional care, if provided in appropriate ways and in appropriate settings, is more humane than allowing the most impaired people in society to continue to fall through all of the safety nets and end up on park benches or in train stations.

The dually diagnosed among today's street and shelter populations present the most difficult challenges for treatment. Nevertheless, new treatment arrangements with collaborative and integrated staffing by professionals from both the psychiatric field and from the alcohol and drug treatment field are being explored.[23] Experts in this emerging field suggest that collaborative agreements between mental health and substance abuse treatment agencies can eliminate the bureaucratic divisions between agencies that presently create barriers to cooperation between mental health workers and substance abuse workers. These experts also urge that funding be flexible enough for agencies to share responsibility for treating individual clients in nontraditional settings using multidisciplinary teams.[24] The rule is flexibility and adaptability to the special needs of the dually diagnosed, including the ability for them to participate in twelve-step support groups similar to AA and NA but specifically designed to permit the use of medication to treat their mental illness.

If the goal is to promote success rather than repeated failure, program planners must be realistic about what they can expect from people who are seriously troubled and have been in crisis for a long time. Offering employment counseling programs in shelters or transitional housing, for example, will do little good unless such counseling is preceded by programs that promote sustained recovery and stability. Planners also need to be realistic about predetermined time-lines for recovery. It is hard to predict how long it will take for seriously incapacitated people in transitional programs to "graduate" to less structured housing and independent living. It is also a reality that some patients will have relapses, either of their addictions or of their mental illness, and that repeated treatment and short-stay hospitalizations will be needed. Relapses and repeated treatment are not measures of failure; relapses are characteristic of chronic diseases and repeated treatment is necessary for successful care.

Finally, policymakers and program planners must be careful of the myths that have developed equating independence with living alone.[25] Recovering alcoholics, drug addicts, and the mentally ill, like other people, need interdependence—loving and supporting relationships—and the success of a program should not always be measured by how quickly clients move into "independent" living, if that also means solitary living.

In short, there are positive and constructive alternatives to the poorly staffed shelters and soup kitchens that, while providing necessary emergency services, do little if anything to address the real needs of most of their clients. These appropriate solutions, however, take commitment, time, and money—and enlightened public and private leadership.

Cost of Treatment

It is difficult to gather good data about the cost of providing various types of effective services for "homeless" alcoholics, drug addicts, and severely mentally ill individuals. Program components like those reviewed above are combined differently in different programs. Programs serve different segments of the "homeless" population, for instance, or may use these strategies for varying lengths of time depending on the individual needs of each client. It is, therefore, difficult to generate a single cost figure for a "good" program.

There are, however, some estimates of the cost of providing certain kinds of services. For example, a feasibility study for the Minneapolis alcohol treatment program for chronic public inebriates determined that detoxification, medical, and psychiatric costs totaled $15,900 per person per year; that legal and social service costs amounted to $6,940 per person per year; and that the total annual cost per person was $22,840.[26] Similarly, the New York City Commission on the Homeless reports that not-for-profit agencies spend $15,000 to $19,000 per year to operate substance abuse beds, including capital costs as well as operating costs.[27]

Staff at the DRC in Philadelphia provided us with more detailed cost figures on a per person basis for a full spectrum of services for alcohol and drug treatment:

1. Emergency shelter—overnight shelter for people not yet in the program: $11.50/night.
2. Detoxification for seven days in a medically supervised, nonhospital setting: $115/day. (In-hospital detoxification is estimated to cost $450–$500/day.)
3. Intermediate service for four to six weeks, including assessment and inpatient or outpatient treatment: $60/day.
4. Long-term service for six to nine months, including dormitory inpatient treatment, substance abuse counseling, life skills and parenting training, and vocational counseling: $90/day.
5. Substance-free living center with outpatient treatment: $75/day.

According to these estimates, the cost at the DRC for an individual would range from $29,800 to slightly over $31,000 for the first year, and would be $27,000 for a second year.[28]

For those who are concerned that the cost of providing appropriate and effective treatment for seriously disabled people who now live in shelters or on the streets is unacceptably high, particularly given current budget and economic constraints, we should point out that, under the current system, patterns of recidivism are such that the "less costly" services are being provided over and over again to the same people. Many service providers report that the most disheartening and frustrating part of running a shelter is seeing the same people coming back again and again. Said another way, "It is ironical, and not cost-effective, to use valuable dollars year after year to provide limited services to the same population. Good business sense dictates that sometimes more money has to be spent up front to save dollars down the line."[29]

The costs for the current system of shelters are enormous. New York City spends between $18,000 and $20,000 per year for sheltering single adults and between $27,375 and $52,000 per year to house families in welfare motels.[30] The 1988 HUD survey found that the national average cost of a night of shelter was $28, or $10,200 per year; the cost per year for sheltering a single man was $8,030 per year, and the cost for a family, $10,585 per year.[31] These costs include the provision of very few services. On an aggregated basis, the U.S. Department of Housing and Urban Development reported in 1988 that $1.6 billion was being spent per year for emergency shelters alone—two-thirds from public, governmental sources and one-third from private sources.[32] Under the federal Stewart B. McKinney Homeless Assistance Act, by the end of fiscal year 1992, the federal government will have spent almost $3.2 billion since 1987 when the act was passed.[33] According to the U.S. General Accounting Office, 69 percent of the $600 million appropriated for McKinney programs in 1990 was spent for food and shelter assistance, 26 percent for all health-related programs, and 5 percent for education and job training. The funds specifically designated for alcohol and drug treatment and for mental health under the act were for demonstration and research projects, not for direct funding of treatment programs in general.[34]

In a cost-benefit analysis of short-term versus long-term care, the secretary of Health and Human Services suggested to Congress that over the long run, it may well be cheaper to provide appropriate treatment services at the outset. "The average alcoholic's treatment could be offset by reductions in other health care costs within two to three years following the start of treatment."[35] A dramatic example of the potential for savings is the report by the DRC that it had provided sufficient treatment to sixteen crack-addicted pregnant women so that their babies were born drug-free. Using an estimate of $100,000 per baby for the in-hospital care of babies born drug-addicted, the DRC program personnel calculated that treating the mothers for their cocaine addiction saved more than $1 million.[36]

The problem is not that government and others are not spending money for programs for the "homeless"; the problem is that most of the money is not being used for the kinds of treatment needed by the severely disabled substance abusers, the mentally ill, and the dually diagnosed who comprise up to 85 percent of this population. There may be additional costs associated with the initial development of needed programs, but there may well be long-term savings, since the current array of "cheaper" services is being provided over and over again to the same people. Regardless, the costs of not developing these needed services will far outstrip the initial costs in terms of the costs to the criminal justice[37] and welfare systems and in terms of human life.

NIMBY

A major obstacle to helping the homeless is the phenomenon commonly known as NIMBY, Not In My Back Yard. Many people claim to have an interest in supporting the development of shelters, half-way houses, and treatment and care facilities for alcoholics and drug addicts, particularly for those who are "homeless," as long as such facilities are "not in my neighborhood." Residents fear a negative impact on property values, and media reports are replete with stories about the angry battles over neighborhood opposition to proposed facilities. Frequently, because of such controversy, no sites for such facilities can be found.

NIMBY is, in part, a product of the politics of the homelessness movement. In portraying the "homeless" as "people just like us" or as the very poor, advocates have tried to impose shelters and other facilities on residential neighborhoods. In doing so, they have played on the guilt of citizens who are accused of not being willing to bear the burden of community support and responsibility for the "deserving poor." In its most extreme form, this battle is waged as an "in your face" exercise—advocates insist that the "homeless" have the right to beg, to use subway or metro stations as public latrines and sleeping places, and to set up shop—panhandling, staying, and sleeping wherever they choose. By denying that substance abuse and mental illness are part of the problem, the movement tries to persuade citizens to disregard these disabilities and levels accusations of selfishness, racism, and elitism at those who do not.

Once again, those who are serious about solving these problems need to be clear about the relevant issues. Shelters and large welfare hotels that house untreated substance abusers and mentally ill people do introduce unwanted and unwelcome conditions into the neighborhoods where they are located. When shelters house severely disabled individuals and provide no real care, these individuals produce litter in the form of empty liquor bottles, used drug paraphernalia, discarded trash, sometimes human waste, and other debris. Panhandling near shelters is annoying; bizarre behavior is frightening; drug transactions can involve danger; explicit sexual activity is inappropriate. To pretend that these things do not happen is yet another form of denial of the diseases of substance abuse and mental illness and their effects on behavior. To expect neighborhood residents or businesses to accept such behavior is naive. Neighborhood opposition is not only understandable, but, quite frankly, appropriate.

If planners and advocates change their attitudes and shift from simply sheltering people to creating treatment and recovery facilities, they can simultaneously be honest about the full range of facilities that are needed and the best locations for them. For example, places where alcoholics, drug addicts, and the mentally ill receive encouragement to enter treatment, such as intake shelters and drop-in shelters, should be located in neighborhoods easily accessible to street people but not in business or restaurant districts or in residential neighborhoods near schools and playgrounds. Substance-free living centers, in contrast, should be in residential neighborhoods, not to impose them on anyone, but for the benefit of the clients who need to be away from skid row–like areas to maintain their sobriety. The residents of these centers, like the mentally ill whose illnesses have been stabilized and who are able to live in the community, are of no threat to their neighbors.

Become Advocates
for a More Enlightened Policy

Even though many claim that the homeless are victims of racism, elitism, gnawing greed, and an unresponsive government, the homeless are really victims of confused thinking, of political agendas, of unintended consequences, of good ideas but poor implementation. Everyone, especially the most troubled members of society, is a victim of the denial that results from fear of facing the truth that in turn prevents people from telling the truth. And so, unimaginable in the late twentieth century in America, our cities and towns have become Calcuttas filled with men and women huddled in doorways, breadlines and soup kitchens, beggars and waifs, human tragedy, disease, and death. It should not be this way; it need not be this way.

All who are concerned with homelessness, especially those who work as professionals or volunteers in the thousands of programs throughout the country, need to raise a new voice of advocacy on behalf of those to whom we are now giving so little that is of genuine and lasting benefit. Concerned citizens need to become advocates for programs that offer concrete help and hope—and the real dignity that comes from recovery and sustained mental health. But to do so, ignorance and denial must be eliminated and the political games that distract from the real issues must be stopped. Policymakers and planners need to take advantage of the good model programs that already exist to address the needs of homeless substance abusers and the homeless mentally ill; unless they do, it is a virtual certainty that the needs of the homeless will continue to go unmet. Finally, society must let go of its unrealistic expectations that a quick fix will solve a problem that, in one form or another, has existed for a long time. There are no easy answers, but if helping others, especially the most helpless, is a measure of a society's decency, Americans cannot delay any longer.

In order to realize these goals, both the media and policymakers at every level of government must be enlisted in developing more enlightened policies. Part of the task will be to educate them about the realities of what is now called homelessness but that really is a combination of serious disabling addictions, mental illness, social isolation caused in part by the stigma attached to these conditions, and the absence of appropriate treatment services. Advocates, the media, and especially policymakers need to ask the following questions when investigating homelessness, and they must seek honest answers to them.

1. How many people are actually homeless, excluding those who might be considered "at risk" for homelessness or those who might be called the "prehomeless?" Does the answer reflect the total number of people who are homeless on a given night or does it represent an aggregation of all instances of homelessness reported throughout a year?

2. What proportion of the homeless population, including members of homeless families, especially mothers, suffer from alcoholism, drug addictions, serious mental illness, or some combination of these three?

3. To what extent are family violence and social isolation, aggravated by substance abuse and mental illness, characteristic of the homeless population?

4. Given the prevalence of alcoholism, drug addiction, and serious mental illness among the homeless, how might providers design a full continuum of treatment and support services, including supported housing, to address these problems?

5. How can planners design substance abuse treatment programs for women with children so that fear of losing their children is not a disincentive for women entering treatment?

6. Are such services currently available? Do the available services provide appropriate treatment and long-term support services before expecting people to make realistic transitions to independent living?

7. What causes homelessness and what has caused the increase in homelessness during the past decade? Given the increased numbers of people at risk for mental illness and substance abuse problems—because of the population bulge of the baby boom on the one hand and various public policies that had the unintended consequence of eliminating previously available services for the residents of skid row or skid row–like neighborhoods on the other—how likely is it that current economic conditions have been the underlying cause of the increase in homelessness? Why did homelessness not decrease after the end of the 1981–1982 recession, and why did it not substantially increase during the much deeper recession of 1991–1992?

8. What, realistically, will an increase in affordable housing do to solve the problem of homelessness if no treatment or support services are available for those who suffer from alcoholism, drug addiction, mental illness, or dual diagnosis?

9. How much will it cost to provide the appropriate kinds of treatment services and long-term supports for the homeless? How much will it cost not to?

10. What are concerned individuals prepared to do to ensure that the public understands the true nature of the problem and overcome its denial about modern homelessness?

Overcome Denial

It has been almost fifteen years since homelessness became sufficiently visible to touch a nerve in the American consciousness and conscience, and this country has responded with little more than Band-Aids; so, to rising frustration, homelessness continues unabated. Denial prevents America's citizenry from facing the truth about the alcoholics, drug addicts, victims of family violence, abused and sick children, mentally ill people, and dually diagnosed people who so desperately need help. Unlike many previous generations of Americans, most people today deny the relationship between disabling addictions and mental illness and the fact of homelessness. Enabled by aggressive political efforts to portray the homeless as "just like us," the public ignores reality despite the overwhelming evidence to the contrary.

Overcoming denial about alcoholism, drug addiction, and mental illness is a challenge for all, whether those suffering from these problems are family members, friends, employees, or strangers on the street. Only by doing so, however, can society offer help and hope to both loved ones and strangers alike. The rapid expansion of treatment opportunities for middle-class patients suggests that people are overcoming their denial when these diseases appear among the middle class. It is time to put aside class prejudices and recognize that those who stay on the streets and live in shelters deserve the same kind of help and treatment. No less than anyone else, the homeless deserve the opportunity to recover and maintain sobriety and stable mental health so they too can fully participate in this interdependent society we call America.

Notes

Chapter 1

1. Frank R. Lipton and Albert Sabatini, "Constructing Support Systems for Homeless Chronic Patients," in *The Homeless Mentally Ill: A Task Force Report of the American Psychiatric Association,* ed. H. Richard Lamb (Washington, DC: American Psychiatric Association, 1984), 156.

2. Analysts have described other research problems in detail. First, frequently there are differences among researchers in how to define homelessness. The usual definition includes those people who use public or private emergency shelters or sleep in public or private spaces that are not designed as shelter, such as train and subway stations or under bridges. Some researchers also attempt to include the "prehome-less," i.e., persons who are doubled up with relatives or friends and people who live in substandard housing. Second, study samples often include only those people who are currently using either shelters or other services such as soup kitchens or clinics. These samples fail to include the "street" people who either do not use such services or only use them intermittently.

3. Mary E. Stefl, "The New Homeless: A National Perspective," in *The Homeless in Contemporary Society,* ed. Richard D. Bingham, Roy E. Green, and Sammis B. White (Newbury Park, CA: Sage Publications, 1989), 48; Interagency Council on the Homeless, *The 1989 Annual Report of the Interagency Council on the Homeless* (Washington, DC: U.S. Government Printing Office, 1989), I, 1; Peter H. Rossi, *Without Shelter: Homelessness in the 1980s* (Washington, DC: Twentieth Century Fund, 1989), 24; and James D. Wright, *Address Unknown: The Homeless in America* (New York: Aldine De Gruyter, 1989), 62.

4. Peter H. Rossi, *Down and Out in America: The Origins of Homelessness* (Chicago, IL: University of Chicago Press, 1989), 121; U.S. Department of Housing and Urban Development, *A Report on the 1988 National Survey of Shelters for the Homeless* (Washington, DC: U.S. Department of Housing and Urban Development, 1989), 11; Wright, *Address Unknown,* 62.

5. Martha R. Burt and Barbara E. Cohen, *America's Homeless: Numbers, Charac-teristics and Programs That Serve Them* (Washington, DC: Urban Institute, 1989), 3; U.S. Department of Housing and Urban Development, *1988 National Survey,* 11; Wright, *Address Unknown,* 66.

6. Burt and Cohen, *America's Homeless,* 24, 26.

7. Ibid., 3.

8. Howard M. Bahr, "Introduction," in *Homelessness in the United States: State Surveys,* ed. Jamshid A. Momeni (New York: Praeger Publishers, 1990), xvii–xviii.

9. For a good summary of research on veterans among the homeless, see Marjorie J. Robertson, "Homeless Veterans: An Emerging Problem," in *The Homeless in Contemporary Society,* ed. Bingham, Green, and White, 64–81. See also Kathleen H.

Dockett, *Street Homeless People in the District of Columbia* (Washington, DC: University of the District of Columbia, 1989), 29, 41; Paul Koegel, M. Audrey Burnam, and Rodger K. Farr, "The Prevalence of Specific Psychiatric Disorders Among Homeless Individuals in the Inner City of Los Angeles," *Archives of General Psychiatry* 45, no. 11 (1988): 1088; National Coalition for the Homeless, *American Nightmare: A Decade of Homelessness in the United States* (New York and Washington, DC: National Coalition for the Homeless, 1989), 2; and Wright, *Address Unknown,* 63–64.

10. Burt and Cohen, *America's Homeless,* 3; Rossi, *Down and Out,* 118; and James D. Wright and Eleanor Weber, *Homelessness and Health* (Washington, DC: McGraw-Hill, 1987), 46.

11. Andrew M. Cuomo, *The Way Home: A New Direction in Social Policy* (New York: New York City Commission on the Homeless, February 1992), B-3; Dockett, *Street Homeless People,* 29; Rossi, *Down and Out,* 131–132. This phenomenon has been confirmed in conversations with several service providers, who report that one of their goals is to reunite these "single women" with their children.

12. Burt and Cohen, *America's Homeless,* 3.

13. Ibid., 40; Wright, *Address Unknown,* 57.

14. Ellen L. Bassuk, Alison S. Lauriat, and Leonore Rubin, "Homeless Families," in *Homelessness: Critical Issues for Policy and Practice,* ed. Jill Kneerim (Boston, MA: The Boston Foundation, 1987), 20–21; William R. Breakey, "Recent Empirical Research on the Homeless Mentally Ill," in *Research Methodologies Concerning Homeless Persons with Serious Mental Illness and/or Substance Abuse Disorders,* ed. Deborah L. Dennis (Proceedings of a two-day conference sponsored by the U.S. Department of Health and Human Services, Alcohol, Drug Abuse, and Mental Health Administration, Washington, DC, December 1987), 36; Housing Authority of Portland, *Resolving Homelessness in Portland and Multnomah County: A Report and Planning Framework* (Portland, OR: Department of Planning, Development and Intergovernmental Relations, November 1989), 4; Tom Robbins, "New York's Homeless Families," in *Housing the Homeless,* ed. Jon Erickson and Charles Wilhelm (Piscataway, NJ: Center for Urban Policy Research, 1986), 27.

15. Burt and Cohen, *America's Homeless,* 74.

16. Tri-County Youth Services Consortium, "A Plan to Resolve Youth Homelessness in Multnomah County" (Draft Report, prepared by Providers of Youth Services, Multnomah County Youth Program Office, February 1991), 6–7.

17. A good summary of the research on the effects of homelessness on children is found in Yvonne Rafferty and Marybeth Shinn, "The Impact of Homelessness on Children," *American Psychologist* 46, no. 11 (November 1991): 1170–1176. See also Stanford Center for the Study of Families, Children and Youth, *Stanford Studies of Homeless Families, Children and Youth* (Palo Alto, CA: Stanford Center for the Study of Families, Children and Youth, November 1991). For research about homeless mothers see Ellen L. Bassuk and Lynn Rosenberg, "Why Does Family Homelessness Occur? A Case-Control Study," *American Journal of Public Health* 78, no. 7 (1988): 783–788; Marybeth Shinn, James R. Knickman, and Beth C. Weitzman, "Social Relationships and Vulnerability to Becoming Homeless Among Poor Families," *American Psychologist* 46, no. 11 (November 1991): 1180–1185.

18. Tri-County Youth Services Consortium, "Youth Homelessness," 5.

19. For a good analysis of homeless youth, see James T. Kennedy et al., "Health Care for Familyless, Runaway Street Kids," in *Under the Safety Net: The Health and Social Welfare of the Homeless in the United States,* ed. Philip W. Brickner et al. (New York: W. W. Norton, 1990), 82–117. See also Momeni, ed., *State Surveys,* 62; Virginia Price, "Runaways and Homeless Street Youth," in *Homelessness: Critical Issues,* ed. Kneerim, 25–26; Marjorie J. Robertson, "Homeless Youth in Hollywood: Patterns of Alcohol Use" (National Institute on Alcohol Abuse and Alcoholism, Washington, DC, 1987, Mimeographed), vi; Wright, *Address Unknown,* 60.

20. Bahr, "Introduction," xxi.

21. Ellen Bassuk, quoted in Leona L. Bachrach, "The Homeless Mentally Ill and Mental Health Services: An Analytical Review of the Literature," in *The Homeless Mentally Ill,* ed. Lamb, 21.

22. Ellen L. Bassuk, "The Homelessness Problem," in *Housing the Homeless,* ed. Erickson and Wilhelm, 258; Gerald J. Bean, Jr., Mary E. Stefl, and Steven R. Howe, "Mental Health and Homelessness: Issues and Findings," *Social Work* (September–October 1987): 412; Pamela J. Fischer and William R. Breakey, "Mental Illness and Substance Abuse in the Contemporary American Homeless Population: Findings from the Baltimore Homeless Study" (Paper presented at Professional Symposium, Recent Findings and New Approaches to the Treatment of Mental Illness and Substance Abuse, Tulsa, OK, 1988), 7–8; Mary Ann Lee et al., "Health Care for Children in Homeless Families," in *Under the Safety Net,* ed. Brickner et al., 121; Rossi, *Down and Out,* 130; and Wright, *Address Unknown,* 66, 68, 74, 86–87.

23. Peter H.Rossi, Gene Fisher, and Georgianna Willis, "The Condition of the Homeless of Chicago" (National Opinion Research Center, Chicago, IL, 1986, Mimeographed paper), 76.

24. Rossi, *Down and Out,* 131–132. See also Cuomo, *The Way Home,* B-3.

25. Robertson, "Homeless Veterans," 76; Rossi, Fisher, and Willis, "Homeless of Chicago," 34; Richard C. Tessler and Deborah L. Dennis, "A Synthesis of NIMH-Funded Research Concerning Persons Who Are Homeless and Mentally Ill" (Program for the Homeless Mentally Ill, Washington, DC: U.S. Department of Health and Human Services, February 9, 1989, Mimeographed), 23; and Wright, *Address Unknown,* 18, 72, 125.

26. Barbara G. Lubran, "Alcohol and Drug Abuse Among the Homeless Population: A National Response," in *Treating Alcoholism and Drug Abuse Among Homeless Men and Women: Nine Community Demonstration Grants,* ed. Milton Argeriou and Dennis McCarty (Binghamton, NY: The Haworth Press, 1990), 12; Wright, *Address Unknown,* 76; Wright and Weber, *Homelessness and Health,* 56.

27. Koegel, Burnam, and Farr, "Psychiatric Disorders Among Homeless Individuals," 1091.

28. Dennis McCarty et al., "Alcoholism, Drug Abuse, and the Homeless," *American Psychologist* 46, no. 11 (November 1991): 1139; Lisa Thomas, Mike Kelly, and Michael Cousineau, "Alcoholism and Substance Abuse," in *Under the Safety Net,* ed. Brickner et al., 205; James D. Wright, "Correlates and Consequences of Alcohol Abuse in the National 'Health Care for the Homeless' Client Population: Final Results" (National Institute on Alcohol Abuse and Alcoholism, Washington, DC, April 1990, Mimeographed), 2.

29. Pamela J. Fischer and William R. Breakey, "The Epidemiology of Alcohol, Drug, and Mental Disorders Among Homeless Persons," *American Psychologist* 46, no. 11 (November 1991): 1118. Alcoholism, defined as "alcohol abuse and dependence," affects about 10 percent of adult Americans. U.S. Department of Health and Human Services, *Seventh Special Report to the Congress on Alcohol and Health from the Secretary of Health and Human Services* (Washington, DC: U.S. Department of Health and Human Services, January 1990), xxi.

30. Fischer and Breakey, "The Epidemiology of Alcohol," 1116; James D. Wright, "Final Results," 2. A wide variety of studies is summarized by Barbara G. Lubran in her chapter, "Alcohol and Drug Abuse," in *Treating Alcoholism and Drug Abuse*, ed. Argeriou and McCarty. The National Institute on Alcohol Abuse and Alcoholism, "Homelessness, Alcohol and Other Drugs" (Proceedings of a conference held by U.S. Department of Health and Human Services in San Diego, CA, February 2–4, 1989) presents a table on page 19 that includes seventy-eight studies and shows that percentages reported for the rate of people who suffer from long-term, chronic alcoholism or serious alcohol abuse range from as low as 2 percent to as high as 86 percent. This range results from variations in methodology, reporting by gender and location of the study, and again suggests attention to local conditions for the purpose of program planning.

31. Wright, "Final Results," 23. See also Fischer and Breakey, "Epidemiology of Alcohol," 1115; McCarty et al., "Alcoholism, Drug Abuse, and the Homeless," 1139; Alan J. Romanoski et al., "Alcoholism and Psychiatric Comorbidity in the Homeless: The Baltimore Study" (Paper presented at the Annual Meeting of the American Public Health Association, Boston, MA, 1988), 11.

32. P. Koegel and M. Audrey Burnam, "Alcoholism Among Homeless Adults in the Inner City of Los Angeles," *Archives of General Psychiatry* 45, no. 11 (1988): 1015–1016.

33. Dee Roth and Jerry Bean, "Alcohol Problems and Homelessness: Findings from the Ohio Study" (Conference paper for meeting on Homeless with Alcohol Related Problems, National Institute on Alcohol Abuse and Alcoholism, Bethesda, MD, July 29–30, 1985), 4–20.

34. Wright and Weber, *Homelessness and Health*. See also Wright, "Final Results," and Wright, *Address Unknown*.

35. James D. Wright et al., "Homelessness and Health: The Effects of Life Style on Physical Well-being Among Homeless People in New York City" (Manuscript for inclusion in: *Social Theory and Social Problems*, ed. M. Lewis and J. Miller, JAI Press, 1987), 20.

36. Lydia Williams, *Mourning in America: Health Problems, Mortality, and Homelessness* (Washington, DC: National Coalition for the Homeless, December 1991), iii, 12; Wright, *Address Unknown*, 62; Wright and Weber, *Homelessness and Health*, 127–129.

37. Wright and Weber, *Homelessness and Health*, 134.

38. See Wright and Weber, *Homelessness and Health*.

39. The health problems of the homeless, the relationship of these problems to alcohol, and the potential for victimization of vulnerable and sick homeless people have been documented extensively in Brickner et al., *Under the Safety Net;* Brickner et al., eds. *Health Care of Homeless People* (New York: Springer Publishing, 1985); U.S.

Department of Health and Human Services, *Sixth Special Report to the U.S. Congress on Alcohol and Health from the Secretary of Health and Human Services* (Rockville, MD: U.S. Department of Health and Human Services, January 1987); Wright, "Final Results," 43–45; Wright and Weber, *Homelessness and Health*.

40. Fischer and Breakey, "The Epidemiology of Alcohol," 1120; National Institute on Alcohol Abuse and Alcoholism, "Homelessness, Alcohol and Other Drugs," 4.

41. See Rossi, *Without Shelter*, 25; and Wright, *Address Unknown*, 67.

42. Gina Kolata, "Twins on the Streets: Homelessness and Addiction," *New York Times*, May 22, 1989, 1.

43. Dr. Donald W. Burnes was a member of the Mayor's Homeless Coordinating Council, Washington, DC, from 1987 to 1989 and attended the meeting described here.

44. Gerald R. Garrett and Russell K. Schutt, "The Homeless Alcoholic, Past and Present," in *Homelessness: Critical Issues*, ed. Kneerim, 29.

45. Fischer and Breakey, "The Epidemiology of Alcohol," 1116. The National Institute on Alcohol Abuse and Alcoholism, "Homelessness, Alcohol and Other Drugs," presents a table on page 19 that includes sixty-six individual studies and shows that the percentages reported for the rate of homeless people who use or abuse drugs range from as low as 1 percent to as high as 70 percent. This range results from variations in methodology, reporting by gender, and location of the study and, again, suggests attention to local conditions for the purpose of program planning. Researchers suggest that those studies that use self-reporting as the method of identification of drug use create serious problems of underreporting of drug use. See Cuomo, *The Way Home*, 26; Dockett, *Street Homeless People*, 60; James K. Steward, "Drug Use Forecasting, Fourth Quarter 1988" (Report for National Institute of Justice Research in Action, Washington, DC: U.S. Department of Justice, June 1989), 9.

46. Cuomo, *The Way Home*, 28, 70.

47. McCarty et al., "Alcoholism, Drug Abuse, and the Homeless," 1139; Wright and Weber, *Homelessness and Health*, 47.

48. Fischer and Breakey, "The Epidemiology of Alcohol," 1120.

49. Elaine Fox, Director, Philadelphia Health Management Corporation. Comments to authors at Interagency Council on the Homeless Workshop, Philadelphia, June 20, 1990; Irving W. Shandler, *Diagnostic and Rehabilitation Center/Philadelphia: Annual Report, Fiscal Year 1989* (Philadelphia, PA: Diagnostic and Rehabilitation Center, 1989), 2; conversations with shelter providers, 1989–1991; Richard W. White, *Rude Awakenings: What the Homeless Crisis Tells Us* (San Francisco, CA: ICS Press, 1992), 15.

50. U.S. General Accounting Office, *Welfare Hotels: Uses, Costs, and Alternatives* (Washington, DC: GAO, January 1989), 29.

51. Shandler, *Annual Report*, 3. See also Douglas J. Besharov, "The Children of Crack: Will We Protect Them?" *Public Welfare* (Fall 1989): 7.

52. David Wood et al., *Over the Brink: Homeless Families in Los Angeles: California Children, California Families* (Los Angeles: Assembly Office of Research, August 1989), 7–8, 18.

53. Committee on Health Care for Homeless People, Institute of Medicine, *Homelessness, Health, and Human Needs* (Washington, DC: National Academy Press, 1988), 60; Fischer and Breakey, "The Epidemiology of Alcohol," 1121;

Norweeta G. Milburn, "Drug Abuse Among Homeless People," in *Homelessness in the United States: Data and Issues,* ed. Jamshid A. Momeni (New York: Praeger Publishers, 1990), 63; Wright, "Final Results," 3.

54. Fischer and Breakey, "The Epidemiology of Alcohol," 1121; Price, "Runaways and Homeless Youth," 25; Tri-County Youth Services Consortium, "A Plan to Resolve Youth Homelessness," 5–6; Wright and Weber, *Homelessness and Health,* 74.

55. U.S. Congress, House Select Committee on Children, Youth and Families, *Law and Policy Affecting Addicted Women and Their Children,* 101st Cong., 2nd sess., May 17, 1990 (Washington, DC: U.S. Government Printing Office, 1990), 6, 74; John M. Raba, "Homelessness and AIDS," in *Under the Safety Net,* ed. Brickner et al., 215–233; Williams, *Mourning in America,* 21; Wright and Weber, *Homelessness and Health,* 75.

56. Ellen L. Bassuk, Leonore Rubin, and Alison S. Lauriat, "Characteristics of Sheltered Homeless Families," *American Journal of Public Health* 76, no. 9 (1986): 1097; McCarty et al., "Alcoholism, Drug Abuse, and the Homeless," 1144–1145; Rossi, Fisher, and Willis, "The Condition of the Homeless of Chicago," 135; Stefl, "The New Homeless: A National Perspective," in *The Homeless in Contemporary Society,* ed. Bingham, Green, and White, 46; U.S. Department of Housing and Urban Development, *1988 National Survey,* 21; U.S. Department of Housing and Urban Development, *A Report on Homeless Assistance Policy and Practice in the Nation's Five Largest Cities* (Washington, DC: U.S. Department of Housing and Urban Development, 1989), 48; Wright, *Address Unknown,* 149.

57. E. Fuller Torrey, quoted in Rael Jean Isaac and Virginia C. Armat, *Madness in the Streets: How Psychiatry and the Law Abandoned the Mentally Ill* (New York: Free Press, 1990), 6–7.

58. E. Fuller Torrey, *Nowhere to Go: The Tragic Odyssey of the Homeless Mentally Ill* (New York: Harper & Row, 1988), 10. It is hard to introduce the subject of mental illness among the homeless without an extensive discussion of the failures of deinstitutionalization; however, we will return to this subject in later chapters.

59. U.S. General Accounting Office, *Homeless Mentally Ill: Problems and Options in Estimating Numbers and Trends* (Washington, DC: GAO, 1988), 42.

60. Burt and Cohen, *America's Homeless,* 136; Fischer and Breakey, "The Epidemiology of Alcohol," 1116; U.S. General Accounting Office, *Homeless Mentally Ill,* 36–42. The National Institute on Alcohol Abuse and Alcoholism, "Homelessness, Alcohol and Other Drugs," presents a summary on page 19 of seventy-two studies that include measures of mental illness showing that percentages reported on the rate of homeless people who suffer from mental illness ranges from as low as 2 percent to as high as 90 percent.

61. National Mental Health Association, "The Role of Community Foundations in Meeting the Needs of Homeless Individuals with Mental Illness" (Conference Report, National Mental Health Association, Alexandria, VA, 1986), 3.

62. H. Richard Lamb, "The Homeless Mentally Ill," in *Homelessness: Critical Issues,* ed. Kneerim, 36.

63. Burt and Cohen, *America's Homeless,* 3.

64. Jennifer Burroughs, "Health Concerns of Homeless Women," in *Under the Safety Net,* ed. Brickner et al., 149; Fischer and Breakey, "The Epidemiology of

Alcohol," 1115, 1123; McCarty et al., "Alcoholism, Drug Abuse, and the Homeless," 1139; Wright, *Address Unknown,* 61.

65. Burt and Cohen, *America's Homeless,* 51; Sonjia Parker Redmond and Joan Brackmann, "Homeless Children and Their Caretakers," in *Data and Issues,* ed. Momeni, 124.

66. Martha R. Burt and Barbara E. Cohen, "A Sociodemographic Profile of the Service-Using Homeless: Findings from a National Survey," in *Data and Issues,* ed. Momeni, 33–34; Dockett, *Street Homeless People,* 88.

67. National Institute on Alcohol Abuse and Alcoholism, "Homelessness, Alcohol and Other Drugs," 3.

68. Fred C. Osher, "Assessing Dual Diagnosis," *Access* 2, no. 2 (June 1990): 6; Tessler and Dennis, "A Synthesis of NIMH-Funded Research," 49. See also Robert E. Drake, Fred C. Osher, and Michael Wallach, "Homelessness and Dual Diagnosis," *American Psychologist* 46, no. 11 (November 1991): 1149–1150; Fischer and Breakey, "The Epidemiology of Alcohol," 1116, 1120; Wright, "Final Results," 33.

69. M. Susan Ridgely et al., *Executive Summary: Chronic Mentally Ill Young Adults with Substance Abuse Problems: A Review of Research, Treatment, and Training Issues* (Baltimore: University of Maryland at Baltimore, 1987), 11.

70. National Resource Center on Homelessness and Mental Illness, *Working with Dually Diagnosed Homeless Persons* (Delmar, NY: Policy Research Associates, July 1990), 1. We will discuss dual diagnosis among the homeless more fully in Chapter 2.

71. Jeffrey C. Wilson and Anthony C. Kouzi, "A Social-Psychiatric Perspective on Homelessness: Results from a Pittsburgh Study," in *Data and Issues,* ed. Momeni, 105.

72. Fischer and Breakey, "Findings from the Baltimore Homeless Study," 13.

73. National Coalition for Jail Reform, *Removing the Chronically Mentally Ill from Jail* (Washington, DC: National Coalition for Jail Reform, 1984), 1.

74. Fischer and Breakey, "Findings from the Baltimore Homeless Study," 7. See also Fischer and Breakey, "The Epidemiology of Alcohol," 1122.

75. Rossi, *Down and Out,* 115. See also Burt and Cohen, "A Sociodemographic Profile," in *Data and Issues,* ed. Momeni, 26.

76. Burt and Cohen, "A Sociodemographic Profile," in *Data and Issues,* ed. Momeni, 33–34; Dockett, *Street Homeless People,* 29, 32; Rossi, *Down and Out,* 115; Tessler and Dennis, "A Synthesis of NIMH-Funded Research," 23; and Wright, *Address Unknown,* 66, 88.

77. Susan Sadd, "Revolving Door Revisited: Public Inebriates' Use of Medical and Non-medical Detoxification Services in New York City" (Conference paper for meeting on Homeless with Alcohol Related Problems, National Institute on Alcohol Abuse and Alcoholism, Bethesda, MD, July 29–30, 1985), 8.

78. Committee on Health Care for Homeless People, Institute of Medicine, *Homelessness, Health, and Human Needs,* 23–25. See also A. Anthony Arce et al., "A Psychiatric Profile of Street People Admitted to an Emergency Shelter," *Hospital and Community Psychiatry* 34, no. 9 (September 1983): 812–817.

79. Burt and Cohen, *America's Homeless,* 3; Cuomo, *The Way Home,* 22; Dockett, *Street Homeless People,* 59; U.S. Department of Housing and Urban Development, *1988 National Survey,* 16; Rossi, *Down and Out,* 94–95; Wright, *Address Unknown,* 73.

80. Lillian Gelberg, Lawrence S. Linn, and Barbara D. Leake, "Mental Health, Alcohol and Drug Use, and Criminal History Among Homeless Adults," *American Journal of Psychiatry* 145, no. 2 (February 1988): 192.

81. Drake, Osher, and Wallach, "Homelessness and Dual Diagnosis," *American Psychologist,* 1150; "Exploring Myths About 'Street People,'" *Access* 2, no. 2 (June 1990): 1; Irving Piliavin et al., "Conditions Contributing to Long-Term Homelessness," (School of Social Work and Institute for Research on Poverty, University of Wisconsin, Madison, WI, 1989, Mimeographed), 14–19.

82. Bassuk, Lauriat, and Rubin, "Homeless Families," 21; Burt and Cohen, *America's Homeless,* 3; Rossi, Fisher, and Willis, "The Condition of the Homeless of Chicago," 62; U.S. Department of Housing and Urban Development, *1988 National Survey,* 16.

83. Bassuk, Lauriat, and Rubin, "Homeless Families," 21. See also Cuomo, *The Way Home,* 75.

84. Dockett, *Street Homeless People,* 45; U.S. Department of Housing and Urban Development, *1988 National Survey,* 16.

85. Deborah L. Dennis et al., "A Decade of Research and Services for Homeless Mentally Ill Persons," *American Psychologist* 46, no. 11 (November 1991): 1134; Wright, *Address Unknown,* 69.

86. According to one national study, two-thirds of the homeless have been in at least one of these institutional settings and almost 20 percent have been in three or all four. See Burt and Cohen, "A Sociodemographic Profile," in *Data and Issues,* ed. Momeni, 33. In addition, Peter Rossi's study in Chicago indicates that only 4 percent of the homeless in his sample do not suffer from unemployment, criminal involvement, mental illness, or poor health. See Rossi, *Down and Out,* 179.

87. Committee on Health Care for Homeless People, Institute of Medicine, *Homelessness, Health, and Human Needs,* 50–56. See also Interagency Council on the Homeless, *1989 Annual Report,* 5–11; National Institute on Alcohol Abuse and Alcoholism, "Homelessness, Alcohol, and Other Drugs," 18–20; Rossi, *Down and Out,* 42–43; Wright and Weber, *Homelessness and Health,* 94.

Chapter 2

1. By the year 2030, there will be 65 million senior citizens, compared with 30 million in 1990. Leon F. Bouvier and Carol J. De Vita, "The Baby Boom—Entering Midlife," *Population Bulletin* 46, no. 3 (November 1991): 27.

2. Landon Y. Jones, *Great Expectations: America and the Baby Boom Generation* (New York: Ballantine Books, 1980), 1; Paul C. Light, *Baby Boomers* (New York: W. W. Norton, 1988), 10.

3. Bouvier and De Vita, "The Baby Boom," 2.

4. Jones, *Great Expectations,* 1.

5. Bouvier and De Vita, "The Baby Boom," 14.

6. Jones, *Great Expectations,* 57.

7. Bouvier and De Vita, "The Baby Boom," 14.

8. Mary E. Stefl, "The New Homeless: A National Perspective," in *The Homeless in Contemporary Society,* ed. Richard D. Bingham, Roy E. Green, and Sammis B. White (Newbury Park, CA: Sage Publications, 1989), 48; Interagency Council on

the Homeless, *The 1989 Annual Report of the Interagency Council on the Homeless* (Washington, DC: U.S. Government Printing Office, 1989), I-1; Peter H. Rossi, *Without Shelter: Homelessness in the 1980s* (Washington, DC: Twentieth Century Fund, 1989), 24; James D. Wright, *Address Unknown: The Homeless in America* (New York: Aldine De Gruyter, 1989), 62; and James D. Wright and Eleanor Weber, *Homelessness and Health* (Washington, DC: McGraw-Hill, 1987), 48.

9. Martha R. Burt and Barbara E. Cohen, *America's Homeless: Numbers, Characteristics and Programs That Serve Them* (Washington, DC: Urban Institute, 1989), 38.

10. Jones, *Great Expectations,* 140.

11. E. J. Dionne, Jr., *Why Americans Hate Politics* (New York: Simon and Schuster, 1991), 38.

12. Ibid.

13. Jones, *Great Expectations,* 107.

14. For an excellent analysis of political polling data of baby boomers, see Light, *Baby Boomers.*

15. Jones, *Great Expectations,* 300.

16. Testimony of Abbie Hoffman at the Trial of the Chicago Seven, quoted in Jones, *Great Expectations,* 120.

17. Jones, *Great Expectations,* 122.

18. Ibid., 132.

19. Ibid., 130.

20. Ibid., 131.

21. Ibid., 79.

22. The clinical and research literature, much of it referenced in following endnotes, tends to use the terms "chronically mentally ill young adults" and "dually diagnosed young adults" interchangeably because there is a high degree of overlap between the two and their behavioral characteristics are very similar.

23. M. Susan Ridgely et al., *Executive Summary: Chronic Mentally Ill Young Adults with Substance Abuse Problems: A Review of Research, Treatment, and Training Issues* (Baltimore: University of Maryland at Baltimore, 1987), 9.

24. U.S. Bureau of the Census, *Current Population Reports,* P-25, no. 1018 (Washington, DC: U.S. Government Printing Office, 1989), Table F.

25. Darrel A. Regier et al., "Comorbidity of Mental Disorders with Alcohol and Other Drug Abuse," *The Journal of the American Medical Association* 264, no. 19 (November 21, 1990): 2513.

26. E. Fuller Torrey, "Thirty Years of Shame: The Scandalous Neglect of the Mentally Ill Homeless," *Policy Review,* no. 48 (Spring 1989): 11. See also Rael Jean Isaac and Virginia C. Armat, *Madness in the Streets: How Psychiatry and the Law Abandoned the Mentally Ill* (New York: Free Press, 1990), for an excellent review of the deinstitutionalization movement.

27. Leona L. Bachrach, "Young Adult Chronic Patients: An Analytical Review of the Literature," in *The Young Adult Chronic Patient: Collected Articles from Hospital and Community Psychiatry,* ed. Hospital and Community Psychiatry Service (Washington, DC: Hospital and Community Psychiatry Service of the American Psychiatric Association, June 1985), 2.

28. S. P. Segal and J. Baumohl, quoted in Bachrach, "Young Adult Chronic Patients," 5.

29. Leona L. Bachrach, "The Homeless Mentally Ill and Mental Health Services: An Analytical Review of the Literature," in *The Homeless Mentally Ill: A Task Force Report of the American Psychiatric Association,* ed. H. Richard Lamb (Washington, DC: American Psychiatric Association, 1984), 16.

30. See Isaac and Armat, *Madness in the Streets,* Part 1.

31. Bert Pepper, Michael C. Kirshner, and Hilary Ryglewicz, "The Young Adult Chronic Patient: Overview of a Population," in *The Young Adult Chronic Patient,* 23.

32. See Isaac and Armat, *Madness in the Streets,* for a full discussion of these issues.

33. M. Susan Ridgely et al., *Chronic Mentally Ill Young Adults with Substance Abuse Problems: Treatment and Training Issues* (Baltimore: University of Maryland at Baltimore, 1987), 39.

34. Stuart R. Schwartz and Stephen M. Goldfinger, "The New Chronic Patient: Clinical Characteristics of an Emerging Subgroup," in *The Young Adult Chronic Patient,* 28.

35. Robert E. Drake, Fred C. Osher, and Michael Wallach, "Homelessness and Dual Diagnosis," *American Psychologist* 46, no. 11 (November 1991): 1150.

36. The following summary is based on the research on the dually diagnosed including: Drake, Osher, and Wallach, "Homelessness and Dual Diagnosis"; Robert E. Drake and Michael A. Wallach, "Dual Diagnosis Among the Chronically Mentally Ill" (Submitted to Hospital and Community Psychiatry, Cambridge, MA: Department of Psychiatry, Harvard Medical School); Hospital and Community Psychiatry Service, ed., *The Young Adult Chronic Patient;* H. Richard Lamb, "The Deinstitutionalization of the Mentally Ill," in *Assisting the Homeless: State and Local Responses in an Era of Limited Resources—M-161,* ed. U.S. Advisory Commission on Intergovernmental Relations (Washington, DC: U.S. Advisory Commission on Intergovernmental Relations, 1988), 24–27; National Institute on Alcohol Abuse and Alcoholism, "Homelessness, Alcohol and Other Drugs" (Proceedings of a conference held by U.S. Department of Health and Human Services, in San Diego, CA, February 2–4, 1989), 4, 16–18, 25; Ridgely et al., *Executive Summary;* Ridgely et al., *Treatment and Training Issues;* Ridgely et al., *Chronic Mentally Ill Young Adults with Substance Abuse Problems: A Review of Relevant Literature and Creation of a Research Agenda* (Baltimore: University of Maryland at Baltimore, 1986).

37. Ridgely et al., *Executive Summary,* 13.

38. Pepper, Kirshner, and Ryglewicz, "Young Adult Chronic Patient," 22.

39. Bachrach, quoted in Ridgely et al., *Review of Relevant Literature,* 39.

40. National Institute on Alcohol Abuse and Alcoholism, "Homelessness, Alcohol and Other Drugs," 25; Ridgely, *Treatment and Training Issues,* 16.

41. Pepper, Kirshner, and Ryglewicz, "Young Adult Chronic Patient," 23.

42. Drake and Wallach, "Dual Diagnosis," 12.

Chapter 3

1. Although the underclass includes Hispanics in the barrios of some major U.S. cities, most of the research and analysis has focused on the African American ghetto. For thorough analyses of the underclass, see Ken Auletta, *The Underclass* (New York: Random House, 1982); Fred R. Harris and Roger W. Wilkins, eds., *Quiet Riots:*

Race and Poverty in the United States (New York: Pantheon Books, 1988); Michael G. H. McGeary and Laurence E. Lynn, Jr., eds. *Urban Change and Poverty* (Washington, DC: National Academy Press, 1988); William Julius Wilson, *The Truly Disadvantaged: The Inner City, the Underclass, and Public Policy* (Chicago: University of Chicago Press, 1987); and William Julius Wilson, *The Declining Significance of Race* (Chicago: University of Chicago Press, 1980).

2. Wilson, *The Truly Disadvantaged*, Part 2.

3. Harris and Wilkens, eds., *Quiet Riots*, 141.

4. Wilson, *The Truly Disadvantaged*, 37.

5. African American births are not reported separately by the National Center for Health Statistics prior to 1959. Authors estimated the number of African American births as 94 percent of all "other" (nonwhite) births for all years prior to 1959; the actual percentage in 1959 was 93.6. The number of African American births for the years 1959 through 1988 are taken directly from the National Center for Health Statistics, "Live Births, Birth Rates, and Fertility Rates, by Race of Child: United States, 1909–88," in *Vital Statistics of the United States, 1988*, vol. 1, *Natality*, DHHS, Pub. No. (PHS) 90–1100 (Washington, DC: U.S. Government Printing Office, 1990), Table I-1.

6. Wilson, *The Truly Disadvantaged*, 65.

7. U.S. Bureau of the Census, quoted in the *Washington Post*, December 10, 1989, A21.

8. Daniel Patrick Moynihan, "The Children of the State," *Washington Post*, November 25, 1990, C1.

9. Sara McLanahan, Irwin Garfinkel, and Dorothy Watson, "Family Structure, Poverty, and the Underclass," in *Urban Change and Poverty*, ed. McGeary and Lynn, 125–126.

10. Marilee C. Rist, "The Shadow Children: Preparing for the Arrival of Crack Babies in School," *Research Bulletin*, no. 9 (July 1990): 2.

11. Jane Koppelman and Judith Miller Jones, "Crack: It's Destroying Fragile Low-Income Families," *Public Welfare* (Fall 1989): 13.

12. U.S. Congress, House Select Committee on Children, Youth and Families, *No Place to Call Home: Discarded Children in America*, 101st Cong., 1st sess., November 1989 (Washington, DC: U.S. Government Printing Office, 1989), 30, 32.

13. National Association of State Alcohol and Drug Abuse Directors, "FY89 State Estimates of Drug Treatment Demand Vs. Supply for Women" (Mimeographed).

14. Rist, "The Shadow Children," 3.

15. Wilson, *The Truly Disadvantaged*, 6.

16. Charles Murray, quoted in Michael B. Katz, *The Undeserving Poor: From the War on Poverty to the War on Welfare* (New York: Pantheon Press, 1989), 153.

17. Auletta, *The Underclass*, xii.

18. Wilson, *The Truly Disadvantaged*, 6.

19. Jonathan Kozol, *Rachel and Her Children: Homeless Families in America* (New York: Crown Publishers, 1988), 10.

20. See discussion about the number of homeless family households, the number of homeless single person households, and the number of homeless individuals in Chapter 1.

21. See, for example, Andrew M. Cuomo, *The Way Home: A New Direction in Social Policy* (New York: New York City Commission on the Homeless, February 1992), B-3.

22. David Wood et al., *Over the Brink: Homeless Families in Los Angeles: California Children, California Families* (Los Angeles: Assembly Office of Research, August 1989), 11.

23. Ellen L. Bassuk, "Homeless Families," *Scientific American* (December 1991): 70.

24. Wood et al., *Over the Brink*, 14.

25. The following paragraphs are based on studies of homeless families including: Ellen L. Bassuk, "The Problem of Homeless Families," in *Community Care for Homeless Families: A Program Design Manual*, ed. Ellen L. Bassuk et al. (Newton Center, MA: The Better Homes Foundation, 1990); Ellen L. Bassuk, Alison S. Lauriat, and Leonore Rubin, "Homeless Families," in *Homelessness: Critical Issues for Policy and Practice*, ed. Jill Kneerim (Boston, MA: The Boston Foundation, 1987); Ellen L. Bassuk and Lynn Rosenberg, "Why Does Family Homelessness Occur? A Case-Control Study," *American Journal of Public Health* 78, no. 7 (1988): 783–788; Cuomo, *The Way Home*; Sonjia Parker Redmond and Joan Brackmann, "Homeless Children and Their Caretakers," in *Homelessness in the United States: Data and Issues*, ed. Jamshid A. Momeni (New York, Praeger Publishers, 1990); Wood et al., *Over the Brink*.

26. National Institute on Alcohol Abuse and Alcoholism, "Homelessness, Alcohol and Other Drugs" (Proceedings of a conference held by U.S. Department of Health and Human Services in San Diego, CA, February 2–4, 1989), 27. See also Cuomo, *The Way Home*, 22; Irving Piliavin et al., "Conditions Contributing to Long-Term Homelessness" (School of Social Work and Institute for Research on Poverty, University of Wisconsin, Madison, WI, 1989, Mimeographed), 20.

27. Bassuk, Lauriat, and Rubin, "Homeless Families," 22. See also Cuomo, *The Way Home*, 22.

28. Bassuk, Lauriat, and Rubin, "Homeless Families," 22.

29. Ibid.

30. Wood et al., *Over the Brink*, 12.

31. Bassuk, Lauriat, and Rubin, "Homeless Families," 22.

32. Joan Morein, Clinical Director at Diagnostic and Rehabilitation Center, Philadelphia, PA, conversation with authors, June 20, 1990.

33. See John J. DiIulio, Jr., "There but for Fortune," *The New Republic*, June 24, 1991, 32; Grace Milgram, *Housing: Low- and Moderate-Income Assistance Programs* (Washington, DC: Congressional Research Service, September 10, 1991), 5.

34. James Brigl, Director of Tenant Services, Fairfax County Department of Housing Development, interview with authors, June 1991.

35. Bassuk, "Homeless Families," 70.

36. Elaine Fox, Director, Philadelphia Health Management Corporation, comments to authors at Interagency Council on the Homeless Workshop, Philadelphia, June 20, 1990; Irving W. Shandler, *Diagnostic and Rehabilitation Center/Philadelphia: Annual Report, Fiscal Year 1989* (Philadelphia, PA: Diagnostic and Rehabilitation Center, 1989), 2; conversations with shelter providers, 1989–1991; Richard W. White, *Rude Awakenings: What the Homeless Crisis Tells Us* (San Francisco, CA: ICS Press, 1992), 15.

37. Pamela J. Fischer and William R. Breakey, "The Epidemiology of Alcohol, Drug, and Mental Disorders Among Homeless Persons," *American Psychologist* 46, no. 11 (November 1991): 1120.

38. Cuomo, *The Way Home,* 68.

39. Ibid., 67, B-3.

40. U.S. General Accounting Office, *Children and Youths: About 68,000 Homeless and 186,000 in Shared Housing at Any Given Time* (Washington, DC: GAO, June 1989), 24.

41. Bassuk, "The Problem of Homeless Families," 7.

42. Redmond and Brackmann, "Homeless Children and Their Caretakers," 126.

43. James D. Wright and Eleanor Weber, *Homelessness and Health* (Washington, DC: McGraw-Hill, 1987), 112.

44. U.S. Congress, House Select Committee on Children, Youth and Families, *No Place to Call Home,* 31.

45. Deborah L. Dennis et al., "A Decade of Research and Services for Homeless Mentally Ill Persons," *American Psychologist* 46, no. 11 (November 1991): 1132; Marybeth Shinn, James R. Knickman, and Beth C. Weitzman, "Social Relationships and Vulnerability to Becoming Homeless Among Poor Families," *American Psychologist* 46, no. 11 (November 1991): 1181.

46. Piliavin et al., "Conditions Contributing to Long-Term Homelessness," 20.

47. M. Susan Ridgely et al., *Chronic Mentally Ill Young Adults with Substance Abuse Problems: A Review of Relevant Literature and Creation of a Research Agenda* (Baltimore: University of Maryland at Baltimore, 1986), 3.

48. Patricia A. Sullivan and Shirley P. Damrosch, "Homeless Women and Children," in *The Homeless in Contemporary Society,* ed. Richard D. Bingham, Roy E. Green, and Sammis B. White (Newbury Park, CA: Sage Publications, 1989), 92–93.

49. Wilson, *The Truly Disadvantaged,* 6.

50. Cuomo, *The Way Home,* 73.

Chapter 4

1. We met with Franklin on three different occasions, using a semi-structured interview format that permitted follow-up questions to confirm information, to clarify certain points, and to obtain as complete a picture as possible about his experiences on the streets and in the Pierce shelter for homeless men. With Franklin's permission, we taped our conversations and had the tapes transcribed. In writing this chapter, we edited the transcriptions to present the information in proper sequence and to eliminate redundancy. Throughout, we tried to remain as faithful as possible to Franklin's own words, making only those changes needed for the reader to understand Franklin's story.

2. Shortly after Franklin stayed at the Pierce shelter, the city stopped serving meals at the shelters because of budget cuts.

3. This is the common name for the shelter run by the Community for Creative Non-Violence (CCNV) because it is located at 2nd and D Streets, N.W., in Washington, DC.

Chapter 5

1. Ellen Baxter and Kim Hopper, *Private Lives/Public Spaces: Homeless Adults on the Streets of New York City* (New York: Community Service Society, 1981), 104; Kathleen H. Dockett, *Street Homeless People in the District of Columbia* (Washington, DC: University of the District of Columbia, 1989), 101, 103; "Exploring Myths About 'Street People,'" *Access* 2, no. 2 (June 1990): 2; Rene Jahiel, "The Situation of Homelessness," in *The Homeless in Contemporary Society,* ed. Richard D. Bingham, Roy E. Green, and Sammis B. White (Newbury Park, CA: Sage Publications, 1989), 107; Peter H. Rossi, *Down and Out in America: The Origins of Homelessness* (Chicago, IL: University of Chicago Press, 1989), 35.

2. Most research has studied the length of time that people have been homeless, not necessarily the length of time they have been in any given shelter, in part because many homeless people are transient, moving from the streets to shelters and from one shelter to another. Nevertheless, we have anecdotal evidence, including newspaper reports, that some homeless people have lived in the same shelter for five years or more. See Andrew M. Cuomo, *The Way Home: A New Direction in Social Policy* (New York: New York City Commission on the Homeless, February 1992), 22. See also discussion of mobility in Chapter 1. In addition, for a discussion on the extent to which shelters create dependence, see Robert E. Drake, Fred C. Osher, and Michael Wallach, "Homelessness and Dual Diagnosis," *American Psychologist* 46, no. 11 (November 1991): 1152.

3. Quoted in Nancy K. Rhoden, "The Limits of Liberty: Deinstitutionalization, Homelessness, and Libertarian Theory," *Emory Law Journal* 31, no. 2 (Spring 1982): 376. See also Ellen Baxter and Kim Hopper, "Shelter and Housing for the Homeless Mentally Ill," in *The Homeless Mentally Ill: A Task Force Report of the American Psychiatric Association,* ed. H. Richard Lamb (Washington, DC: American Psychiatric Association, 1984), 123.

4. U.S. Department of Housing and Urban Development, *A Report on the 1988 National Survey of Shelters for the Homeless* (Washington, DC: U.S. Department of Housing and Urban Development, 1989), 2; U.S. Department of Housing and Urban Development, *A Report to the Secretary on the Homeless and Emergency Shelters* (Washington, DC: U.S. Department of Housing and Urban Development, 1984), 34.

5. U.S. Department of Housing and Urban Development, *1988 National Survey,* 17, 24.

6. Ibid., 17.

7. Only 26 percent of McKinney funds are dedicated to all health-related services. See U.S. General Accounting Office, *Homelessness: McKinney Act Programs and Funding Through Fiscal Year 1990* (Washington, DC: GAO, May 1991), 2–3.

8. U.S. Department of Housing and Urban Development, *1988 National Survey,* 20.

9. Deborah L. Dennis et al., "A Decade of Research and Services for Homeless Mentally Ill Persons," *American Psychologist* 46, no. 11 (November 1991): 1133; Susan Sadd and Douglas W. Young, "Nonmedical Treatment of Indigent Alcoholics: A Review of Recent Research Findings," *Alcohol Health and Research World* 2, no. 3

(1987): 48–49; Friedner D. Wittman, "Homeless with Alcohol-related Problems: Proceedings of a Meeting to Provide Research Recommendations to the National Institute on Alcohol Abuse and Alcoholism, Bethesda, MD, July 29–30, 1985" (Berkeley, CA: Pacific Institute for Research and Evaluation, 1985), 15.

10. Martha R. Burt and Barbara E. Cohen, *Feeding the Homeless: Does the Prepared Meals Provision Help?* vol. 1 (Washington, DC: Urban Institute Press, 1988), 61–62.

11. Pam Wynn, quoted in Lydia Williams, *Mourning in America: Health Problems, Mortality, and Homelessness* (Washington, DC: National Coalition for the Homeless, December 1991), ii.

12. Ellen L. Bassuk, Leonore Rubin, and Alison S. Lauriat, "Characteristics of Sheltered Homeless Families," *American Journal of Public Health* 76, no. 9 (1986): 1097; Dennis McCarty et al., "Alcoholism, Drug Abuse, and the Homeless," *American Psychologist* 46, no. 11 (November 1991): 1144–1145; Peter H. Rossi, Gene Fisher, and Georgianna Willis, "The Condition of the Homeless of Chicago" (Chicago, IL: National Opinion Research Center, 1986), 135; Mary E. Stefl, "The New Homeless: A National Perspective," in *The Homeless in Contemporary Society*, ed. Bingham, Green, and White, 46; U.S. Department of Housing and Urban Development, *A Report on Homeless Assistance Policy and Practice in the Nation's Five Largest Cities* (Washington, DC: U.S. Department of Housing and Urban Development, 1989), 48; James D. Wright, *Address Unknown: The Homeless in America* (New York: Aldine De Gruyter, 1989), 149.

13. Dockett, *Street Homeless People*, 101.

14. Fred C. Osher, "Assessing Dual Diagnosis," *Access* 2, no. 2 (June 1990): 6.

15. Martha R. Burt and Barbara E. Cohen, *America's Homeless: Numbers, Characteristics and Programs That Serve Them* (Washington, DC: Urban Institute, 1989), 67–73.

16. U.S. Department of Housing and Urban Development, *1988 National Survey*, 6.

17. U.S. Conference of Mayors, *A Status Report on Hunger and Homelessness in America's Cities: 1991* (Washington, DC: U.S. Conference of Mayors, 1991), 25.

18. Steven Banks, Legal Aid Society, Testimony before Congress, quoted in U.S. General Accounting Office, *Welfare Hotels: Uses, Costs, and Alternatives* (Washington, DC: GAO, January 1989), 27.

19. Cuomo, *The Way Home*, 10.

20. U.S. Congress, House Committee on Government Operations, *Mismanagement in Programs for the Homeless: Washington, DC, as a Case Study*, 102nd Cong., 1st sess., 1991, H. Rept. 102–366 (Washington, DC: U.S. Government Printing Office, 1991), 2.

21. Gregg Barak, *Gimme Shelter: A Social History of Homelessness in Contemporary America* (New York: Praeger Publishers, 1991), 122.

22. Burt and Cohen, *America's Homeless*, 5.

23. Paul A. Toro and Dennis M. McDonell, "Beliefs, Attitudes, and Knowledge About Homelessness: A Survey of the General Public," *American Journal of Community Psychology* 20, no. 1 (1992): 60.

24. In light of prolonged unemployment and the slow recovery from the 1990–1992 recession, food banks and clothes closets, particularly in rural areas, are helping large numbers of very poor people. It is important to keep in mind the distinction

between the very poor who need various kinds of help and the homeless who, more often than not, need help of a very different kind.

25. Barak, *Gimme Shelter,* 104–106.

26. Ellen L. Bassuk and Alison S. Lauriat, "The Politics of Homelessness," in *The Homeless Mentally Ill: A Task Force Report,* ed. Lamb, 311–312.

27. Grace Milgram, "Glossary," in *The Cranston-Gonzalez National Affordable Housing Act: Key Provisions and Analysis,* prepared by Morton Schussheim (Washington, DC: Congressional Research Service, 1991), 68.

28. U.S. Conference of Mayors, *A Status Report: 1991,* 37.

29. U.S. General Accounting Office, *Homelessness: Transitional Housing Shows Initial Success but Long-term Effects Unknown* (Washington, DC: GAO, September 1991).

30. Treatment programs for substance abuse and programs for the mentally ill all have as ultimate goals empowering individuals by enhancing their self-esteem and promoting their independence, but such programs achieve these goals by directly confronting the substance abuse or mental illness, not by ignoring them.

31. Thomas Nees, Executive Director, Community of Hope, Washington, DC, conversation with authors, Spring 1988.

32. Even various provisions of the federal McKinney Act that provide funds for transitional housing require that the services for addressing the problems of the seriously mentally ill, chronic substance abusers, and those with AIDS among homeless persons or families must be provided "from matching funds from other sources," i.e., not from funds received under the McKinney Act.

33. Jane Plapinger, Kostas Gounis, and Susan Barrow, "Finding a Place to Call Home," *Access* 1, no. 1 (March 1989): 3. See also Anna's story in Chapter 1.

34. Cuomo, *The Way Home,* 75.

35. Andrew M. Cuomo, quoted in Mitchel Levitas, "Homeless in America," *New York Times Magazine,* Sunday, June 10, 1990.

36. McCarty et al., "Alcoholism, Drug Abuse, and the Homeless," 1143; National Institute on Alcohol Abuse and Alcoholism, "Homelessness, Alcohol and Other Drugs" (Proceedings of a conference held by U.S. Department of Health and Human Services in San Diego, CA, February 2–4, 1989), 54; U.S. Department of Housing and Urban Development, *Five Cities,* 61.

37. National Institute on Alcohol Abuse and Alcoholism, "Homelessness, Alcohol and Other Drugs," 54. See also Hope Burness Gleicher et al., "Staff Organization, Retention, and Burnout," in *Under the Safety Net: The Health and Social Welfare of the Homeless in the United States,* ed. Philip W. Brickner et al. (New York: W. W. Norton, 1990), 278.

38. The CAGE is a device using four matter-of-fact questions to make an initial assessment of potential problems with alcohol. The questions relate to: cutting down, annoyance by criticism, guilty feelings, and eyeopeners. See U.S. Department of Health and Human Services, *Sixth Special Report to the U.S. Congress on Alcohol and Health from the Secretary of Health and Human Services* (Rockville, MD: U.S. Department of Health and Human Services, January 1987), 111.

39. Leona L. Bachrach, "The Homeless Mentally Ill and Mental Health Services: An Analytical Review of the Literature," in *The Homeless Mentally Ill: A Task Force Report,* ed. Lamb, 43.

40. Stewart B. McKinney Homeless Assistance Amendments Act of 1990 (P.L. 101–645).

41. U.S. General Accounting Office, *Homelessness: Too Early to Tell What Kinds of Prevention Assistance Work Best* (Washington, DC: GAO, April 1990), 11.

42. Ibid., 21.

43. Very few homeless families, i.e., women with children, have been found living on the streets or in places other than shelters, hotels, or motels. See Burt and Cohen, *America's Homeless,* 42; Dockett, *Street Homeless People,* 26; Rossi, *Down and Out,* 117.

44. National Mental Health Association and Families for the Homeless. *Homeless in America* (Washington, DC: Acropolis Books, 1988), 7.

45. Thomas L. Kenyon with Justine Blau, *What You Can Do to Help the Homeless* (New York: Simon and Schuster/Fireside, 1991), 13.

46. Ibid., 9.

47. U.S. Conference of Mayors, *A Status Report on Hunger and Homelessness in America's Cities: 1990* (Washington, DC: U.S. Conference of Mayors, 1990), 49–53.

48. William Raspberry, "Walking Away from the Homeless," *Washington Post,* September 6, 1991, A21.

Chapter 6

1. John Steinbeck, *The Grapes of Wrath* (New York: Penguin Books, 1989 edition), 555–556.

2. Henry Miller, *On the Fringe: The Dispossessed in America* (Lexington, MA: Lexington Books, 1991), 25.

3. In fact, the colony of Georgia was originally designed by the British as a penal colony for some of these criminals, but criminals did not reside exclusively in Georgia.

4. Andrew W. Dobelstein, *Politics, Economics, and Public Welfare* (Englewood Cliffs, NJ: Prentice-Hall, 1986), 64.

5. Ibid.

6. The terms almshouse and poorhouse are used interchangeably in the literature. Sometimes a distinction is made between the almshouse or poorhouse, which cared for the infirm and elderly, and the workhouse, which housed able-bodied men who were put to work.

7. Michael B. Katz, *In the Shadow of the Poorhouse: A Social History of Welfare in America* (New York: Basic Books, 1986), 19.

8. Ibid., 29.

9. Ibid., 19.

10. Dobelstein, *Politics, Economics, and Public Welfare,* 64.

11. National Law Center on Homelessness and Poverty, *Go Directly to Jail: A Report Analyzing Local Anti-Homeless Ordinances* (Washington, DC: National Law Center on Homelessness and Poverty, 1991).

12. Miller, *On the Fringe,* 26.

13. Ibid., 32.

14. Ibid., 31.

15. Katz, *Poorhouse*, 6.

16. Ibid., 9.

17. Ibid., 16.

18. Ibid., 16–17.

19. Ibid., 16.

20. Miller, *On the Fringe*, 33.

21. Ibid., 36–37.

22. Ibid., 38.

23. Charles Hoch and Robert A. Slayton, *New Homeless and Old: Community and the Skid Row Hotel* (Philadelphia, PA: Temple University Press, 1989), 40.

24. Katz, *Poorhouse*, 92.

25. Miller, *On the Fringe*, 39.

26. Charles Hoch, "A Brief History of the Homeless Problem in the United States," in *The Homeless in Contemporary Society*, ed. Richard D. Bingham, Roy E. Green, and Sammis B. White (Newbury Park, CA: Sage Publications, 1989), 21.

27. See Chapter 4.

28. Miller, *On the Fringe*, 41.

29. Nels Anderson, quoted in National Institute on Alcohol Abuse and Alcoholism, "Homelessness, Alcohol and Other Drugs" (Proceedings of a conference held by U.S. Department of Health and Human Services in San Diego, CA, February 2–4, 1989), 2. One researcher added a fourth line to this aphorism, "The homeless researcher ponders and wanders." Ibid., 11.

30. Hoch and Slayton, *New Homeless and Old*, 42–44.

31. In our work with the homeless, we encountered individuals who fit the description of each of the types described by Hoch and Slayton.

32. Earl Rubington, "The Chronic Drunkenness Offender on Skid Row," in *Alcohol, Science and Society Revisited*, ed. Edith Lisansky Gomberg, Helene Raskin White, and John A. Carpenter (Ann Arbor, MI: University of Michigan Press, 1982), 323.

33. Hoch and Slayton, *New Homeless and Old*, 54.

34. Ibid., 56.

35. Miller, *On the Fringe*, 44.

36. Hoch and Slayton, *New Homeless and Old*, 47–61.

37. Quoted in James D. Wright, *Address Unknown: The Homeless In America* (New York: Aldine De Gruyter, 1989), 30.

38. Miller, *On the Fringe*, 47–48.

39. Dennis McCarty et al., "Alcoholism, Drug Abuse, and the Homeless," *American Psychologist* 46, no. 11 (November 1991): 1139; Lisa Thomas, Mike Kelly, and Michael Cousineau, "Alcoholism and Substance Abuse," in *Under the Safety Net: The Health and Social Welfare of the Homeless in the United States*, ed. Philip W. Brickner et al. (New York: W.W. Norton, 1990), 205; James D. Wright, "Correlates and Consequences of Alcohol Abuse in the National 'Health Care for the Homeless' Client Population: Final Results" (National Institute on Alcohol Abuse and Alcoholism, Washington, DC, April 1990, Mimeographed), 2.

40. Leonard U. Blumberg, Thomas E. Shipley, Jr., and Stephen F. Barsky, *Liquor and Poverty: Skid Row as a Human Condition* (New Brunswick, NJ: Rutgers Center of Alcohol Studies, 1978), 122–127; Hoch and Slayton, *New Homeless and Old*, 24, 32.

41. Katz, *Poorhouse*, 100–103.

42. The term "snake pits" derives from a 1946 novel by Mary Jane Ward entitled *The Snake Pit* that was condensed by *Reader's Digest* and made into a popular movie by the same name.

43. Katz, *Poorhouse,* 67–68.

44. Ibid., 68.

45. Hoch and Slayton, *New Homeless and Old,* 74.

46. Ruth Ellen Wasem, *Homelessness: Issues and Legislation in the 102nd Congress* (Washington, DC: Congressional Research Service, Updated January 3, 1992), 1.

47. Katz, *Poorhouse,* 128.

48. Hoch and Slayton, *New Homeless and Old,* 79.

49. Miller, *On the Fringe,* 76.

50. Michael B. Katz, *The Undeserving Poor: From the War on Poverty to the War on Welfare* (New York: Pantheon Books, 1989), 75.

51. Paul Taylor, "War's Veterans See Their Nation Losing Faith in Its Future," *Washington Post,* December 3, 1991, A7.

52. Ibid. The cost of World War II must be remembered; more than 400,000 Americans were killed and almost 700,000 were injured during this four-year war.

53. Nathan Glazer, *The Limits of Social Policy* (Cambridge, MA: Harvard University Press, 1988), 1.

54. David Hamilton, "Poverty Is Still With Us—And Worse," in *Quiet Riots: Race and Poverty in the United States,* ed. Fred R. Harris and Roger W. Wilkins (New York: Pantheon Books, 1988), 29.

55. E. Fuller Torrey, *Nowhere to Go: The Tragic Odyssey of the Homeless Mentally Ill* (New York: Harper and Row, 1988), 138.

56. Rubington, "Chronic Drunkenness Offender on Skid Row," 331. In Chapter 9 we will discuss the unintended consequences of decriminalization and the extent to which voluntary enrollment in alcohol detox facilities permitted individuals more frequent opportunities to leave, return to the streets, and enroll again, thus the term "spinning door."

57. U.S. Conference of Mayors, *A Status Report on Hunger and Homelessness in America's Cities: 1991* (Washington, DC: U.S. Conference of Mayors, 1991), 60.

58. Ibid., 21.

59. National Law Center on Homelessness and Poverty, *Go Directly to Jail,* 55.

60. Michael J. Dear and Brendan Gleeson, "Community Attitudes Toward the Homeless," *Urban Geography* 12, no. 2 (1990): 171.

61. L. Christopher Awalt, "Brother, Don't Spare a Dime." *Newsweek,* September 30, 1991, 13.

Chapter 7

1. Drew Altman et al., "Health Care for the Homeless," *Transaction Social Science and Modern Society* 26, no. 4 (May/June 1989): 4–5.

2. Nicholas Lemann, "How the Seventies Changed America," *American Heritage* (July/August 1991), 41.

3. Jay Lewis, "The Federal Role in Alcoholism Research, Treatment and Prevention," in *Alcohol, Science and Society Revisited,* ed. Edith Lisansky Gomberg, Helene

Raskin White, and John A. Carpenter (Ann Arbor, MI: University of Michigan Press, 1982), 386.

4. Thomas Byrne Edsall and Mary D. Edsall, *Chain Reaction: The Impact of Race, Rights, and Taxes on American Politics* (New York: W. W. Norton, 1991), 129.

5. Ibid., 141.

6. See Edsall and Edsall, *Chain Reaction*.

7. The New York City lawsuit, *Callahan v. Carey,* which sought and obtained "shelter on demand," was actually filed in 1979, but Snyder's well-publicized activity in the nation's capital drew more national attention.

8. Mary Ellen Hombs and Mitch Snyder, *Homelessness in America: A Forced March to Nowhere* (Washington, DC: The Community for Creative Non-Violence, 1982), 129, 131.

9. In 1982, one Reagan administration official claimed that "no one is living on the streets"; in 1983, presidential adviser Edwin Meese stated that soup kitchens were a "free lunch" for persons not truly in need; and President Reagan said in 1984 that some of those living on the street were there "by their own choice." See Maria Foscarinis, "The Politics of Homelessness: A Call to Action," *American Psychologist* 46, no. 11 (November 1991): 1234.

10. Quoted in Gregg Barak, *Gimme Shelter: A Social History of Homelessness in Contemporary America* (New York: Praeger Publishers, 1991), ix.

11. Victoria Rader, *Signal Through the Flames: Mitch Snyder and America's Homeless* (Kansas City: Sheed and Ward, 1986), 44. Much of the biographical information about Mitch Snyder in this and the following paragraphs is taken from this excellent volume about Snyder, the development of the Community for Creative Non-Violence, and the centrality of its role in making homelessness a national issue.

12. Hombs and Snyder, *A Forced March to Nowhere,* 4.

13. Rader, *Signal Through the Flames,* 59.

14. Taken from Snyder's oral testimony as reported in Hombs and Snyder, *A Forced March to Nowhere,* 130–131.

15. Rader, *Signal Through the Flames,* ix.

16. Ibid., 5.

17. Hombs and Snyder, *A Forced March to Nowhere,* 60.

18. Rader, *Signal Through the Flames,* 30.

19. Ibid., 31.

20. A *Washington Post* article quoted in Rader, *Signal Through the Flames,* 30.

21. Over the years, many came to view Snyder as both a hero and the foremost leader of the activist homelessness movement. Others came to regard him as a mentally disturbed middle-class individual who needed psychiatric treatment. Regardless of his reputation as a hero and leader of the movement, his premature death by suicide suggests that he was a deeply troubled man.

22. Rader, *Signal Through the Flames,* 250.

23. Walter Goodman, "Critic's Notebook: TV Journalists' Urge to Prettify the News," *New York Times,* February 19, 1992.

24. Robert S. Lichter and Linda S. Lichter, "The Visible Poor: Media Coverage of the Homeless: 1986–1989," *Media Monitor* 3, no. 3 (March 1989).

25. Ibid., 6.

26. Cynthia M. Taeuber and Paul M. Siegel, "Counting the Nation's Homeless Population in the 1990 Census," in *Conference Proceedings for Enumerating Homeless Persons: Methods and Data Issues* (Conference Cosponsored by the Bureau of the Census, the U.S. Department of Housing and Urban Development, and the Interagency Council for the Homeless, Washington, DC, March 19, 1991), 97.

27. Ibid.

28. Ellen Baxter and Kim Hopper, *Private Lives/Public Spaces: Homeless Adults on the Streets of New York City* (New York: Community Service Society, February 1981), 6–7.

29. U.S. Department of Housing and Urban Development, *A Report to the Secretary on the Homeless and Emergency Shelters* (Washington, DC: U.S. Department of Housing and Urban Development, May 1984), 7.

30. Irene Shifren Levine, quoted in U.S. General Accounting Office, *Homelessness: A Complex Problem and the Federal Response,* HRD 85-40 (Washington, DC: GAO, 1985), 4.

31. Peter H. Rossi, *Down and Out in America: The Origins of Homelessness* (Chicago, IL: University of Chicago Press, 1989), 11.

32. Barak, *Gimme Shelter,* 27.

33. Kim Hopper and Jill Hamberg, *The Making of America's Homeless: From Skid Row to New Poor* (New York: Community Service Society, 1984) 9.

34. Quoted in Barak, *Gimme Shelter,* 28.

35. Paul A. Toro and Dennis M. McDonell, "Beliefs, Attitudes, and Knowledge About Homelessness: A Survey of the General Public," *American Journal of Community Psychology* 20, no. 1 (1992): 74.

36. Howard M. Bahr, "Introduction," in *Homelessness in the United States: State Surveys,* ed. Jamshid A. Momeni (New York: Praeger Publishers, 1990), xix–xx.

37. Joel Blau, *The Visible Poor: Homelessness in the United States* (New York: Oxford University Press, 1992), 20.

38. Hombs and Snyder, *A Forced March to Nowhere,* xvi; U.S. Department of Housing and Urban Development, *1984 Report to the Secretary,* 18.

39. Hombs and Snyder, *A Forced March to Nowhere,* 129.

40. Quoted in John Scanlon, "Homelessness: Describing the Symptoms, Prescribing a Cure," *The Heritage Foundation Backgrounder,* no. 729 (October 2, 1989): 4.

41. U.S. General Accounting Office, *Homeless Mentally Ill: Problems and Options in Estimating Numbers and Trends* (Washington, DC: GAO, 1988), 30–31.

42. Rossi, *Down and Out,* 70.

43. David C. Schwartz and John H. Glascock, *Combatting Homelessness: A Resource Book,* quoted in Spencer Rich, "Millions of Families Said to Be on the Brink of Homelessness," *Washington Post,* August 9, 1989, A19. See also Barak, *Gimme Shelter,* 4.

44. Toro and McDonell, "Beliefs, Attitudes, and Knowledge About Homelessness," 74.

45. Ibid., 75.

46. See note 8.

47. Anna Kondratas, "Ending Homelessness: Policy Challenges," *American Psychologist* 46, no. 11 (November 1991): 1226.

48. Burt and Cohen, *America's Homeless*, 2.

49. Peter H. Rossi, "Critical Methodological Issues in Research on Homeless Persons," in *Research Methodologies Concerning Homeless Persons with Serious Mental Illness and/or Substance Abuse Disorders*, ed. Deborah L. Dennis (Proceedings of a two-day conference sponsored by the Alcohol, Drug Abuse Mental Health Administration, U.S. Department of Health and Human Services, Washington, DC, December 1987), 42.

50. Heritage Foundation, *Rethinking Policy on Homelessness*. The Heritage Lectures No. 194 (Washington, DC: The Heritage Foundation, 1988), 58.

51. Burt and Cohen, *America's Homeless*, 22.

52. Ibid., 27.

53. Burt suggested that increasing poverty among portions of the American population is linked to an increase in the size of the homeless population. See Martha R. Burt, *Over the Edge: The Growth of Homelessness in the 1980s* (New York: Russell Sage Foundation, 1992), 3, 5–9.

54. Spencer Rich, "'Hidden Homeless' May Elude Census," *Washington Post*, June 8, 1989, A21.

55. Barbara Vobejda, "Fanning Out to Find, Count the Homeless," *Washington Post*, March 18, 1990, A18.

56. Ibid.

57. Mitch Snyder, Letter to the Editor, *Washington Post*, April 15, 1990.

58. Cynthia Taeuber, "Fact Sheet for 1990 Decennial Census Counts of Persons in Emergency Shelters for the Homeless and Visible in Street Locations," *U.S. Department of Commerce News* (April 12, 1991), 1–2. In a subsequent publication, the Census Bureau reported confidence about their count within shelters; officials felt less confident about the street enumeration. See Taeuber and Siegel, "Counting the Nation's Homeless," 102. If, as they suggested, the shelter count was accurate and the street count was an undercount by as much as 50 percent, their total enumeration, corrected for this undercount, would have been about 279,000. If their total enumeration was an undercount by 50 percent, their total count, corrected for the undercount, would have been about 457,000. The higher of these counts is close to the low end of the Urban Institute's estimate.

59. Barbara Vobejda, "Census Spotted Nearly 230,000 Homeless People," *Washington Post*, April 13, 1991, A3.

60. Cynthia Taeuber, "Census Bureau Releases 1990 Decennial Counts for Persons Enumerated in Emergency Shelters and Observed on Streets," *U.S. Department of Commerce News*, CB 91–117 (April 12, 1991), 1.

61. Rossi, "Critical Methodological Issues," 41.

62. Congressman Charles E. Schumer, in U.S. Congress, House Committee on the Budget, Ad Hoc Task Force on the Homeless and Housing, *Homelessness During Winter 1988–1989: Prospects for Change* (Serial No. AH 100-4), 100th Cong., 2nd sess., December 20, 1988 (Washington, DC: U.S. Government Printing Office, 1989), 3.

63. Hombs and Snyder, *A Forced March to Nowhere*, 8.

64. Thomas L. Kenyon with Justine Blau, *What You Can Do to Help the Homeless* (New York: Simon and Schuster/Fireside, 1991), 15–16.

65. Ibid., 111.

66. See Chapter 3.

67. Jonathan Kozol, *Rachel and Her Children: Homeless Families in America* (New York: Crown Publishers, 1988), 1.

68. David Whitman, "Shattering Myths About the Homeless," *U.S. News and World Report* (March 20, 1989), 28.

69. Janelle Goetcheus, "Healing the Homeless: They Need Medical Care, Shelter, Solace," *Washington Post,* October 15, 1991, Health Section, 6.

70. See Linda Wheeler, "Parents of 14 Accused of Misusing Public Funds," *Washington Post,* March 12, 1990, B3.

71. Goodman, "Critic's Notebook."

72. Hombs and Snyder, *A Forced March to Nowhere,* xvii.

73. Baxter and Hopper, *Private Lives/Public Spaces,* i.

74. Blau, *The Visible Poor,* ix.

75. Barak, *Gimme Shelter,* 21.

76. James D. Wright, *Address Unknown: The Homeless in America* (New York: Aldine De Gruyter, 1989), 67.

77. Peter H. Rossi, *Without Shelter: Homelessness in the 1980s* (Washington, DC: Twentieth Century Fund, 1989), 25.

78. Martha R. Burt and Barbara E. Cohen, *America's Homeless: Numbers, Characteristics and Programs That Serve Them* (Washington, DC: Urban Institute, 1989), 148.

79. Ibid., 149, 152–153. See also Martha R. Burt and Barbara E. Cohen, *State Activities and Programs for the Homeless: A Review of Six States* (Washington, DC: Urban Institute Press, 1988); U.S. General Accounting Office, *Homelessness: HUD's and FEMA's Progress in Implementing the McKinney Act* (Washington, DC: GAO, May 1989); and U.S. General Accounting Office, *Homelessness: Implementation of Food and Shelter Programs Under the McKinney Act* (Washington, DC: GAO, December 1987).

80. Ellen L. Bassuk and Alison S. Lauriat, "The Politics of Homelessness," in *The Homeless Mentally Ill: A Task Force Report of the American Psychiatric Association,* ed. H. Richard Lamb (Washington, DC: American Psychiatric Association, 1984), 305.

81. Frank R. Lipton, Albert Sabatini, and Peter Micheels, "Characteristics and Service Needs of the Homeless Mentally Ill," in *Treating the Homeless: Urban Psychiatry's Challenge,* ed. Billy E. Jones (Washington, DC: American Psychiatric Press, 1986), 38.

82. Toro and McDonell, "Beliefs, Attitudes, and Knowledge About Homelessness," 54.

83. Ellen L. Bassuk, "Homeless Families," *Scientific American* (December 1991), 74.

84. Quoted in Richard W. White, *Rude Awakenings: What the Homeless Crisis Tells Us* (San Francisco, CA: ICS Press, 1992), 6.

85. Ibid.

86. Ronald L. Rogers and Chandler Scott McMillin, *Free Someone You Love from Alcohol and Other Drugs* (New York: The Putnam Publishing Group, 1992), 19.

87. U.S. Department of Health and Human Services, *Seventh Special Report to the Congress on Alcohol and Health from the Secretary of Health and Human Services* (Washington, DC: U.S. Department of Health and Human Services, January 1990), 36.

88. National Council on Alcoholism and Drug Dependence, Inc. "NCADD Fact Sheet: Alcoholism and Alcohol Related Problems," revised November 1990, 1–2.

89. Ibid., 1.

90. National Council on Alcoholism and Drug Dependence, Inc., "NCADD Fact Sheet: Alcoholism, Other Drug Addictions and Related Problems Among Women," June 1990, 2.

91. Dorothy P. Rice et al., *The Economic Costs of Alcohol and Drug Abuse and Mental Illness: 1985* (Washington, DC: U.S. Department of Health and Human Services, 1990), 2.

92. Ibid.

93. U.S. Department of Health and Human Services, *Crack Babies* (Draft Report, Office of the Inspector General, Washington, DC: U.S. Department of Health and Human Services, February 1990), 1, 4.

Chapter 8

1. Dee Roth et al., *Homelessness in Ohio: A Study of People in Need: Statewide Report.* (Columbus, OH: Ohio Deptartment of Mental Health, 1985), 2.

2. Andrew M. Cuomo, *The Way Home: A New Direction in Social Policy* (New York: New York City Commission on the Homeless, February 1992), 6–7.

3. Victoria Rader, *Signal Through the Flames: Mitch Snyder and America's Homeless* (Kansas City: Sheed and Ward, 1986), 147–148.

4. Quoted in Martha R. Burt, *Over the Edge: The Growth of Homelessness in the 1980s* (New York: Russell Sage Foundation, 1992), 4.

5. See Chapter 2.

6. Leon F. Bouvier and Carol J. De Vita, "The Baby Boom—Entering Midlife," *Population Bulletin* 46, no. 3 (November 1991): 19.

7. Burt, *Over the Edge,* 35.

8. Bouvier and De Vita, "The Baby Boom," 21.

9. Irving Welfeld, *Where We Live: A Social History of American Housing* (New York: Simon and Schuster, 1988), 13.

10. Grace Milgram, *Housing Assistance in the United States* (Washington, DC: Congressional Research Service, December 5, 1991), 3.

11. Barbara Vobejda, "Average Household Shrinks as More in U.S. Live Alone," *Washington Post,* May 1, 1991, A1.

12. Burt, *Over the Edge,* 35.

13. Ibid., 49.

14. Michael S. Carliner, "Homelessness: A Housing Problem," in *The Homeless in Contemporary Society,* ed. Richard D. Bingham, Roy E. Green, and Sammis B. White (Newbury Park, CA: Sage Publications, 1989), 119.

15. Milgram, *Housing Assistance in the United States,* 2.

16. See Linda Wheeler, "Parents of 14 Accused of Misusing Public Funds," *Washington Post,* March 12, 1990, B3. This story was described in Chapter 7, page 126.

17. Cuomo, *The Way Home,* 75.

18. Kim Hopper and Jill Hamberg, *The Making of America's Homeless: From Skid Row to New Poor* (New York: Community Service Society, 1984), 71.

19. Ibid. See also Chester Hartman, "The Housing Part of the Homelessness Problem," in *Homelessness: Critical Issues for Policy and Practice,* ed. Jill Kneerim (Boston, MA : The Boston Foundation, 1987), 19.

20. Hopper and Hamberg, *The Making of America's Homeless,* 34. See also Carliner, "Homelessness: A Housing Problem," 120; Chester Hartman, "The Housing Part of the Homelessness Problem," 17; U.S. General Accounting Office, *Homelessness: A Complex Problem and the Federal Response,* HRD 85-40 (Washington, DC: GAO, 1985), 25.

21. Hartman, "The Housing Part of the Homelessness Problem," 17.

22. Leonard U. Blumberg, Thomas E. Shipley, Jr., and Stephen F. Barsky, *Liquor and Poverty: Skid Row as a Human Condition* (New Brunswick, NJ: Rutgers Center of Alcohol Studies, 1978), xi–xii. See also Leonard U. Blumberg, Thomas E. Shipley, Jr., and Irving W. Shandler, *Skid Row and Its Alternatives* (Philadelphia: Temple University Press, 1973), 204.

23. Blumberg, Shipley, and Shandler, *Skid Row and Its Alternatives,* 197–198.

24. Irving W. Shandler. Interview with authors, Philadelphia, PA, June 20, 1990.

25. Quoted in Mary Ellen Hombs and Mitch Snyder, *Homelessness in America: A Forced March to Nowhere* (Washington, DC: The Community for Creative Non-Violence, 1982), 2.

26. James D. Wright, *Address Unknown: The Homeless in America* (New York: Aldine De Gruyter, 1989), 135.

27. David Wood et al., *Over the Brink: Homeless Families in Los Angeles: California Children, California Families* (Los Angeles: Assembly Office of Research, August 1989), 10, 14.

28. James D. Wright and Eleanor Weber, *Homelessness and Health* (Washington, DC: McGraw-Hill, 1987), 9.

29. Hopper and Hamberg, *The Making of America's Homeless,* 63. See Chapter 6 for a full discussion of "homelessness" during the postwar period.

30. Ellen L. Bassuk and H. Richard Lamb, "Homelessness and the Implementation of Deinstitutionalization," in *The Mental Health Needs of Homeless Persons,* ed. Ellen L Bassuk (San Francisco: Jossey-Bass, 1986), 13; Burt, *Over the Edge,* 90.

31. Peter H. Rossi, *Down and Out in America: The Origins of Homelessness* (Chicago, IL: University of Chicago Press, 1989), 109.

32. Burt, *Over the Edge,* 86.

33. Ibid., 217. In her study, Burt hypothesized that this finding is probably due to the common relationship of both factors to cost of living, i.e., as a city's cost of living rises, both the level of benefits and the rate of homelessness increase. What Burt did not examine is the finding from her data that the increases in benefit levels, although correlated with increases in cost of living, do not keep people from becoming homeless—as benefit levels increase, there is simultaneously more homelessness. Intuitively, it seems unlikely that increased benefit levels cause more homelessness.

34. U.S. General Accounting Office, *Homelessness: A Complex Problem,* 19.

35. Peter H. Rossi, Gene Fisher, and Georgianna Willis, "The Condition of the Homeless of Chicago" (Chicago, IL: National Opinion Research Center, 1986), 87.

36. Cuomo, *The Way Home*, 89. The authors found that the depressed rental market slowed eviction rates in Fairfax County, VA, where county officials reported fewer families applying for shelter space as a consequence of eviction.

37. Hombs and Snyder, *A Forced March to Nowhere*, 6, 13.

38. Joel Blau, *The Visible Poor: Homelessness in the United States* (New York: Oxford University Press, 1992), 47.

39. Ibid., 181, 188.

40. Ibid., 177.

41. Gregg Barak, *Gimme Shelter: A Social History of Homelessness in Contemporary America* (New York: Praeger Publishers, 1991), xi.

42. Ibid., 175.

43. Ibid., 62.

44. Ibid., 183.

45. Hombs and Snyder, *A Forced March to Nowhere*, 129, 131.

46. Ellen L. Bassuk and Alison S. Lauriat, "The Politics of Homelessness," in *The Homeless Mentally Ill: A Task Force Report of the American Psychiatric Association*, ed. H. Richard Lamb (Washington, DC: American Psychiatric Association, 1984), 306.

47. H. Richard Lamb, Leona L. Bachrach, and Frederic I. Kass, eds., *Treating the Homeless Mentally Ill: A Task Force Report of the American Psychiatric Association* (Washington, DC: American Psychiatric Association, 1992), 5.

48. Peter H. Rossi, *Without Shelter: Homelessness in the 1980s* (Washington, DC: Twentieth Century Fund, 1989), 25.

49. Charles Hoch and Robert Slayton, *New Homeless and Old: Community and the Skid Row Hotel* (Philadelphia, PA: Temple University Press, 1989), 253.

50. Wright and Weber, *Homelessness and Health*, 99.

51. Ibid., 113.

52. Ibid., 73, 75.

53. Ibid., 127–134.

54. Ibid., 55.

55. Ibid., 56.

56. Wright, *Address Unknown*, 97.

57. Ibid., 100.

58. Ibid., 102.

59. Ibid., 105.

60. Ibid., 155.

61. Ibid., 153.

62. Ibid., 99.

63. Committee on Health Care for Homeless People, Institute of Medicine, *Homelessness, Health, and Human Needs* (Washington, DC: National Academy Press, 1988), 51.

64. Ibid., 50.

65. Ibid.

66. See James D. Wright, "Correlates and Consequences of Alcohol Abuse in the National 'Health Care for the Homeless' Client Population: Final Results" (National Institute on Alcohol Abuse and Alcoholism, Washington, DC, April 1990, Mimeographed), 49–50.

67. Wright, *Address Unknown,* 135.

68. Ibid.

69. Charles A. Kiesler, "Homelessness and Public Policy Priorities," *American Psychologist* 46, no. 11 (November 1991): 1246.

70. Rossi, *Down and Out,* 208–209.

71. Wright, *Address Unknown,* 140–148.

72. National Coalition for the Homeless, "Tips for Doing Homeless Voter Registration Drives," *Safety Network* 11, no. 2 (February 1992): 2.

73. See Hoch and Slayton, *New Homeless and Old,* 216.

74. Burt, *Over the Edge,* 226. See also 219–224 for her discussion of other recommendations.

75. Martha R. Burt and Barbara E. Cohen, "A Sociodemographic Profile of the Service-Using Homeless: Findings from a National Survey," in *Homelessness in the United States: Data and Issues,* ed. Jamshid A. Momeni (New York: Praeger Publishers, 1990), 26, 33–34; Rossi, *Down and Out,* 115; and Wright, *Address Unknown,* 66, 88.

76. Pamela J. Fischer and William R. Breakey, "The Epidemiology of Alcohol, Drug, and Mental Disorders Among Homeless Persons," *American Psychologist* 46, no. 11 (November 1991): 1124.

Chapter 9

1. Marsha A. Martin, "The Implications of NIMH-Supported Research for Homeless Mentally Ill Racial and Ethnic Minority Persons" (New York: November 1986, unpublished paper), 10.

2. William R. Breakey, "Treating the Homeless," *Alcohol Health and Research World* 2, no. 3 (1987): 47.

3. Ibid.

4. Erving Goffman, *Stigma: Notes on the Management of Spoiled Identity* (New York: Prentice-Hall, 1963), 1.

5. James D. Wright, *Address Unknown: The Homeless in America* (New York: Aldine De Gruyter, 1989), 110. See also James D. Wright and Eleanor Weber, *Homelessness and Health* (Washington, DC: McGraw-Hill, 1987), 95.

6. Breakey, "Treating the Homeless," 45.

7. Victoria Rader, *Signal Through the Flames: Mitch Snyder and America's Homeless* (Kansas City: Sheed and Ward, 1986), 28, 31.

8. Robert Morgan et al., "Alcoholism and the Homeless," in *Health Care of Homeless People,* ed. Philip W. Brickner et al. (New York: Springer Publishing, 1985), 145.

9. Richard A. Rawson, "Cut the Crack: The Policymaker's Guide to Cocaine Treatment," *Policy Review,* no. 51 (Winter 1990): 10.

10. Breakey, "Treating the Homeless," 45–46.

11. Martha R. Burt, *Over the Edge: The Growth of Homelessness in the 1980s* (New York: Russell Sage Foundation, 1992), 226.

12. U.S. Bureau of the Census, *Current Population Reports,* P-25, no. 1018 (Washington, DC: U.S. Government Printing Office, 1989), Table F.

13. The Yale Center is now the Rutgers Center of Alcohol Studies.

14. Robin Room, "Alcohol, Science and Social Control," in *Alcohol, Science, and Society Revisited,* ed. Edith Lisansky Gomberg, Helene Raskin White, and John A. Carpenter (Ann Arbor, MI: University of Michigan Press, 1982), 371; Earl Rubington, "The Chronic Drunkenness Offender on Skid Row," in *Alcohol, Science, and Society Revisited,* ed. Gomberg, White, and Carpenter, 326.

15. Peter Finn, "Decriminalization of Public Drunkenness: Response of the Health Care System," *Journal of Studies on Alcohol* 46, no. 1 (1985): 18.

16. Rubington, "The Chronic Drunkenness Offender on Skid Row," 327.

17. U.S. Department of Health and Human Services, *Seventh Special Report to the Congress on Alcohol and Health from the Secretary of Health and Human Services* (Washington, DC: U.S. Department of Health and Human Services, January 1990), ix.

18. Rubington, "The Chronic Drunkenness Offender on Skid Row," 328.

19. Ibid., 329.

20. Richard J. Frances and John E. Franklin, *Treatment of Alcoholism and Addictions* (Washington, DC: American Psychiatric Press, 1989), xv, 13.

21. Charlotte A. Schoenborn, "Exposure to Alcoholism in the Family: United States, 1988," *Advance Data,* no. 205 (September 30, 1991): 1.

22. U.S. Department of Health and Human Services, *Sixth Special Report to the U.S. Congress on Alcohol and Health from the Secretary of Health and Human Services* (Rockville, MD: U.S. Department of Health and Human Services, January 1987), 121.

23. Ibid.

24. National Institute on Alcohol Abuse and Alcoholism, "Homelessness, Alcohol and Other Drugs" (Proceedings of a conference held by U.S. Department of Health and Human Services in San Diego, CA, February 2–4, 1989), 29.

25. National Coalition for the Homeless, *Addiction on the Streets* (Washington, DC: National Coalition for the Homeless, February 1992), 20.

26. There is evidence that many homeless people knowingly use alcohol detox facilities and increasingly hospital emergency rooms not for the treatment but as a better way of getting in out of the elements. See Gerald R. Garrett and Russell K. Schutt, "The Homeless Alcoholic, Past and Present," in *Homelessness: Critical Issues for Policy and Practice,* ed. Jill Kneerim (Boston, MA: The Boston Foundation, 1987), 31; Frank R. Lipton, Albert Sabatini, and Peter Micheels, "Characteristics and Service Needs of the Homeless Mentally Ill," in *Treating the Homeless: Urban Psychiatry's Challenge,* ed. Billy E. Jones (Washington, DC: American Psychiatric Press, 1986), 36; National Institute on Alcohol Abuse and Alcoholism, "Homelessness, Alcohol and Other Drugs," 6, 21.

27. Quoted in Ricardo Castillo, "Shelter from the Storm Building on the Horizon," *Washington Post,* May 2, 1992, A3.

28. Marcia Slocum Greene, "D.C. Rehabilitating Drug Treatment System," *Washington Post,* March 13, 1992: B1.

29. Quoted in Marcia Slocum Greene, "Addicts Swamp City Facilities," *Washington Post,* October 14, 1991, B1.

30. Pamela J. Fischer and William R. Breakey, "The Epidemiology of Alcohol, Drug, and Mental Disorders Among Homeless Persons," *American Psychologist* 46, no. 11 (November 1991): 1120.

31. National Council on Alcoholism and Drug Dependence, Inc., "NCADD Fact Sheet: Alcoholism, Other Drug Addictions and Related Problems Among Women," June 1990, 2.

32. National Association of State Alcohol and Drug Abuse Directors, "FY89 State Estimates of Drug Treatment Demand Vs. Supply for Women" (Mimeographed).

33. National Institute on Drug Abuse, *National Drug and Alcoholism Treatment Unit Survey (NDATUS): 1989 Main Findings Report* (Rockville, MD: U.S. Department of Health and Human Services, 1990), 14, 18.

34. National Coalition for the Homeless, *Addiction on the Streets,* 23.

35. E. Fuller Torrey, *Nowhere to Go: The Tragic Odyssey of the Homeless Mentally Ill* (New York: Harper & Row, 1988), 139. See also E. Fuller Torrey, "Thirty Years of Shame: The Scandalous Neglect of the Mentally Ill Homeless," *Policy Review,* no. 48 (Spring 1989): 11; U.S. General Accounting Office, *Homelessness: A Complex Problem and the Federal Response,* HRD 85-40 (Washington, DC: GAO, 1985), 20.

36. Rael Jean Isaac and Virginia C. Armat, *Madness in the Streets: How Psychiatry and the Law Abandoned the Mentally Ill* (New York: Free Press, 1990), 140.

37. Ibid.

38. Marjorie J. Robertson, "Homeless Veterans: An Emerging Problem," in *The Homeless in Contemporary Society,* ed. Richard D. Bingham, Roy E. Green, and Sammis B. White (Newbury Park, CA: Sage Publications, 1989), 75, 77.

39. Ibid., 69. Robertson indicated that one-third of all homeless veterans are Vietnam veterans. Using this statistic, we estimate that some 41,000 Vietnam veterans are homeless. This estimate is based on data reported here and in Chapters 1 and 7; in the following explanation we refer to the endnotes in Chapters 1 and 7 that contain the multiple citations for these data.

Since 23 percent of all homeless individuals are family members, the remaining 77 percent are single adults (Chapter 1, note 13). By using the estimation that 81 percent of all single homeless adults are male (Chapter 1, note 10), we calculate that 62.37 percent of all homeless individuals are single men. Approximately one-third of all single homeless men are veterans (Chapter 1, note 9), and approximately one-third of all homeless veterans are Vietnam veterans (see above). Therefore, we calculate that approximately 6.9 percent of all homeless individuals are Vietnam veterans. Assuming a total homeless population of 600,000 (Chapter 7, note 48), some 41,000 Vietnam veterans are homeless.

40. Torrey, *Nowhere to Go,* 150–152.

41. U.S. General Accounting Office, *Homelessness: A Complex Problem and the Federal Response,* 20.

42. Torrey, "Thirty Years of Shame," 11.

43. Torrey, *Nowhere to Go,* 143, 147–148.

44. Ibid., 97.

45. Irene S. Levine and Cille Kennedy, "The Homeless Mentally Ill: A Consultation Challenge," *Consultation* (Spring 1985): 57.

46. Ellen L. Bassuk and H. Richard Lamb, "Homelessness and the Implementation of Deinstitutionalization," in *The Mental Health Needs of Homeless Persons,* ed. Ellen L. Bassuk (San Francisco: Jossey-Bass, 1986), 11–12.

47. Vivian B. Brown et al., "The Dual Crisis: Mental Illness and Substance Abuse: Present and Future Directions," *American Psychiatrist* 44, no. 3 (March 1989): 568.

48. Jeffrey C. Wilson and Anthony C. Kouzi, "A Social-Psychiatric Perspective on Homelessness: Results from a Pittsburgh Study," in *Homelessness in the United States: Data and Issues,* ed. Jamshid A. Momeni (New York: Praeger Publishers, 1990), 106.

49. Frances and Franklin, *Treatment of Alcoholism and Addictions,* 54.

50. Ibid.

51. U.S. Bureau of the Census, *Current Population Reports,* Table F.

52. Darrel A. Regier et al., "Comorbidity of Mental Disorders with Alcohol and Other Drug Abuse," *The Journal of the American Medical Association* 264, no. 19 (November 21, 1990): 2513.

53. Our calculations are similar to estimates reported by Morton J. Schussheim, *Bethel: A Model Community for Housing and Treating the Mentally Ill* (Washington, DC: Congressional Research Service, October 31, 1990), 1. Schussheim based his estimates on "One-Month Prevalence of Mental Disorders in the United States," *Archives of General Psychiatry* 4 (November 1988).

54. Richard W. White, *Rude Awakenings: What the Homeless Crisis Tells Us* (San Francisco, CA: ICS Press, 1992), 22.

55. Torrey, *Nowhere to Go,* 10–11.

56. Rubington, "The Chronic Drunkenness Offender on Skid Row," 328.

57. Torrey, *Nowhere to Go,* 29–30. For a concise and chronological review of the legal issues surrounding the rights of the mentally ill, see Virginia C. Armat and Roger Peele, "The Need-for-Treatment Standard in Involuntary Civil Commitment," in *Treating the Homeless Mentally Ill: A Task Force Report of the American Psychiatric Association,* ed. H. Richard Lamb, Leona L. Bachrach, and Frederic I. Kass (Washington, DC: American Psychiatric Association, 1992), 183–202.

58. Thomas Szasz, quoted in Isaac and Armat, *Madness in the Streets,* 34.

59. E. Fuller Torrey, quoted in The Heritage Foundation, *Rethinking Policy on Homelessness,* The Heritage Lectures No. 194 (Washington, DC: The Heritage Foundation, 1988), 40.

60. Lamb, Bachrach, and Kass, eds., *Treating the Homeless Mentally Ill,* 3.

61. Roger Peele et al., "The Legal System and the Homeless," in *The Homeless Mentally Ill: A Task Force Report of the American Psychiatric Association,* ed. H. Richard Lamb (Washington, DC: American Psychiatric Association, 1984), 262–263.

62. Ibid., 268.

63. Ibid., 264.

64. Ibid.

65. Ibid., 266.

66. Quoted in Isaac and Armat, *Madness in the Streets,* 144.

67. Ibid.

68. Peele et al., "The Legal System and the Homeless," 269.

69. Isaac and Armat, *Madness in the Streets,* 249.

70. Ibid., 265.

71. Peele et al., "The Legal System and the Homeless," 264–265.

72. Ibid., 265.

73. H. Richard Lamb, "The Deinstitutionalization of the Mentally Ill," in *Assisting the Homeless: State and Local Responses in an Era of Limited Resources— M-161,* U.S. Advisory Commission on Intergovernmental Relations (Washington, DC: U.S. Advisory Commission on Intergovernmental Relations, 1988), 23.

74. See Mark J. Stern, "The Emergence of the Homeless as a Public Problem," in *Housing the Homeless,* ed. Jon Erickson and Charles Wilhelm (Piscataway, NJ: Center for Urban Policy Research, 1986), 118–121, for a full discussion of these ideas.

75. Michael B. Katz, *In the Shadow of the Poorhouse: A Social History of Welfare in America* (New York: Basic Books, 1986), 67–68.

Chapter 10

1. Richard W. White, *Rude Awakenings: What the Homeless Crisis Tells Us* (San Francisco, CA: ICS Press, 1992), 268.

2. Vernon E. Johnson, *Intervention: How to Help Someone Who Doesn't Want Help* (Minneapolis: Johnson Institute Books, 1986), 65.

3. Susan Stone, *Breaking the Cycle of Homelessness: The Portland Model* (Portland, OR: Office of the Mayor, September 1988), 56–57.

4. Employee assistance programs (EAPs) have become a standard feature in many places of business. In such programs, employees are encouraged by management or labor or both to participate in substance abuse treatment and aftercare programs to address on-the-job difficulties resulting from their addiction problems.

5. Stephen P. Newton and Charles P. Duffey, "Old Town Portland and an Old-time Problem," *Alcohol Health and Research World* 2, no. 3 (1987): 63.

6. Ibid., 64.

7. Stone, *The Portland Model,* 35–36.

8. Ibid., 37.

9. Ibid., 52.

10. Edward Geffner, interview with the authors, February 22, 1990.

11. H. Richard Lamb, Leona L. Bachrach, and Frederic I. Kass, eds., *Treating the Homeless Mentally Ill: A Task Force Report of the American Psychiatric Association* (Washington, DC: American Psychiatric Association, 1992), 145–146.

12. Friedner D. Wittman and Patricia A. Madden, *Alcohol Recovery Programs for Homeless People: A Survey of Current Programs in the US* (Berkeley, CA: Pacific Institute for Research and Evaluation, Prevention Research Center, 1988), 46. When we visited Portland, we observed the CHIERS program in operation and were impressed by the humane care provided to the extremely inebriated individuals being brought to the Hooper Detox facility.

13. Deborah L. Dennis et al., "A Decade of Research and Services for Homeless Mentally Ill Persons," *American Psychologist* 46, no. 11 (November 1991). See Chapter 5, note 9.

14. For example, the Diagnostic and Rehabilitation Center in Philadelphia, the Manhattan Bowery Project in New York, and the Portland Model.

15. Irving W. Shandler, *Diagnostic and Rehabilitation Center/Philadelphia: Annual Report, Fiscal Year 1989* (Philadelphia, PA: Diagnostic and Rehabilitation Center, 1989), 4–6. See National Institute on Alcohol Abuse and Alcoholism, "Homelessness, Alcohol and Other Drugs" (Proceedings of a conference held by U.S. Department of Health and Human Services in San Diego, CA, February 2–4, 1989), 34–37, for a description of a similar program in Los Angeles.

16. Richard A. Rawson, "Cut the Crack: The Policymaker's Guide to Cocaine Treatment," *Policy Review,* no. 51 (Winter 1990): 11.

17. National Institute on Alcohol Abuse and Alcoholism, "Homelessness, Alcohol and Other Drugs," 5.

18. The success of Oxford House, Inc., started in 1975 by a recovering alcoholic, prompted the creation of a $100,000 revolving loan fund as part of the 1988 federal Anti-Drug Abuse Act. Under the act, the funds are available to each state to provide start-up loans for establishing group houses for recovering people; the act also includes provisions for overcoming zoning restrictions that prohibit group housing. According to the National Coalition for the Homeless, by the end of 1990, only fourteen out of twenty-five states surveyed reported that they had made use of this program. See National Coalition for the Homeless, *Addiction on the Streets* (Washington, DC: National Coalition for the Homeless, February 1992), 37–38.

19. National Institute on Alcohol Abuse and Alcoholism, "Homelessness, Alcohol and Other Drugs," 48–49. See also Friedner D. Wittman, "Housing Models for Alcohol Programs Serving Homeless People" (Paper presented at National Conference on Homelessness, Alcohol, and Other Drugs, San Diego, CA, February 1989); and Wittman and Madden, *Alcohol Recovery Programs for Homeless People.*

20. National Institute on Alcohol Abuse and Alcoholism, "Homelessness, Alcohol and Other Drugs," 48–51.

21. Federal Task Force on Homelessness and Severe Mental Illness, *Outcasts on Main Street* (Washington, DC: U.S. Department of Health and Human Services and the Interagency Council on the Homeless, 1992), 43–44.

22. Rudyard N. Propst, "A Normal Life for the Mentally Ill," in *Homelessness: Critical Issues for Policy and Practice,* ed. Jill Kneerim (Boston, MA: The Boston Foundation, 1987), 39–42; E. Fuller Torrey, "Thirty Years of Shame: The Scandalous Neglect of the Mentally Ill Homeless," *Policy Review,* no. 48 (Spring 1989): 15.

23. See Vivian B. Brown et al., "The Dual Crisis: Mental Illness and Substance Abuse: Present and Future Directions," *American Psychiatrist* 44, no. 3 (March 1989); Kate B. Carey, "Emerging Treatment Guidelines for Mentally Ill Chemical Abusers," *Hospital and Community Psychiatry* 40, no. 4 (April 1989).

24. Susan E. Axelroad and Gail Toff, "Outreach Services for Homeless Mentally Ill People" (Proceedings of the First of Four Knowledge Development Meetings on Issues Affecting Homeless Mentally Ill People, the Intergovernmental Health Policy Project, George Washington University, Washington, DC, May 1987), 6–7; Deborah L. Dennis, ed. *Research Methodologies Concerning Homeless Persons With Serious Mental Illness and/or Substance Abuse Disorders* (Proceedings of a two-day conference sponsored by the Alcohol, Drug Abuse Mental Health Administration, U.S. Department of Health and Human Services, Washington, DC, December 1987), 58.

25. Mary Ann Allard and Paul J. Carling, *Providing Housing and Supports for People with Psychiatric Disabilities: A Technical Assistance Manual for Applicants for the Robert Wood Johnson Foundation and U.S. Department of Housing and Urban Development Program for the Chronically Mentally Ill* (Manual prepared for the National Institute of Mental Health. Washington, DC: April 1986), 29.

26. Mark L. Willenbring et al., "Community Treatment of the Chronic Public Inebriate I: Implementation," in *Treating Alcoholism and Drug Abuse Among*

Homeless Men and Women: Nine Community Demonstration Grants, ed. Milton Argeriou and Dennis McCarty (Binghamton, NY: The Haworth Press, 1990), 80.

27. Andrew M. Cuomo, *The Way Home: A New Direction in Social Policy* (New York: New York City Commission on the Homeless, February 1992), 108.

28. Telephone conversation with DRC staff, July 2, 1992.

29. Irving W. Shandler and Thomas E. Shipley, "Policy, Funding, Resources Are Needed," *Alcohol Health and Research World* 2, no. 3 (1987): 88.

30. Cuomo, *The Way Home,* 72–73, 106.

31. U.S. Department of Housing and Urban Development, *A Report on the 1988 National Survey of Shelters for the Homeless* (Washington, DC: U.S. Department of Housing and Urban Development, 1989), 19.

32. U.S. Department of Housing and Urban Development, *1988 National Survey,* 17, 24.

33. U.S. General Accounting Office, *Homelessness: McKinney Act Programs and Funding Through Fiscal Year 1990* (Washington, DC: GAO, May 1991), 14–15; Ruth Ellen Wasem, *Homelessness: Issues and Legislation in the 102nd Congress* (Washington, DC: Congressional Research Service, Updated January 3, 1992), 9.

34. U.S. General Accounting Office, *Homelessness: McKinney Act Programs and Funding Through Fiscal Year 1990,* 2–3.

35. U.S. Department of Health and Human Services, *Sixth Special Report to the U.S. Congress on Alcohol and Health from the Secretary of Health and Human Services* (Rockville, MD: U.S. Department of Health and Human Services, January 1987), 134.

36. Irving Shandler, interview with authors, Philadelphia, PA, June 20, 1990.

37. In 1984, the National Coalition for Jail Reform estimated that it cost $15,000 per year to house one inmate and between $50,000 and $70,000 to build each new jail cell, and these costs have undoubtedly risen in the past eight years. See National Coalition for Jail Reform, *Removing the Chronically Mentally Ill from Jail* (Washington, DC: National Coalition for Jail Reform, 1984), 2.

Bibliography

Allard, Mary Ann, and Paul J. Carling. *Providing Housing and Supports for People with Psychiatric Disabilities: A Technical Assistance Manual for Applicants for the Robert Wood Johnson Foundation and U.S. Department of Housing and Urban Development Program for the Chronically Mentally Ill.* Manual prepared for the National Institute of Mental Health. Washington, DC: April 1986.

Altman, Drew, Ellen L. Bassuk, William R. Breakey, A. Alan Fischer, Charles R. Halpern, Gloria Smith, Louisa Stark, Nathan Stark, Bruce C. Vladeck, and Phyllis Wolfe. "Health Care for the Homeless." *Transaction Social Science and Modern Society* 26, no. 4 (May/June 1989): 4–5.

Arce, A. Anthony, Marilyn Tadlock, Michael J. Vergare, and Stuart Shapiro. "A Psychiatric Profile of Street People Admitted to an Emergency Shelter." *Hospital and Community Psychiatry* 34, no. 9 (September 1983): 812–817.

Argeriou, Milton, and Dennis McCarty, eds. *Treating Alcoholism and Drug Abuse Among Homeless Men and Women: Nine Community Demonstration Grants.* Binghamton, NY: The Haworth Press, 1990.

Armat, Virginia C., and Roger Peele. "The Need-for-Treatment Standard in Involuntary Civil Commitment." In *Treating the Homeless Mentally Ill: A Task Force Report of the American Psychiatric Association,* edited by H. Richard Lamb, Leona L. Bachrach, and Frederic I. Kass (Washington, DC: American Psychiatric Association, 1992).

Auletta, Ken. *The Underclass.* New York: Random House, 1982.

Awalt, L. Christopher. "Brother, Don't Spare a Dime." *Newsweek,* September 30, 1991, 13.

Axleroad, Susan E., and Gail Toff. "Outreach Services for Homeless Mentally Ill People." Proceedings of the First of Four Knowledge Development Meetings on Issues Affecting Homeless Mentally Ill People. The Intergovernmental Health Policy Project, George Washington University, Washington, DC, May 1987.

Bachrach, Leona L. "The Homeless Mentally Ill and Mental Health Services: An Analytical Review of the Literature." In *The Homeless Mentally Ill: A Task Force Report of the American Psychiatric Association,* edited by H. Richard Lamb. Washington, DC: American Psychiatric Association, 1984.

———. "Young Adult Chronic Patients: An Analytical Review of the Literature." In *The Young Adult Chronic Patient: Collected Articles from Hospital and Community Psychiatry,* compiled by Hospital and Community Psychiatry Service. Washington, DC: Hospital and Community Psychiatry Service of the American Psychiatric Association, June 1985.

Bahr, Howard M. "Introduction." In *Homelessness in the United States: State Surveys,* edited by Jamshid A. Momeni. New York: Praeger Publishers, 1990.

Barak, Gregg. *Gimme Shelter: A Social History of Homelessness in Contemporary America.* New York: Praeger Publishers, 1991.

Bassuk, Ellen L. "Homeless Families: Single Mothers and Their Children in Boston Shelters." In *The Mental Health Needs of Homeless Persons,* edited by Ellen L. Bassuk. San Francisco: Jossey-Bass, 1986.

———. "The Homelessness Problem." In *Housing the Homeless,* edited by Jon Erickson and Charles Wilhelm. Piscataway, NJ: Center for Urban Policy Research, 1986.

———. "The Problem of Homeless Families." In *Community Care for Homeless Families: A Program Design Manual,* edited by Ellen L. Bassuk, Rebecca W. Carman, and Linda F. Weinreb. Newton Center, MA: The Better Homes Foundation, 1990.

———. "Homeless Families." *Scientific American,* December 1991, 66–74.

Bassuk, Ellen L., and H. Richard Lamb. "Homelessness and the Implementation of Deinstitutionalization." In *The Mental Health Needs of Homeless Persons,* edited by Ellen L. Bassuk. San Francisco: Jossey-Bass, 1986.

Bassuk, Ellen L., and Alison S. Lauriat. "The Politics of Homelessness." In *The Homeless Mentally Ill: A Task Force Report of the American Psychiatric Association,* edited by H. Richard Lamb. Washington, DC: American Psychiatric Association, 1984.

Bassuk, Ellen L., Alison S. Lauriat, and Leonore Rubin. "Homeless Families." In *Homelessness: Critical Issues for Policy and Practice,* edited by Jill Kneerim. Boston, MA: The Boston Foundation, 1987.

Bassuk, Ellen L., and Lynn Rosenberg. "Why Does Family Homelessness Occur? A Case-Control Study." *American Journal of Public Health* 78, no. 7 (1988): 783–788.

Bassuk, Ellen L., Leonore Rubin, and Alison S. Lauriat. "Characteristics of Sheltered Homeless Families." *American Journal of Public Health* 76, no. 9 (1986): 1097–1101.

Bassuk, Ellen L., ed. *The Mental Health Needs of Homeless Persons.* San Francisco: Jossey-Bass, 1986.

Bassuk, Ellen L., Rebecca W. Carman, and Linda F. Weinreb, eds. *Community Care for Homeless Families: A Program Design Manual.* Newton Center, MA: The Better Homes Foundation, 1990.

Baxter, Ellen, and Kim Hopper. *Private Lives/Public Spaces: Homeless Adults on the Streets of New York City.* New York: Community Service Society, 1981.

———. "Shelter and Housing for the Homeless Mentally Ill." In *The Homeless Mentally Ill: A Task Force Report of the American Psychiatric Association,* edited by H. Richard Lamb. Washington, DC: American Psychiatric Association, 1984.

Bean, Gerald J., Jr., Mary E. Stefl, and Steven R. Howe. "Mental Health and Homelessness: Issues and Findings." *Social Work* (September–October 1987): 411–416.

Besharov, Douglas J. "The Children of Crack: Will We Protect Them?" *Public Welfare* (Fall 1989), 7–15.

Bingham, Richard D., Roy E. Green, and Sammis B. White, eds. *The Homeless in Contemporary Society.* Newbury Park, CA: Sage Publications, 1989.

Blau, Joel. *The Visible Poor: Homelessness in the United States.* New York: Oxford University Press, 1992.

Blumberg, Leonard U., Thomas E. Shipley, Jr., and Stephen F. Barsky. *Liquor and Poverty: Skid Row as a Human Condition.* New Brunswick, NJ: Rutgers Center of Alcohol Studies, 1978.

Blumberg, Leonard U., Thomas E. Shipley, Jr., and Irving W. Shandler. *Skid Row and Its Alternatives.* Philadelphia: Temple University Press, 1973.

Bouvier, Leon F., and Carol J. De Vita. "The Baby Boom—Entering Midlife." *Population Bulletin* 46, no. 3 (November 1991): 27.

Breakey, William R. "Treating the Homeless." *Alcohol Health and Research World* 2, no. 3 (1987): 42–47.

———. "Recent Empirical Research on the Homeless Mentally Ill." In *Research Methodologies Concerning Homeless Persons with Serious Mental Illness and/or Substance Abuse Disorders,* edited by Deborah L. Dennis. Proceedings of a two-day conference sponsored by the U.S. Department of Health and Human Services. Washington, DC: Alcohol, Drug Abuse Mental Health Administration, December 1987.

Brickner, Philip W., Linda Keen Scharer, Barbara Conanan, Alexander Elvy, and Marianne Savarese, eds. *Health Care of Homeless People.* New York: Springer Publishing, 1985.

Brickner, Philip W., Linda Keen Scharer, Barbara Conanan, Marianne Savarese, and Brian C. Scanlan, eds. *Under the Safety Net: The Health and Social Welfare of the Homeless in the United States.* New York: W. W. Norton, 1990.

Brown, Vivian B., M. Susan Ridgely, Bert Pepper, and Irene S. Levine. "The Dual Crisis: Mental Illness and Substance Abuse: Present and Future Directions." *American Psychiatrist* 44, no. 3 (March 1989): 565–569.

Burroughs, Jennifer. "Health Concerns of Homeless Women." In *Under the Safety Net: The Health and Social Welfare of the Homeless in the United States,* edited by Philip W. Brickner, Linda Keen Scharer, Barbara Conanan, Marianne Savarese, and Brian C. Scanlan. New York: W. W. Norton, 1990.

Burt, Martha R. *Over the Edge: The Growth of Homelessness in the 1980s.* New York: Russell Sage Foundation, 1992.

Burt, Martha R., and Barbara E. Cohen. *Feeding the Homeless: Does the Prepared Meals Provision Help?* 2 vols. Washington, DC: Urban Institute Press, 1988.

———. *State Activities and Programs for the Homeless: A Review of Six States.* Washington, DC: Urban Institute Press, 1988.

———. *America's Homeless: Numbers, Characteristics and Programs That Serve Them.* Washington, DC: Urban Institute, 1989.

———. "A Sociodemographic Profile of the Service-Using Homeless: Findings from a National Survey." In *Homelessness in the United States: Data and Issues,* edited by Jamshid A. Momeni. New York: Praeger Publishers, 1990.

Carey, Kate B. "Emerging Treatment Guidelines for Mentally Ill Chemical Abusers." *Hospital and Community Psychiatry* 40, no. 4 (April 1989): 341–349.

Carliner, Michael S. "Homelessness: A Housing Problem." In *The Homeless in Contemporary Society,* edited by Richard D. Bingham, Roy E. Green, and Sammis B. White. Newbury Park, CA: Sage Publications, 1989.

Castillo, Ricardo. "Shelter from the Storm Building on the Horizon." *Washington Post,* May 2, 1992, A3.

Committee on Health Care for Homeless People, Institute of Medicine. *Homelessness, Health, and Human Needs.* Washington, DC: National Academy Press, 1988.

Cuomo, Andrew M. *The Way Home: A New Direction in Social Policy.* New York: New York City Commission on the Homeless, February 1992.

Dear, Michael J., and Brendan Gleeson. "Community Attitudes Toward the Homeless." *Urban Geography* 12, no. 2 (1990): 155–176.

Dennis, Deborah L., John C. Buchner, Frank R. Lipton, and Irene S. Levine. "A Decade of Research and Services for Homeless Mentally Ill Persons." *American Psychologist* 46, no. 11 (November 1991): 1129–1138.

Dennis, Deborah L., ed. *Research Methodologies Concerning Homeless Persons with Serious Mental Illness and/or Substance Abuse Disorders.* Proceedings of a two-day conference sponsored by the Alcohol, Drug Abuse Mental Health Administration, U.S. Department of Health and Human Services, Washington, DC, December 1987.

DiIulio, John J., Jr. "There but for Fortune." *The New Republic,* June 24, 1991, 27–36.

Dionne, E. J., Jr. *Why Americans Hate Politics.* New York: Simon and Schuster, 1991.

Dobelstein, Andrew W. *Politics, Economics, and Public Welfare.* Englewood Cliffs, NJ: Prentice Hall, 1986.

Dockett, Kathleen H. *Street Homeless People in the District of Columbia.* Washington, DC: University of the District of Columbia, 1989.

Drake, Robert E., Fred C. Osher, and Michael Wallach. "Homelessness and Dual Diagnosis." *American Psychologist* 46, no. 11 (November 1991): 1149–1158.

Drake, Robert E., and Michael A. Wallach. "Dual Diagnosis Among the Chronically Mentally Ill." Submitted to Hospital and Community Psychiatry. Cambridge, MA: Department of Psychiatry, Harvard Medical School.

Edsall, Thomas Byrne, and Mary D. Edsall. *Chain Reaction: The Impact of Race, Rights, and Taxes on American Politics.* New York: W. W. Norton, 1991.

Erickson, Jon, and Charles Wilhelm, eds. *Housing the Homeless.* Piscataway, NJ: Center for Urban Policy Research, 1986.

"Exploring Myths About 'Street People.'" *Access* 2, no. 2 (June 1990): 1–3.

Federal Task Force on Homelessness and Severe Mental Illness. *Outcasts on Main Street.* Washington, DC: U.S. Department of Health and Human Services and the Interagency Council on the Homeless, 1992.

Finn, Peter. "Decriminalization of Public Drunkenness: Response of the Health Care System." *Journal of Studies on Alcohol* 46, no. 1 (1985): 7–23.

Fischer, Pamela J., and William R. Breakey. "Mental Illness and Substance Abuse in the Contemporary American Homeless Population: Findings from the Baltimore Homeless Study." Paper presented at Professional Symposium, Recent Findings and New Approaches to the Treatment of Mental Illness and Substance Abuse. Tulsa, OK: 1988.

———. "The Epidemiology of Alcohol, Drug, and Mental Disorders Among Homeless Persons." *American Psychologist* 46, no. 11 (November 1991): 1115–1128.

Foscarinis, Maria. "The Politics of Homelessness: A Call to Action." *American Psychologist* 46, no. 11 (November 1991): 1232–1238.

Frances, Richard J., and John E. Franklin. *Treatment of Alcoholism and Addictions.* Washington, DC: American Psychiatric Press, 1989.

Garrett, Gerald R., and Russell K. Schutt. "The Homeless Alcoholic, Past and Present." In *Homelessness: Critical Issues for Policy and Practice,* edited by Jill Kneerim. Boston, MA: The Boston Foundation, 1987.

Gelberg, Lillian, Lawrence S. Linn, and Barbara D. Leake. "Mental Health, Alcohol and Drug Use, and Criminal History Among Homeless Adults." *American Journal of Psychiatry* 145, no. 2 (February 1988): 191–196.

Glazer, Nathan. *The Limits of Social Policy*. Cambridge, MA: Harvard University Press, 1988.

Gleicher, Hope Burness, Karen McGee, Marianne Savarese, and Angela Kennedy. "Staff Organization, Retention, and Burnout." In *Under the Safety Net: The Health and Social Welfare of the Homeless in the United States*, edited by Philip W. Brickner, Linda Keen Scharer, Barbara Conanan, Marianne Savarese, and Brian C. Scanlan. New York: W. W. Norton, 1990.

Goetcheus, Janelle. "Healing the Homeless: They Need Medical Care, Shelter, Solace." *Washington Post*, October 15, 1991, Health Section, 6.

Goffman, Erving. *Stigma: Notes on the Management of Spoiled Identity*. New York: Prentice-Hall, 1963.

Gomberg, Edith Lisansky, Helene Raskin White, and John A. Carpenter, eds. *Alcohol, Science and Society Revisited*. Ann Arbor, MI: University of Michigan Press, 1982.

Goodman, Walter. "Critic's Notebook: TV Journalists' Urge to Prettify the News." *New York Times*, February 19, 1992.

Greene, Marcia Slocum. "Addicts Swamp City Facilities." *Washington Post*, October 14, 1991, B1.

———. "D.C. Rehabilitating Drug Treatment System." *Washington Post*, March 13, 1992, B1.

Hamilton, David. "Poverty Is Still with Us—And Worse." In *Quiet Riots: Race and Poverty in the United States*, edited by Fred R. Harris and Roger W. Wilkins. New York: Pantheon Books, 1988.

Harrington, Michael. *The Other America: Poverty in the United States*. Baltimore: Penguin Books, 1963.

Harris, Fred R., and Roger W. Wilkins, eds. *Quiet Riots: Race and Poverty in the United States*. New York: Pantheon Books, 1988.

Hartman, Chester. "The Housing Part of the Homelessness Problem." In *Homelessness: Critical Issues for Policy and Practice*, edited by Jill Kneerim. Boston, MA: The Boston Foundation, 1987.

Heritage Foundation. *Rethinking Policy on Homelessness*. The Heritage Lectures No. 194. Washington, DC: The Heritage Foundation, 1988.

Hoch, Charles. "A Brief History of the Homeless Problem in the United States." In *The Homeless in Contemporary Society*, edited by Richard D. Bingham, Roy E. Green, and Sammis B. White. Newbury Park, CA: Sage Publications, 1989.

Hoch, Charles, and Robert A. Slayton. *New Homeless and Old: Community and the Skid Row Hotel*. Philadelphia, PA: Temple University Press, 1989.

Hombs, Mary Ellen, and Mitch Snyder. *Homelessness in America: A Forced March to Nowhere*. Washington, DC: The Community For Creative Non-Violence, 1982.

Hopper, Kim, and Jill Hamberg. *The Making of America's Homeless: From Skid Row to New Poor*. New York: Community Service Society, 1984.

Hospital and Community Psychiatry Service. *The Young Adult Chronic Patient: Collected Articles from Hospital and Community Psychiatry*. Washington, DC:

Hospital and Community Psychiatry Service of the American Psychiatric Association, June 1985.

Housing Authority of Portland. *Resolving Homelessness in Portland and Multnomah County: A Report and Planning Framework.* Portland, OR: Department of Planning, Development and Intergovernmental Relations, November 1989.

Interagency Council on the Homeless. *The 1989 Annual Report of the Interagency Council on the Homeless.* Washington, DC: U.S. Government Printing Office, 1989.

Isaac, Rael Jean, and Virginia C. Armat. *Madness in the Streets: How Psychiatry and the Law Abandoned the Mentally Ill.* New York: Free Press, 1990.

Jahiel, Rene. "The Situation of Homelessness." In *The Homeless in Contemporary Society,* edited by Richard D. Bingham, Roy E. Green, and Sammis B. White. Newbury Park, CA: Sage Publications, 1989.

Johnson, Vernon E. *Intervention: How to Help Someone Who Doesn't Want Help.* Minneapolis: Johnson Institute Books, 1986.

Jones, B. E., ed. *Treating the Homeless: Urban Psychiatry's Challenge.* Washington, DC: American Psychiatry Press, 1986.

Jones, Landon Y. *Great Expectations: America and the Baby Boom Generation.* New York: Ballantine Books, 1980.

Katz, Michael B. *In the Shadow of the Poorhouse: A Social History of Welfare in America.* New York: Basic Books, 1986.

————. *The Undeserving Poor: From the War on Poverty to the War on Welfare.* New York: Pantheon Press, 1989.

Kennedy, James T., Joseph Petrone, Robert W. Deisher, Jed Emerson, Pauline Heslop, Deirdre Bastible, and Marc Arkovitz. "Health Care for Familyless, Runaway Street Kids." In *Under the Safety Net: The Health and Social Welfare of the Homeless in the United States,* edited by Philip W. Brickner, Linda Keen Scharer, Barbara Conanan, Marianne Savarese, and Brian C. Scanlan. New York: W. W. Norton, 1990.

Kenyon, Thomas L., with Justine Blau. *What You Can Do to Help the Homeless.* New York: Simon and Schuster/Fireside, 1991.

Kiesler, Charles A. "Homelessness and Public Policy Priorities." *American Psychologist* 46, no. 11 (November 1991): 1245–1252.

Kneerim, Jill, ed. *Homelessness: Critical Issues for Policy and Practice.* Boston: The Boston Foundation, 1987.

Koegel, Paul, and M. Audrey Burnam. "Alcoholism Among Homeless Adults in the Inner City of Los Angeles." *Archives of General Psychiatry* 45, no. 11 (1988): 1011–1018.

Koegel, Paul, M. Audrey Burnam, and Rodger K. Farr. "The Prevalence of Specific Psychiatric Disorders Among Homeless Individuals in the Inner City of Los Angeles." *Archives of General Psychiatry* 45, no. 11 (1988): 1085–1092.

Kolata, Gina. "Twins on the Streets: Homelessness and Addiction." *New York Times,* May 22, 1989, 1.

Kondratas, Anna. "Ending Homelessness: Policy Challenges." *American Psychologist* 46, no. 11 (November 1991): 1226–1231.

Koppelman, Jane, and Judith Miller Jones. "Crack: It's Destroying Fragile Low-Income Families." *Public Welfare* (Fall 1989), 13–15.

Kozol, Jonathan. *Rachel and Her Children: Homeless Families in America.* New York: Crown Publishers, 1988.

Lamb, H. Richard. "The Homeless Mentally Ill." In *Homelessness: Critical Issues for Policy and Practice,* edited by Jill Kneerim. Boston, MA: The Boston Foundation, 1987.

————. "The Deinstitutionalization of the Mentally Ill." In *Assisting the Homeless: State and Local Responses in an Era of Limited Resources—M-161.* U.S. Advisory Commission on Intergovernmental Relations. Washington, DC: U.S. Advisory Commission on Intergovernmental Relations, 1988.

Lamb, H. Richard, ed. *The Homeless Mentally Ill: A Task Force Report of the American Psychiatric Association.* Washington, DC: American Psychiatric Association, 1984.

Lamb, H. Richard, Leona L. Bachrach, and Frederic I. Kass, eds. *Treating the Homeless Mentally Ill: A Task Force Report of the American Psychiatric Association.* Washington, DC: American Psychiatric Association, 1992.

Lee, Mary Ann, Karen Haught, Irwin Redlener, Almeta Fant, Elaine Fox, and Stephen A. Somers. "Health Care for Children in Homeless Families." In *Under the Safety Net: The Health and Social Welfare of the Homeless in the United States,* edited by Philip W. Brickner, Linda Keen Scharer, Barbara Conanan, Marianne Savarese, and Brian C. Scanlan. New York: W. W. Norton, 1990.

Lemann, Nicholas. "How the Seventies Changed America." *American Heritage,* July/August 1991, 39–49.

Levine, Irene S., and Cille Kennedy. "The Homeless Mentally Ill: A Consultation Challenge." *Consultation* (Spring 1985): 52–63.

Levitas, Mitchel. "Homeless in America." *New York Times Magazine,* June 10, 1990, 45.

Lewis, Jay. "The Federal Role in Alcoholism Research, Treatment and Prevention." In *Alcohol, Science and Society Revisited,* edited by Edith Lisansky Gomberg, Helene Raskin White, and John A. Carpenter. Ann Arbor, MI: University of Michigan Press, 1982.

Lewis, Oscar. *The Children of Sanchez: Autobiography of a Mexican Family.* New York: Random House, 1961.

Lichter, Robert S., and Linda S. Lichter. "The Visible Poor: Media Coverage of the Homeless: 1986–1989." *Media Monitor* 3, no. 3 (March 1989).

Light, Paul C. *Baby Boomers.* New York: W. W. Norton, 1988.

Lipton, Frank R., and Albert Sabatini. "Constructing Support Systems for Homeless Chronic Patients." In *The Homeless Mentally Ill: A Task Force Report of the American Psychiatric Association,* edited by H. Richard Lamb. Washington, DC: American Psychiatric Association, 1984.

Lipton, Frank R., Albert Sabatini, and Peter Micheels. "Characteristics and Service Needs of the Homeless Mentally Ill." In *Treating the Homeless: Urban Psychiatry's Challenge,* edited by Billy E. Jones. Washington, DC: American Psychiatric Press, 1986.

Lubran, Barbara G. "Alcohol and Drug Abuse Among the Homeless Population: A National Response." In *Treating Alcoholism and Drug Abuse Among Homeless Men and Women: Nine Community Demonstration Grants,* edited by Milton Argeriou and Dennis McCarty. Binghamton, NY: The Haworth Press, 1990.

Martin, Marsha A. "The Implications of NIMH-Supported Research for Homeless Mentally Ill Racial and Ethnic Minority Persons." New York: November 1986, unpublished paper.

McCarty, Dennis, Milton Argeriou, Robert B. Huebner, and Barbara Lubran. "Alcoholism, Drug Abuse, and the Homeless." *American Psychologist* 46, no. 11 (November 1991): 1139–1148.

McGeary, Michael G. H., and Laurence E. Lynn, Jr., eds. *Urban Change and Poverty.* Washington, DC: National Academy Press, 1988.

McLanahan, Sara, Irwin Garfinkel, and Dorothy Watson. "Family Structure, Poverty, and the Underclass." In *Urban Change and Poverty,* edited by Michael G. H. McGeary and Laurence E. Lynn, Jr. Washington, DC: National Academy Press, 1988.

Milburn, Norweeta G. "Drug Abuse Among Homeless People." In *Homelessness in the United States: Data and Issues,* edited by Jamshid A. Momeni. New York: Praeger Publishers, 1990.

Milgram, Grace. "Glossary." In *The Cranston-Gonzalez National Affordable Housing Act: Key Provisions and Analysis,* prepared by Morton J. Schussheim. Washington, DC: Congressional Research Service, 1991.

———. *Housing: Low- and Moderate-Income Assistance Programs.* Washington, DC: Congressional Research Service, September 10, 1991.

———. *Housing Assistance in the United States.* Washington, DC: Congressional Research Service, December 5, 1991.

Miller, Henry. *On the Fringe: The Dispossessed in America.* Lexington, MA: Lexington Books, 1991.

Momeni, Jamshid A., ed. *Homelessness in the United States: Data and Issues.* New York: Praeger Publishers, 1990.

Momeni, Jamshid A., ed. *Homelessness in the United States: State Surveys.* New York: Praeger Publishers, 1990.

Morgan, Robert, Edward I. Geffner, Elizabeth Kiernan, and Stephanie Cowles. "Alcoholism and the Homeless." In *Health Care of Homeless People,* edited by Philip W. Brickner, Linda Keen Scharer, Barbara Conanan, Alexander Elvy, and Marianne Savarese. New York: Springer Publishing, 1985.

Moynihan, Daniel Patrick. "The Children of the State." *Washington Post,* November 25, 1990, C1.

Mulkern, Virginia, and Rebecca Spence. "Alcohol Abuse/Alcoholism Among Homeless Persons: A Review of the Literature." Boston, MA: Human Services Research Institute, November 1984.

———. "Illicit Drug Use Among Homeless Persons: A Review of the Literature." Boston, MA: Human Services Research Institute, November 1984.

National Association of State Alcohol and Drug Abuse Directors. "FY89 State Estimates of Drug Treatment Demand Vs. Supply for Women." Mimeographed.

National Center for Health Statistics. "Live Births, Birth Rates, and Fertility Rates, by Race of Child: United States, 1909–88." *Vital Statistics of the United States, 1988,* vol. 1, *Natality,* DHHS, Pub. No. (PHS) 90-1100. Washington, DC: U.S. Government Printing Office, 1990, Table 1-1.

National Coalition for Jail Reform. *Removing the Chronically Mentally Ill from Jail.* Washington, DC: National Coalition for Jail Reform, 1984.

National Coalition for the Homeless. *American Nightmare: A Decade of Homelessness in the United States.* New York and Washington, DC: National Coalition for the Homeless, December 1989.

———. *Addiction on the Streets.* Washington, DC: National Coalition for the Homeless, February 1992.

———. "Tips for Doing Homeless Voter Registration Drives." *Safety Network* 11, no. 2 (February 1992): 2.

National Council on Alcoholism and Drug Dependence, Inc. "NCADD Fact Sheet: Alcoholism, Other Drug Addictions and Related Problems Among Women." New York: National Council on Alcoholism and Drug Dependence, Inc., June 1990.

———. "NCADD Fact Sheet: Alcoholism and Alcohol Related Problems." New York: National Council on Alcoholism and Drug Dependence, Inc., revised November 1990.

National Institute on Alcohol Abuse and Alcoholism. "Homelessness, Alcohol and Other Drugs." Proceedings of a conference held by U.S. Department of Health and Human Services in San Diego, CA, February 2–4, 1989.

National Institute on Drug Abuse. *National Drug and Alcoholism Treatment Unit Survey (NDATUS): 1989 Main Findings Report.* Rockville, MD: U.S. Department of Health and Human Services, 1990.

National Law Center on Homelessness and Poverty. *Go Directly to Jail: A Report Analyzing Local Anti-Homeless Ordinances.* Washington, DC: National Law Center on Homelessness and Poverty, 1991.

National Mental Health Association. "The Role of Community Foundations in Meeting the Needs of Homeless Individuals with Mental Illness." Conference Report. Alexandria, VA: National Mental Health Association, 1986.

National Mental Health Association and Families for the Homeless. *Homeless in America.* Washington, DC: Acropolis Books, 1988.

National Resource Center on Homelessness and Mental Illness. *Working with Dually Diagnosed Homeless Persons.* Delmar, NY: Policy Research Associates, July 1990.

Newton, Stephen P., and Charles P. Duffey. "Old Town Portland and an Oldtime Problem." *Alcohol Health and Research World* 2, no. 3 (1987): 62–64.

Osher, Fred C. "Assessing Dual Diagnosis." *Access* 2, no. 2 (June 1990): 6.

Peele, Roger, Bruce Gross, Bernard Arons, and Mokarram Jafri. "The Legal System and the Homeless." In *The Homeless Mentally Ill: A Task Force Report of the American Psychiatric Association,* edited by H. Richard Lamb. Washington, DC: American Psychiatric Association, 1984.

Pepper, Bert, Michael C. Kirshner, and Hilary Ryglewicz. "The Young Adult Chronic Patient: Overview of a Population." In *The Young Adult Chronic Patient: Collected Articles from Hospital and Community Psychiatry,* compiled by Hospital and Community Psychiatry Service. Washington, DC: Hospital and Community Psychiatry Service of the American Psychiatric Association, June 1985.

Piliavin, Irving, Michael Sosin, Herb Westerfelt, and Ross Matsueda. "Conditions Contributing to Long-Term Homelessness." School of Social Work and Institute for Research on Poverty, University of Wisconsin, Madison, WI, 1989.

Plapinger, Jane, Kostas Gounis, and Susan Barrow. "Finding a Place to Call Home." *Access* 1, no. 1 (March 1989): 3.

Price, Virginia. "Runaways and Homeless Street Youth." In *Homelessness: Critical Issues for Policy and Practice,* edited by Jill Kneerim. Boston, MA: The Boston Foundation, 1987.

Propst, Rudyard N. "A Normal Life for the Mentally Ill." In *Homelessness: Critical Issues for Policy and Practice,* edited by Jill Kneerim. Boston, MA: The Boston Foundation, 1987.

Raba, John M. "Homelessness and AIDS." In *Under the Safety Net: The Health and Social Welfare of the Homeless in the United States,* edited by Philip W. Brickner, Linda Keen Scharer, Barbara Conanan, Marianne Savarese, and Brian C. Scanlan. New York: W. W. Norton, 1990.

Rader, Victoria. *Signal Through the Flames: Mitch Snyder and America's Homeless.* Kansas City: Sheed and Ward, 1986.

Rafferty, Yvonne, and Marybeth Shinn. "The Impact of Homelessness on Children." *American Psychologist* 46, no. 11 (November 1991): 1170–1179.

Raspberry, William. "Walking Away from the Homeless." *Washington Post,* September 6, 1991, A21.

Rawson, Richard A. "Cut the Crack: The Policymaker's Guide to Cocaine Treatment." *Policy Review,* no. 51 (Winter 1990): 10–19.

Redmond, Sonjia Parker, and Joan Brackmann. "Homeless Children and Their Caretakers." In *Homelessness in the United States: Data and Issues,* edited by Jamshid A. Momeni. New York: Praeger Publishers, 1990.

Regier, Darrel A., Mary E. Farmer, Donald S. Rae, Ben Z. Locke, Samuel J. Keith, Lewis L. Judd, and Frederick K. Goodwin. "Comorbidity of Mental Disorders with Alcohol and Other Drug Abuse." *The Journal of the American Medical Association* 264, no. 19 (November 21, 1990): 2511–2518.

Rhoden, Nancy K. "The Limits of Liberty: Deinstitutionalization, Homelessness, and Libertarian Theory." *Emory Law Journal* 31, no. 2 (Spring 1982): 359–440.

Rice, Dorothy P., Sander Kelman, Leonard S. Miller, and Sarah Dunmeyer. *The Economic Costs of Alcohol and Drug Abuse and Mental Illness: 1985.* Washington, DC: U.S. Department of Health and Human Services, 1990.

Rich, Spencer. "'Hidden Homeless' May Elude Census." *Washington Post,* June 8, 1989, A21.

———. "Millions of Families Said to Be on the Brink of Homelessness." *Washington Post,* August 9, 1989, A19.

Ridgely, M. Susan, Howard H. Goldman, and John A. Talbott. *Chronic Mentally Ill Young Adults with Substance Abuse Problems: A Review of Relevant Literature and Creation of a Research Agenda.* Baltimore, MD: University of Maryland at Baltimore, 1986.

Ridgely, M. Susan, Caroline T. McNeil, and Howard H. Goldman. "Alcohol and Other Drug Abuse Among Homeless Individuals: An Annotated Bibliography." Contract NO ADM-281-88-0003, NIAAA. Rockville, MD: ROW Sciences, October 1988.

Ridgely, M. Susan, Fred C. Osher, Howard H. Goldman, and John A. Talbott. *Executive Summary: Chronic Mentally Ill Young Adults with Substance Abuse Problems: A Review of Research, Treatment, and Training Issues.* Baltimore, MD: University of Maryland at Baltimore, 1987.

Ridgely, M. Susan; Fred C. Osher, and John A. Talbott. *Chronic Mentally Ill Young Adults with Substance Abuse Problems: Treatment and Training Issues.* Baltimore, MD: University of Maryland at Baltimore, 1987.

Rist, Marilee C. "The Shadow Children: Preparing for the Arrival of Crack Babies in School." *Research Bulletin,* no. 9 (July 1990): 1–6.

Robbins, Tom. "New York's Homeless Families." In *Housing the Homeless,* edited by Jon Erickson and Charles Wilhelm. Piscataway, NJ: Center for Urban Policy Research, 1986.

Robertson, Marjorie J. "Homeless Veterans: An Emerging Problem." In *The Homeless in Contemporary Society,* edited by Richard D. Bingham, Roy E. Green, and Sammis B. White. Newbury Park, CA: Sage Publications, 1989.

———. "Homeless Youth in Hollywood: Patterns of Alcohol Use." National Institute on Alcohol Abuse and Alcoholism, Washington, DC, 1987.

Rogers, Ronald L., and Chandler Scott McMillin. *Free Someone You Love from Alcohol and Other Drugs.* New York: The Putnam Publishing Group, 1992.

Romanoski, Alan J., Gerald Nestadt, Alan Ross, Pamela J. Fischer, and William R. Breakey. "Alcoholism and Psychiatric Comorbidity in the Homeless: The Baltimore Study." Paper presented at the Annual Meeting of the American Public Health Association. Boston, MA:, 1988.

Room, Robin. "Alcohol, Science and Social Control." In *Alcohol, Science, and Society Revisited,* edited by Edith Lisansky Gomberg, Helene Raskin White, and John A. Carpenter. Ann Arbor, MI: University of Michigan Press, 1982.

Rossi, Peter H. "Critical Methodological Issues in Research on Homeless Persons." In *Research Methodologies Concerning Homeless Persons with Serious Mental Illness and/or Substance Abuse Disorders,* edited by Deborah L. Dennis. Proceedings of a two-day conference sponsored by the Alcohol, Drug Abuse Mental Health Administration. Washington, DC: U.S. Department of Health and Human Services, December 1987.

———. *Down and Out in America: The Origins of Homelessness.* Chicago, IL: University of Chicago Press, 1989.

———. *Without Shelter: Homelessness in the 1980s.* Washington, DC: Twentieth Century Fund, 1989.

Rossi, Peter H., Gene Fisher, and Georgianna Willis. "The Condition of the Homeless of Chicago." Chicago, IL: National Opinion Research Center, 1986.

Roth, Dee, and Jerry Bean. "Alcohol Problems and Homelessness: Findings from the Ohio Study." Conference Paper for meeting on the Homeless with Alcohol Related Problems. Bethesda, MD: National Institute on Alcohol Abuse and Alcoholism, July 29–30, 1985.

Roth, Dee, Jerry Bean, Nancy Lust, and Traian Saveanu. *Homelessness in Ohio: A Study of People in Need—Statewide Report.* Columbus, Ohio: Ohio Dept. of Mental Health, 1985.

Rubington, Earl. "The Chronic Drunkenness Offender on Skid Row." In *Alcohol, Science, and Society Revisited,* edited by Edith Lisansky Gomberg, Helene Raskin White, and John A. Carpenter. Ann Arbor, MI: University of Michigan Press, 1982.

Ryan, William. *Blaming the Victim.* New York: Vintage Books, 1976.

Sadd, Susan. "Revolving Door Revisited: Public Inebriates' Use of Medical and Non-medical Detoxification Services in New York City." Prepared for conference on the Homeless with Alcohol Related Problems. Bethesda, MD: National Institute on Alcohol Abuse and Alcoholism, July 29–30, 1985.

Sadd, Susan, and Douglas W. Young. "Nonmedical Treatment of Indigent Alcoholics: A Review of Recent Research Findings." *Alcohol Health and Research World* 2, no. 3 (1987): 48–49.

Scanlon, John. "Homelessness: Describing the Symptoms, Prescribing a Cure." *The Heritage Foundation Backgrounder*, no. 729 (October 2, 1989): 1–13.

Schoenborn, Charlotte A. "Exposure to Alcoholism in the Family: United States, 1988." *Advance Data*, no. 205 (September 30, 1991).

Schussheim, Morton J. *Bethel: A Model Community for Housing and Treating the Mentally Ill.* Washington, DC: Congressional Research Service, October 31, 1990.

———. *The Cranston-Gonzalez National Affordable Housing Act: Key Provisions and Analysis.* Washington, DC: Congressional Research Service, 1991.

Schwartz, Stuart R., and Stephen M. Goldfinger. "The New Chronic Patient: Clinical Characteristics of an Emerging Subgroup." In *The Young Adult Chronic Patient: Collected Articles from Hospital and Community Psychiatry,* compiled by Hospital and Community Psychiatry Service. Washington, DC: Hospital and Community Psychiatry Service of the American Psychiatric Association, June 1985.

Shandler, Irving W. *Diagnostic and Rehabilitation Center/Philadelphia: Annual Report, Fiscal Year 1989.* Philadelphia, PA: Diagnostic and Rehabilitation Center, 1989.

Shandler, Irving W., and Thomas E. Shipley. "Policy, Funding, Resources Are Needed." *Alcohol Health and Research World* 2, no. 3 (1987): 88.

Shinn, Marybeth, James R. Knickman, and Beth C. Weitzman. "Social Relationships and Vulnerability to Becoming Homeless Among Poor Families." *American Psychologist* 46, no. 11 (November 1991): 1180–1187.

Snyder, Mitch. Letter to the Editor, *Washington Post,* April 15, 1990.

Stanford Center for the Study of Families, Children and Youth. *Stanford Studies of Homeless Families, Children and Youth.* Palo Alto, CA: Stanford Center for the Study of Families, Children and Youth, November 1991.

Stefl, Mary E. "The New Homeless: A National Perspective." In *The Homeless in Contemporary Society,* edited by Richard D. Bingham, Roy E. Green, and Sammis B. White. Newbury Park, CA: Sage Publications, 1989.

Steinbeck, John. *The Grapes of Wrath.* New York: Penguin Books, 1989 edition.

Stern, Mark J. "The Emergence of the Homeless as a Public Problem." In *Housing the Homeless,* edited by Jon Erickson and Charles Wilhelm. Piscataway, NJ: Center for Urban Policy Research, 1986.

Steward, James K. "Drug Use Forecasting, Fourth Quarter 1988." National Institute of Justice Research in Action. Washington, DC: U.S. Department of Justice, June 1989.

Stone, Susan. *Breaking the Cycle of Homelessness: The Portland Model.* Portland, Oregon: Office of the Mayor, September 1988.

Sullivan, Patricia A., and Shirley P. Damrosch. "Homeless Women and Children." In *The Homeless in Contemporary Society,* edited by Richard D. Bingham, Roy E. Green, and Sammis B. White. Newbury Park, CA: Sage Publications, 1989.

Taeuber, Cynthia. "Census Bureau Releases 1990 Decennial Counts for Persons Enumerated in Emergency Shelters and Observed on Streets." *U.S. Department of Commerce News,* CB 91-117, April 12, 1991.

————. "Fact Sheet for 1990 Decennial Census Counts of Persons in Emergency Shelters for the Homeless and Visible in Street Locations." *U.S. Department of Commerce News,* April 12, 1991.

Taeuber, Cynthia M., and Paul M. Siegel. "Counting the Nation's Homeless Population in the 1990 Census." In *Conference Proceedings for Enumerating Homeless Persons: Methods and Data Issues.* Conference cosponsored by the Bureau of the Census, the U.S. Department of Housing and Urban Development, and the Interagency Council for the Homeless, Washington, DC, March 19, 1991.

Taylor, Paul. "War's Veterans See Their Nation Losing Faith in Its Future." *Washington Post,* December 3, 1991, A7.

Tessler, Richard C., and Deborah L. Dennis. "A Synthesis of NIMH-Funded Research Concerning Persons Who Are Homeless and Mentally Ill." Program for the Homeless Mentally Ill. Washington, DC: U.S. Department of Health and Human Services, February 9, 1989.

Thomas, Lisa, Mike Kelly, and Michael Cousineau. "Alcoholism and Substance Abuse." In *Under the Safety Net: The Health and Social Welfare of the Homeless in the United States,* edited by Philip W. Brickner, Linda Keen Scharer, Barbara Conanan, Marianne Savarese, and Brian C. Scanlan. New York: W. W. Norton, 1990.

Toro, Paul A., and Dennis M. McDonell. "Beliefs, Attitudes, and Knowledge About Homelessness: A Survey of the General Public." *American Journal of Community Psychology* 20, no. 1 (1992): 53–80.

Torrey, E. Fuller. *Nowhere to Go: The Tragic Odyssey of the Homeless Mentally Ill.* New York: Harper & Row, 1988.

————. "Thirty Years of Shame: The Scandalous Neglect of the Mentally Ill Homeless." *Policy Review,* no. 48 (Spring 1989): 10–15.

Tri-County Youth Services Consortium. "A Plan to Resolve Youth Homelessness in Multnomah County." Draft Report, prepared by Providers of Youth Services. Multnomah County Youth Program Office, February 1991.

Tucker, William. *The Excluded Americans: Homelessness and Housing Policies.* Washington, DC: Regnery Gateway, 1990.

U.S. Advisory Commission on Intergovernmental Relations. *Assisting the Homeless: State and Local Responses in an Era of Limited Resources—M-161.* Washington, DC: U.S. Advisory Commission on Intergovernmental Relations, 1988.

U.S. Bureau of the Census. *1950 Census of Population—Table 94.* vol. 2. Washington, DC: U.S. Government Printing Office, 1953.

————. "Projections of the Population of the United States by Age, Sex, and Race: 1988 to 2080." *Current Population Reports,* Series P-25, no. 1018, January 1989.

————. "United States Population Estimates, by Age, Sex, Race, and Hispanic Origin: 1980 to 1988." *Current Population Reports,* Series P-25, no. 1045, January 1990.

U.S. Conference of Mayors. *A Status Report on Hunger and Homelessness in America's Cities: 1990.* Washington, DC: U.S. Conference of Mayors, 1990.

————. *A Status Report on Hunger and Homelessness in America's Cities: 1991.* Washington, DC: U.S. Conference of Mayors, 1991.

U.S. Congress. House. Committee on the Budget. Ad Hoc Task Force on the Homeless and Housing. *Homelessness During Winter 1988–1989: Prospects for Change.* Serial No. AH 100-4. 100th Cong., 2nd sess., December 20, 1988. Washington, DC: U.S. Government Printing Office, 1989.

———. Committee on Government Operations. *Mismanagement in Programs for the Homeless: Washington, D.C., as a Case Study.* 102nd Cong., 1st sess., 1991. H. Rept. 102-366. Washington, DC: U.S. Government Printing Office, 1991.

———. Select Committee on Children, Youth and Families. *No Place to Call Home: Discarded Children in America.* 101st Cong., 1st sess., November 1989. Washington, DC: U.S. Government Printing Office, 1989.

———. *Getting Straight: Overcoming Treatment Barriers for Addicted Women and Their Children.* 101st Cong., 2nd sess., April 23, 1990. Washington, DC: U.S. Government Printing Office, 1990.

———. *Law and Policy Affecting Addicted Women and Their Children.* 101st Cong., 2nd sess., May 17, 1990. Washington, DC: U.S. Government Printing Office, 1990.

U.S. Department of Health and Human Services. *Sixth Special Report to the U.S. Congress on Alcohol and Health from the Secretary of Health and Human Services.* Rockville, MD: U.S. Department of Health and Human Services, January 1987.

———. *Seventh Special Report to the Congress on Alcohol and Health from the Secretary of Health and Human Services.* Washington, DC: U.S. Department of Health and Human Services, January 1990.

———. *Crack Babies.* Draft Report, Office of the Inspector General. Washington, DC: U.S. Department of Health and Human Services, February 1990.

U.S. Department of Housing and Urban Development. *A Report to the Secretary on the Homeless and Emergency Shelters.* Washington, DC: U.S. Department of Housing and Urban Development, 1984.

———. *A Report on the 1988 National Survey of Shelters for the Homeless.* Washington, DC: U.S. Department of Housing and Urban Development, 1989.

———. *A Report on Homeless Assistance Policy and Practice in the Nation's Five Largest Cities.* Washington, DC: U.S. Department of Housing and Urban Development, August 1989.

U.S. General Accounting Office. *Homelessness: A Complex Problem and the Federal Response,* HRD 85-40. Washington, DC: GAO, 1985.

———. *Homelessness: Implementation of Food and Shelter Programs Under the McKinney Act.* Washington, DC: GAO, December 1987.

———. *Homeless Mentally Ill: Problems and Options in Estimating Numbers and Trends.* Washington, DC: GAO, 1988.

———. *Welfare Hotels: Uses, Costs, and Alternatives.* Washington, DC: GAO, January 1989.

———. *Homelessness: HUD's and FEMA's Progress in Implementing the McKinney Act.* Washington, DC: GAO, May 1989.

———. *Children and Youths: About 68,000 Homeless and 186,000 in Shared Housing at Any Given Time.* Washington, DC: GAO, June 1989.

———. *Homelessness: Too Early to Tell What Kinds of Prevention Assistance Work Best.* Washington, DC: GAO, April 1990.

———. *Homelessness: McKinney Act Programs and Funding Through Fiscal Year 1990.* Washington, DC: GAO, May 1991.

———. *Homelessness: Transitional Housing Shows Initial Success but Long-term Effects Unknown.* Washington, DC: GAO, September 1991.

Vobejda, Barbara. "Fanning Out to Find, Count the Homeless." *Washington Post,* March 18, 1990, A1–A20.

———. "Census Spotted Nearly 230,000 Homeless People." *Washington Post,* April 13, 1991, A3.

———. "Average Household Shrinks as More in U.S. Live Alone." *Washington Post,* May 1, 1991, A1.

Wasem, Ruth Ellen. *Homelessness: Issues and Legislation in the 102nd Congress.* Washington, DC: Congressional Research Service, Updated January 3, 1992.

Welfeld, Irving. *Where We Live: A Social History of American Housing.* New York: Simon and Schuster, 1988.

Wheeler, Linda. "Parents of 14 Accused of Misusing Public Funds." *Washington Post,* March 12, 1990, B3.

White, Richard W. *Rude Awakenings: What the Homeless Crisis Tells Us.* San Francisco, CA: ICS Press, 1992.

Whitman, David. "Shattering Myths About the Homeless." *U.S. News and World Report,* March 20, 1989, 27–28.

Willenbring, Mark L., Joseph A. Whelan, James S. Dahlquist, and Michael E. O'Neal. "Community Treatment of the Chronic Public Inebriate I: Implementation." In *Treating Alcoholism and Drug Abuse Among Homeless Men and Women: Nine Community Demonstration Grants,* edited by Milton Argeriou and Dennis McCarty. Binghamton, NY: The Haworth Press, 1990.

Williams, Lydia. *Mourning in America: Health Problems, Mortality, and Homelessness.* Washington, DC:National Coalition for the Homeless, December 1991.

Wilson, Jeffrey C., and Anthony C. Kouzi. "A Social-Psychiatric Perspective on Homelessness: Results from a Pittsburgh Study." In *Homelessness in the United States: Data and Issues,* edited by Jamshid A. Momeni. New York: Praeger Publishers, 1990.

Wilson, William Julius. *The Declining Significance of Race.* Chicago, IL: University of Chicago Press, 1980.

———. *The Truly Disadvantaged: The Inner City, the Underclass, and Public Policy.* Chicago: University of Chicago Press, 1987.

Wittman, Friedner D. "Homeless with Alcohol-related Problems: Proceedings of a Meeting to Provide Research Recommendations to the National Institute on Alcohol Abuse and Alcoholism, Bethesda, MD. July 29–30, 1985." Prepared for the National Institute on Alcohol Abuse and Alcoholism. Berkeley, CA: Pacific Institute for Research and Evaluation, 1985.

———. "Housing Models for Alcohol Programs Serving Homeless People." Paper presented at National Conference on Homelessness, Alcohol, and Other Drugs, San Diego, CA, February 1989.

Wittman, Friedner D., and Patricia A. Madden. *Alcohol Recovery Programs for Homeless People: A Survey of Current Programs in the US.* Berkeley, CA: Pacific Institute for Research and Evaluation, Prevention Research Center, 1988.

Wood, David, Steven Schlossman, Toshi Hayashi, and R. Burciaga Valdez. *Over the Brink: Homeless Families in Los Angeles: California Children, California Families.* Los Angeles: Assembly Office of Research, August 1989.

Wright, James D. *Address Unknown: The Homeless in America.* New York: Aldine De Gruyter, 1989.

————. "Correlates and Consequences of Alcohol Abuse in the National 'Health Care for the Homeless' Client Population: Final Results." National Institute on Alcohol Abuse and Alcoholism, Washington, DC, April 1990.

Wright, James D., Peter H. Rossi, Janet W. Knight, Eleanor Weber-Burdin, Richard C. Tessler, Christine E. Stewart, Marianne Geronimo, and Julie Lam. "Homelessness and Health: The Effects of Life Style on Physical Well-being Among Homeless People in New York City." Manuscript for inclusion in *Social Theory and Social Problems,* edited by M. Lewis and J. Miller. JAI Press, 1987.

Wright, James D., and Eleanor Weber. *Homelessness and Health.* Washington, DC: McGraw-Hill, 1987.

About the Book and Authors

When homelessness became increasingly visible in the early 1980s, most Americans were reluctant to admit what was obvious: that the homeless people they encountered were seriously troubled and chronically disabled by alcoholism, drug addiction, and mental illness. The media, policymakers, and the American public, persuaded by advocates for the homeless, came to believe that the homeless were simply victims of the hardships of poverty and the lack of affordable housing, both of which were exacerbated by economic recession and the unresponsiveness of government. Policies were created in the belief that emergency shelters, soup kitchens, job training, and transitional housing would help the homeless regain their independence.

A Nation in Denial challenges these accepted notions. It presents a comprehensive and readable review of the scientific evidence that up to 85 percent of all homeless adults suffer the ravages of substance abuse and mental illness, resulting in the social isolation that has been the hallmark of homelessness in the United States since colonial days. The authors provide new insights into the causes of increased homelessness in the early 1980s, linking the population explosion of the baby boom to increases in the numbers of Americans at risk for substance abuse problems, mental illness, and homelessness; assessing the relationship between the inner-city drug epidemic and increases in family homelessness; and reviewing the failed policies of deinstitutionalization, decriminalization of alcoholism, and the gentrification of both skid row neighborhoods and substance-abuse treatment centers—policies that sent thousands out into the streets and shelters. Weaving together solid demographic and epidemiological research with personal accounts of homeless individuals, this unique study not only provides a new understanding of homelessness and prompts a serious reexamination of current policies but also proposes more honest and effective ways for helping America's most disabled and destitute citizens.

Alice S. Baum has worked in education, politics, and public policy related to poor and disadvantaged children and as a drug and alcohol counselor for homeless people. **Donald W. Burnes** has served as an education policy analyst and as the executive director of a direct-services program for the poor and the homeless. He also served on the Washington, D.C., Mayor's Homeless Coordinating Council.

Index